POSTCARD HISTORY SERIES

DeKalb County

IN VINTAGE POSTCARDS

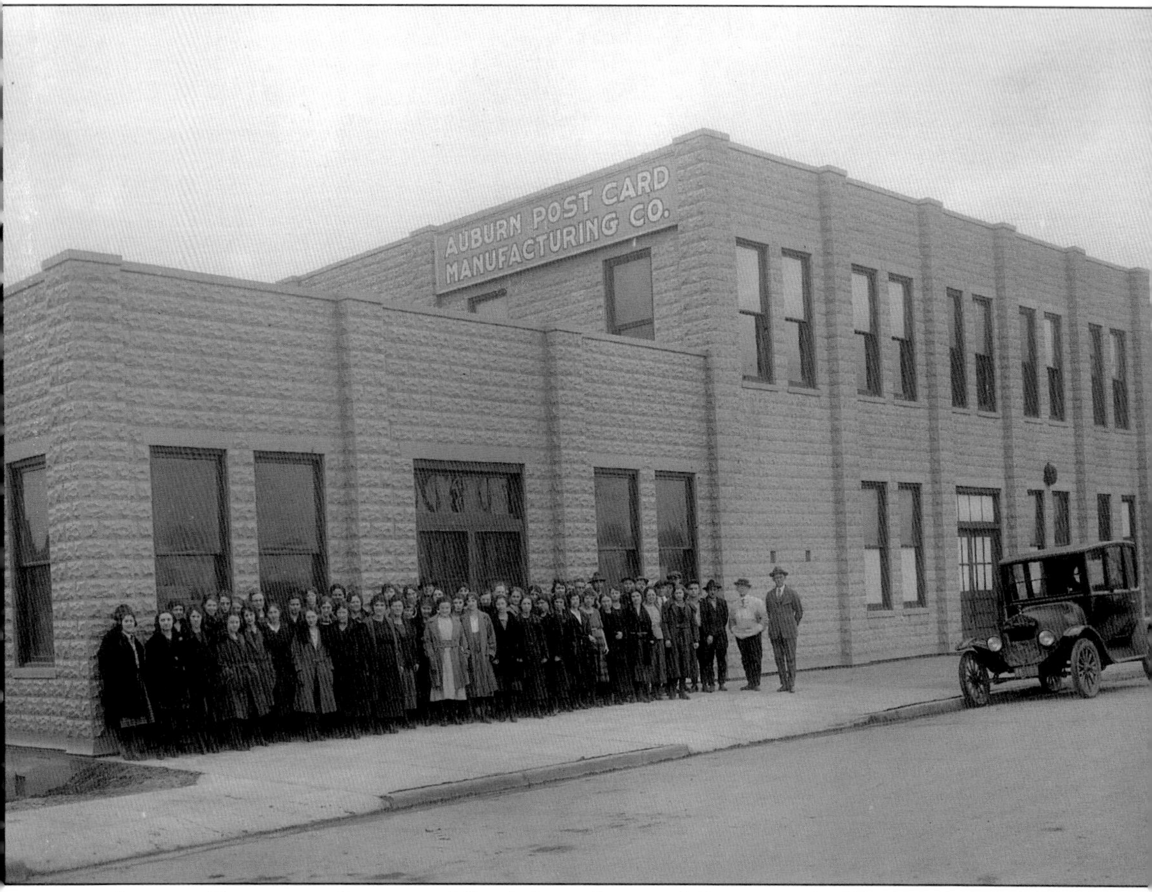

AUBURN POSTCARD COMPANY. The Auburn Postcard Company Building and its employees are pictured here.

POSTCARD HISTORY SERIES

DeKalb County

IN VINTAGE POSTCARDS

John Martin Smith

ARCADIA
PUBLISHING

ISBN 978-0-7385-1917-3

Published by Arcadia Publishing
Charleston SC, Chicago IL, Portsmouth NH, San Francisco CA

Printed in the United States of America

Library of Congress Catalog Card Number: 2001093314

For all general information contact Arcadia Publishing at:
Telephone 843-853-2070
Fax 843-853-0044
E-mail sales@arcadiapublishing.com
For customer service and orders:
Toll-Free 1-888-313-2665

Visit us on the Internet at www.arcadiapublishing.com

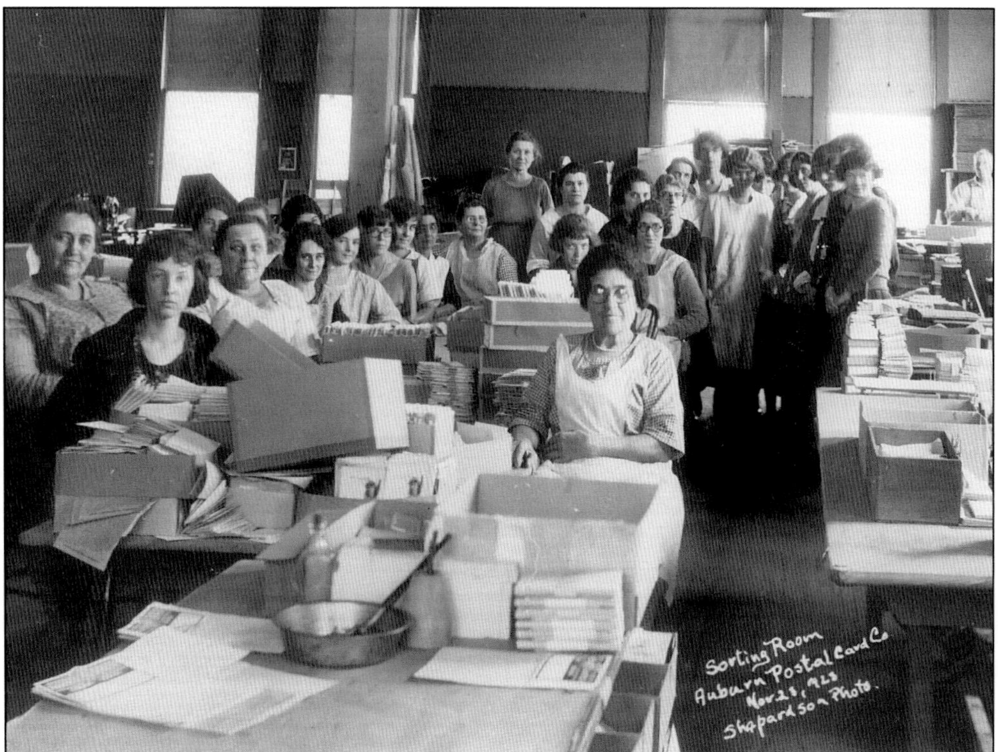

Making Postcards. This is an image of Auburn Postcard Company employees (same as Noble and Steuben).

Contents

ACKNOWLEDGMENTS

The author is indebted to several people who have contributed to the production of this book:

My wife, Barbara Clark Smith, has participated in the collection of these postcards for nearly 40 years. I thank her for her patient search through thousands of postcards at antique shows and antique malls to find those relevant to Northeastern Indiana.

My son and law partner, Thompson Smith, has made law office facilities available to assist in the production of this book. His paralegal, Tricia Hertsel, has done the computer input and organization. My secretary of 32 years, Sharon George, has also assisted.

Arcadia editor, Ann Fugman, has been of great assistance in getting the book into print in accordance with the high standards of Arcadia. The quiet behind-the-scenes efforts of a good editor always makes an author look good!

Lastly, I am indebted to those photographers and merchants who had the foresight and vision to create and distribute the original postcards. While postcards have a fleeting, ephemeral quality to them, those "packrats" who have collected and saved them have provided us a legacy of our towns that would have otherwise been lost after the click of the camera and the thunk of the postmark!

John Martin Smith

INTRODUCTION

After my grandfather died in 1961 we found a box of old postcards which were exchanged between my grandmother Viola Smith and her sister Iona. They both lived in Butler, Indiana, but several blocks apart.

I arranged them in chronological order and scanned the messages. Some were post marked the same day.

With a little research and questions to my father, Walter M. Smith, who served as Postmaster in Butler from 1950 to 1976, I found that beginning in 1907 there was mail delivery twice each day in the town. Therefore, the sisters could exchange messages the same day—i.e. "Can you and Carl come for supper at 6PM? Iona—Yes, I will bring an apple pie, Viola"

Some of the cards had floral and holiday scenes on the front and others had real photographs of buildings located in Butler. Postage was 1¢. I later sorted out the scenes of buildings and started looking for others. At antique shops, flea markets, antique malls, and auctions I found more postcards from Butler. This search then expanded to all of Northeastern Indiana. Over a period of about thirty years I have accumulated hundreds of postcards. One of the best sources now is Ebay on the internet. Since most of the postcards were sent away from their place of origin, many are listed for sale from places far from Northeast Indiana. This source has enabled me to augment the collection presented here.

The history of the use of postcards centers around United States Postal Laws and Regulations. The printed format of postcards also enables one to generally date postcards. The sequence is as follows:

1893–1898 Pioneer Cards

These cards are quite rare and are sometimes labeled as "Souvenir Postcards."

1898–1901 Private Mailing Cards

These cards are labeled "Private Mailing Card" on the address side and usually also state "Authorized by Act of Congress of May 19, 1898."

1901–1907 Undivided Backs

Postal regulations did not permit a message on the back – just the address. This was also true of the Pioneer and Private Mailing Cards.

1907–1915 Divided Backs

On March 1, 1907, the United States Postal Service approved the divided back card which permitted the address on the right side and a message on the left side of the back. This change made the use of postcards much more prevalent as a means of communication.

1915–1930s White Borders

A change in printing techniques resulted in a printed image with a narrow white border.

1935–1955 Linens

These cards were printed on cardboard stock with a "linen" like surface. The publisher started with a photograph but modified it to make an idyllic image that was also colorized.

1945–Present Chromes

These cards are printed in color on a slick stock.

The foregoing date categories overlap considerably. Sometimes the same basic photographs were used for several postcard versions. Pre-linen cards were frequently colorized in various ways. For example, a black and white image would be overprinted with a brick color on a brick building. The Auburn Postcard Company was known for its "Blue Sky" cards which were a black and white image with the sky overprinted in light blue.

From about 1900–1915, many cards were "Real Photo" cards. That term is used to describe a photograph printed by the photographer directly onto postcard stock. Sometimes only a single postcard was made. Usually, the number of cards printed was limited. Real photo cards are sought by collectors due to their relative rarity and sharp, clear image. Real photo cards were also issued in the 1940s and 1950s. A real photo card and a printed card can be distinguished quite easily by magnifying the image—a printed card will have a pattern of small dots to create the contrast, whereas a real photo card will have a solid image.

The bulk of the images in this book date from 1910–1915, which was the golden era of postcard production. It is likely that the local use of postcards waned after the telephone came into general use. As automobile travel increased, postcards were used by tourists to send a photograph and message back home. Many people also collected postcards which led to friends and relatives sending them postcards for their collections.

There were several local postcard companies in Bryan, Ohio; Fort Wayne, Indiana; and Auburn, Indiana. The Auburn Postcard Company was a major national publisher of postcards. The Whitten-Dennison Post Card Company moved to Auburn from Maine in 1910. They built a small factory on East Seventh Street adjacent to Cedar Creek which employed five women. The name of the company was changed to Auburn Post Card Manufacturing Company in 1913, and to Auburn Greeting Card Company in 1929. In 1933, D.E. Messenger acquired the company and changed the name to Messenger Corporation, which is still in operation at 318 E. Seventh Street and is a major printer of religious calendars and printed materials for the funeral home industry.

How were the subjects of postcards chosen? Generally, they were chosen by local merchants on the basis of what would sell in their drugstore, restaurant, or bookstore. In some cases the scenes selected were designed to show off the town. The most common are scenes of the courthouses and principle streets. They were ordered in quantities of 500–1,000, so the merchant wanted to make sure that they would sell.

The images selected for this book are designed to present a representative selection of images for Kendallville and Noble County. The space and format of the book did not permit the use of all cards in our collection for this county. In some cases, the messages on the back are as interesting as the image on the front. I have incorporated some of these in my interpretations. The bold type in my captions repeats the caption of the card. If the date is not contained in the caption and the card is postmarked, the postmarked date is stated "*c.* 19—." If the card is not postmarked, or if the postmark is not readable, no date is stated. I then supplement the caption with other information when appropriate. Some images simply speak for themselves, so I refrain from any further comment.

While not originally intended to document a town or place historically, I find that they are a great source of local history and images that is otherwise unavailable. As persons restore buildings to their original design, a postcard may be the only source of a period image of that particular building.

I sincerely hope that my readers enjoy and use the image and captions contained herein to appreciate their heritage and sense of place.

John Martin Smith

One

Ashley

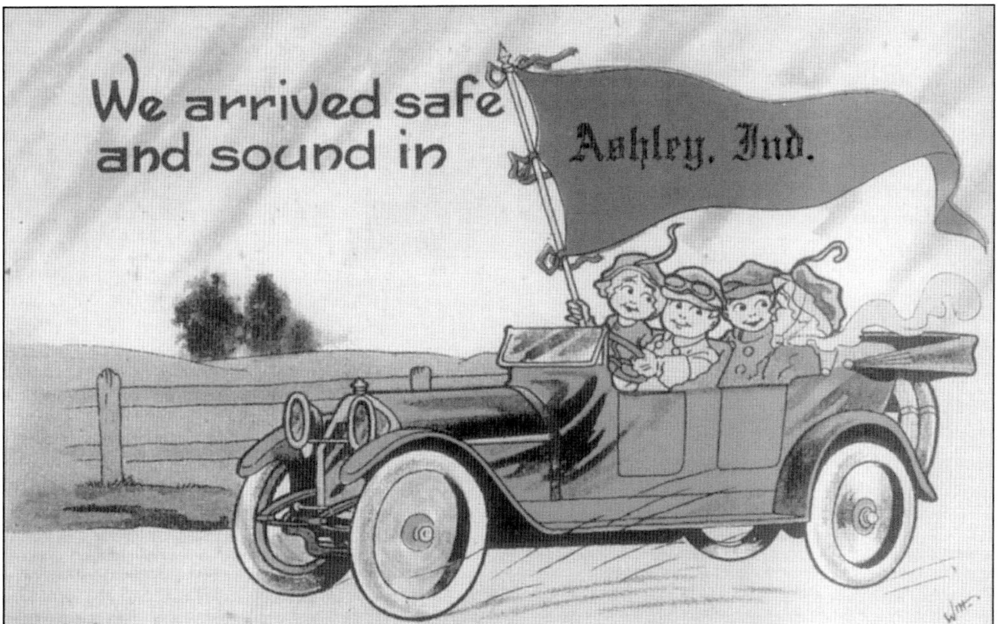

We Arrived Safe and Sound in Ashley, Indiana. This is a stock "comic" postcard. These were a standard image upon which the name of the town was overprinted. Each chapter in this book will start with a comic postcard.

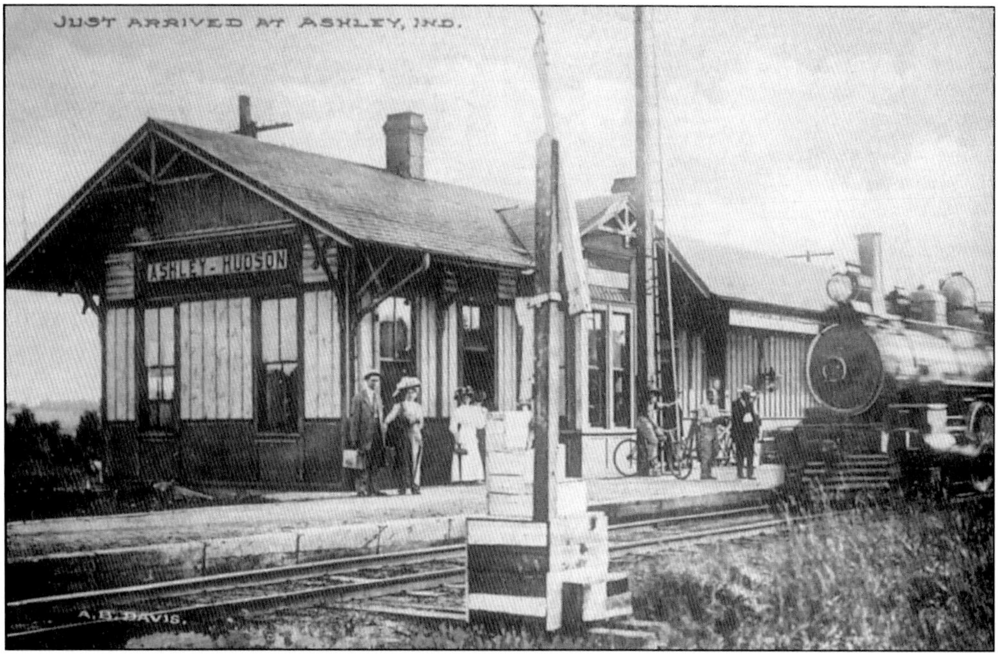

JUST ARRIVED AT ASHLEY, INDIANA. The Wabash Railroad platted Ashley as a town and then sold lots. The depot served both Ashley and Hudson.

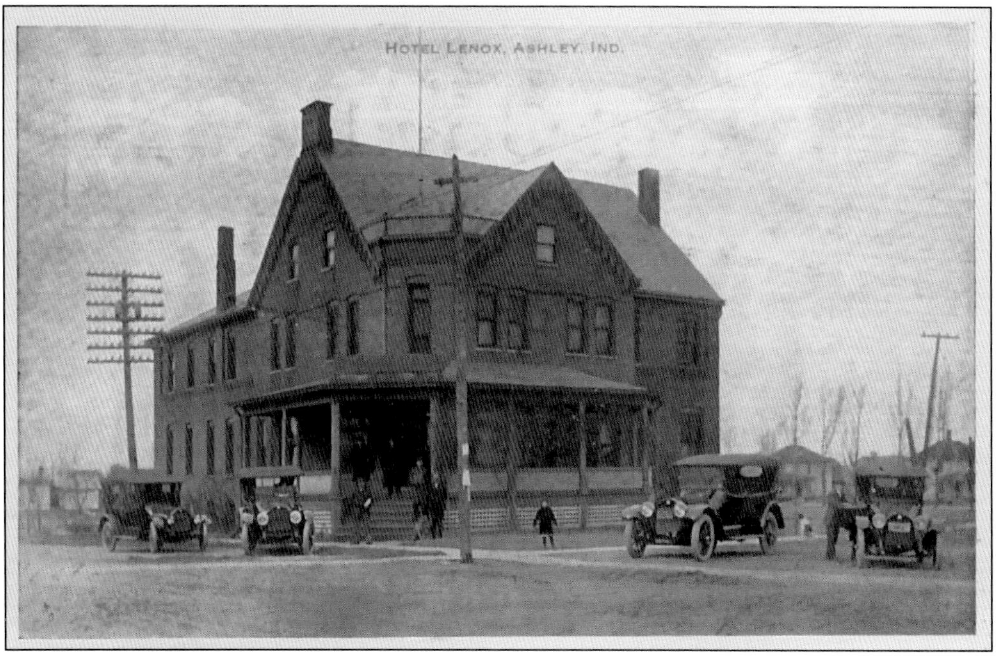

HOTEL LENOX, ASHLEY, INDIANA. The hotel was an impressive building for the small town of Ashley.

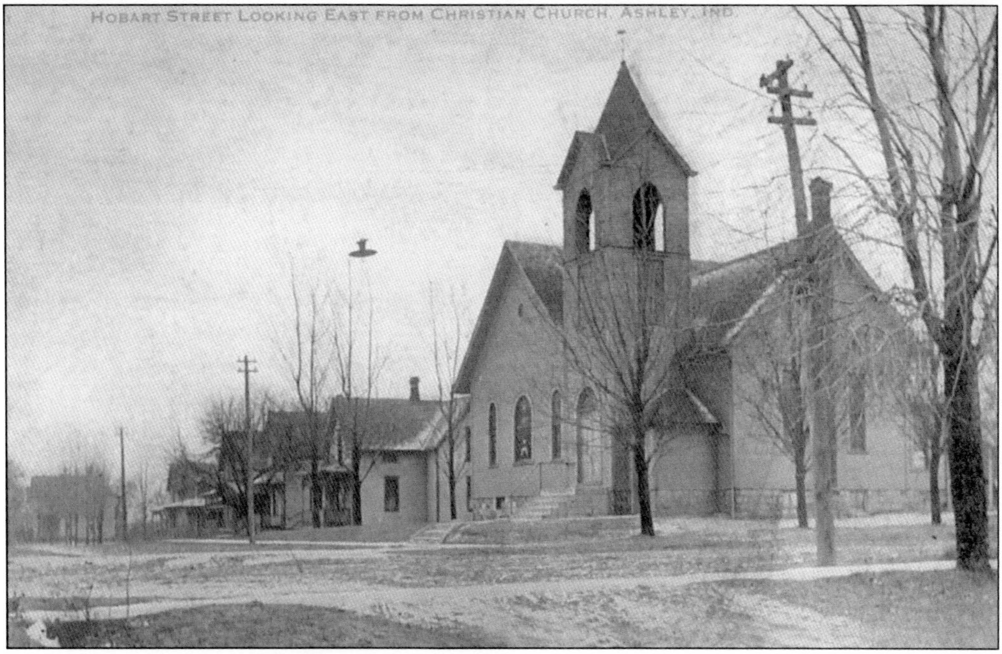

HOBART STREET LOOKING EAST FROM CHRISTIAN CHURCH, ASHLEY, INDIANA. The streets are dirt, but the sidewalks are concrete or stone.

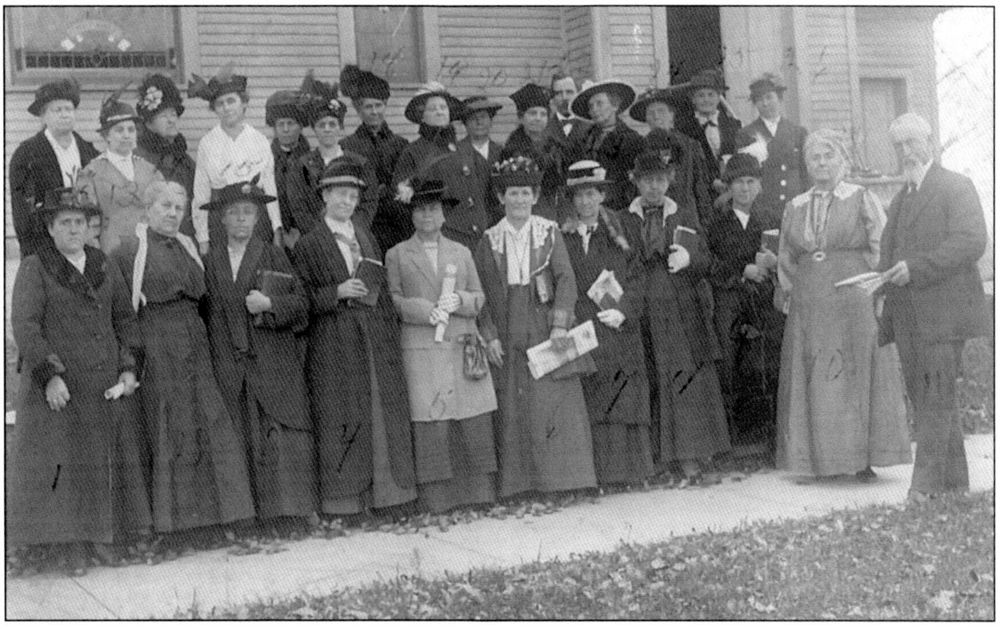

MEMBERS OF THE ASHLEY CHRISTIAN CHURCH. All of the ladies are dressed in their "Sunday Best." The gentleman is probably the minister.

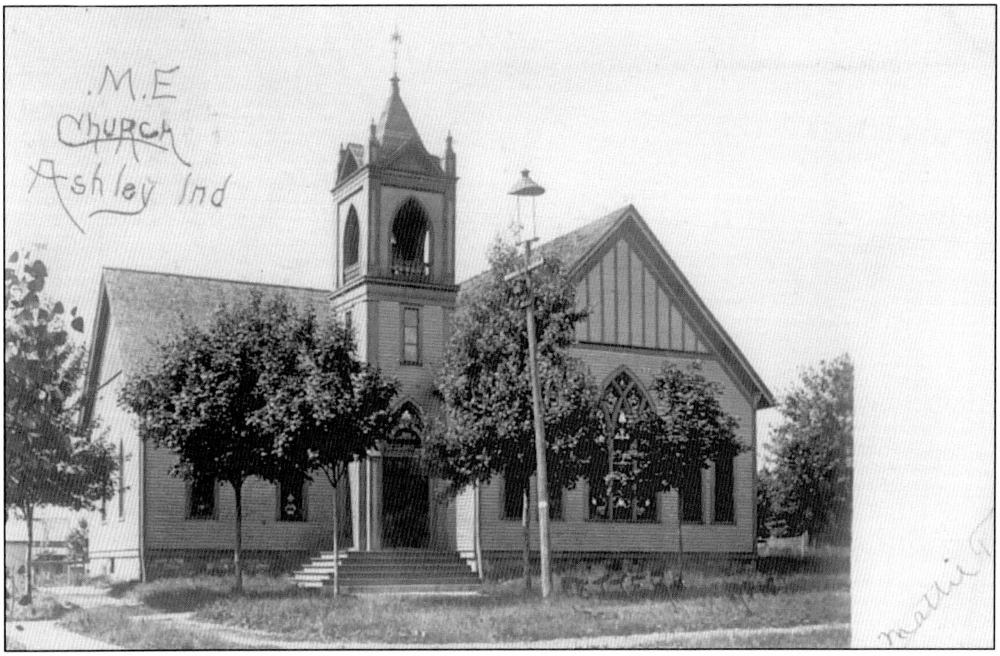

M.E. CHURCH, ASHLEY, INDIANA. M.E. stood for Methodist Episcopal.

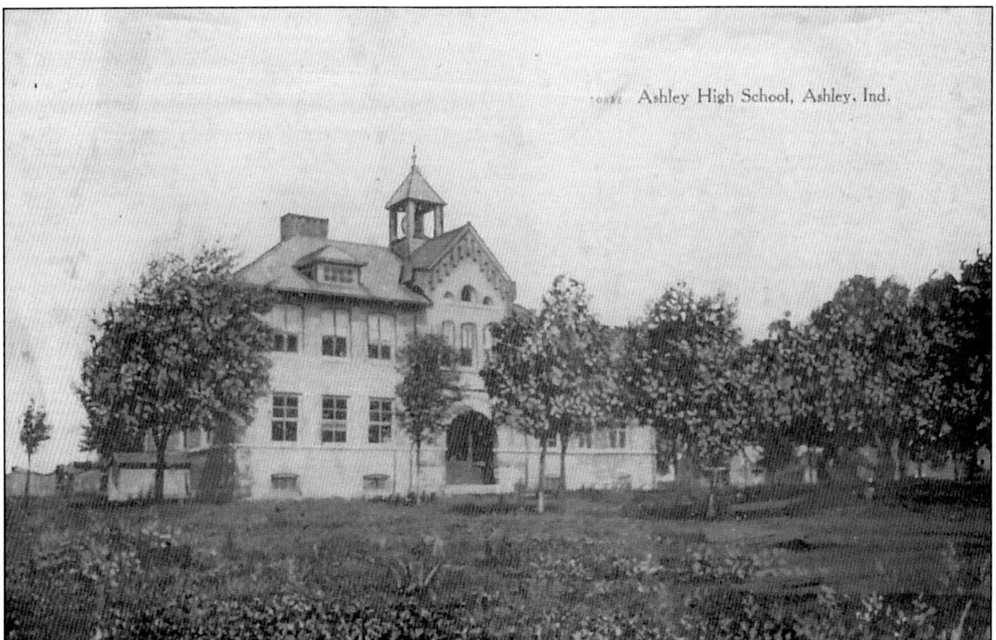

ASHLEY HIGH SCHOOL, ASHLEY, INDIANA. Each town had an impressive school building.

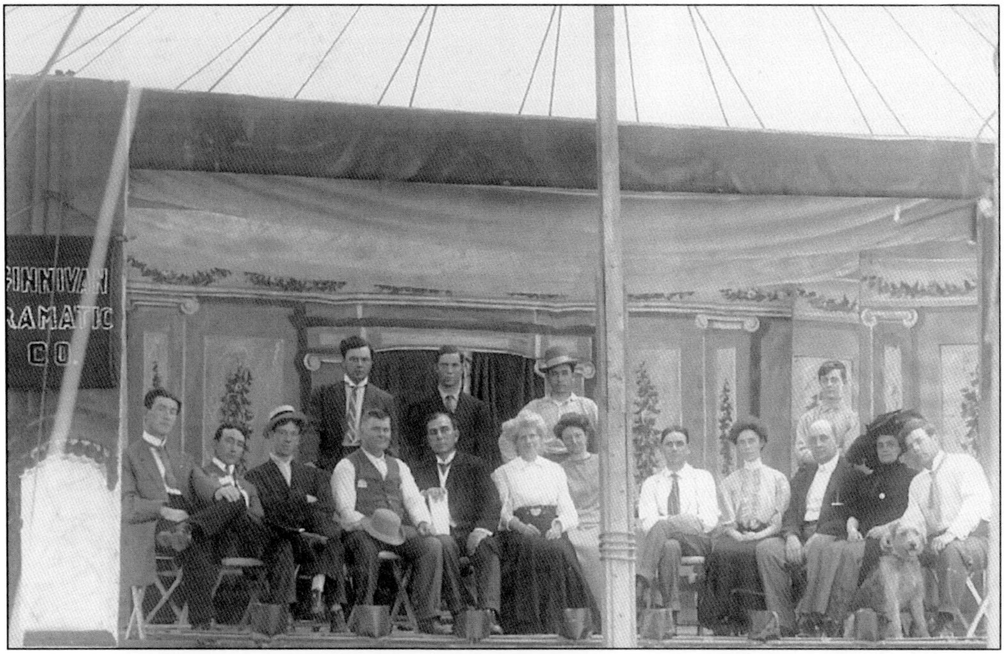

Ginnivan Dramatic Co. The Ginnivan Dramatic Co. was headquartered in Ashley. It traveled the Midwest, putting on dramatic presentations in tents. The postcard is postmarked Edgerton, Ohio, and the message states: "My Dear Grace I did not write you yesterday that is the first I have missed a day the reason is that I could not get a piano here and had to drive back to Butler and that took up the day. I bought a piano of my own love to all. Frank."

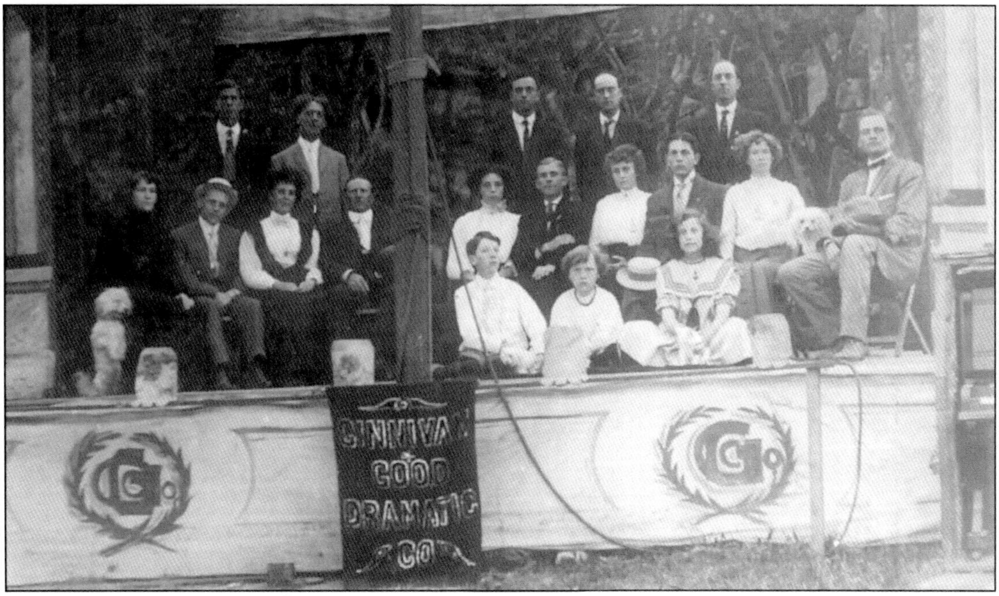

Ginnivan Good Dramatic Co. This was a separate troupe. Note the small dog to the left of the stage. The message states: "My Dear Grace this finds all O.K. bus is fare. Think it will pick up tonight. This is picture of Joes bunch they have had 2 losing weeks. Love to all. and write letters often. Yours Frank."

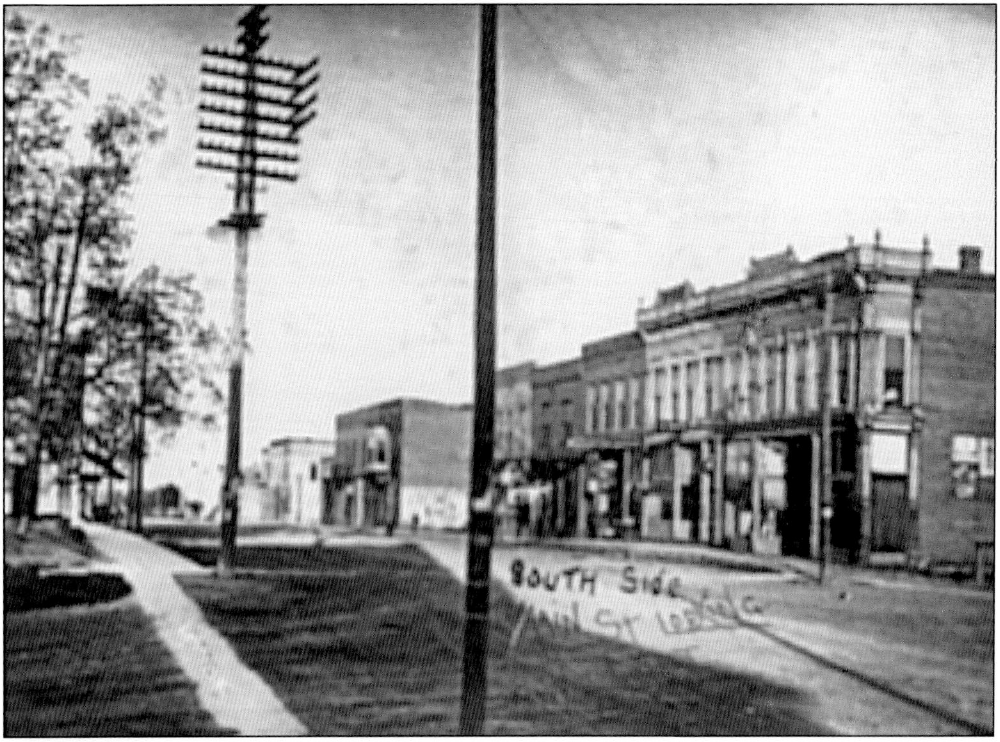

SOUTH SIDE MAIN STREET, ASHLEY, INDIANA.

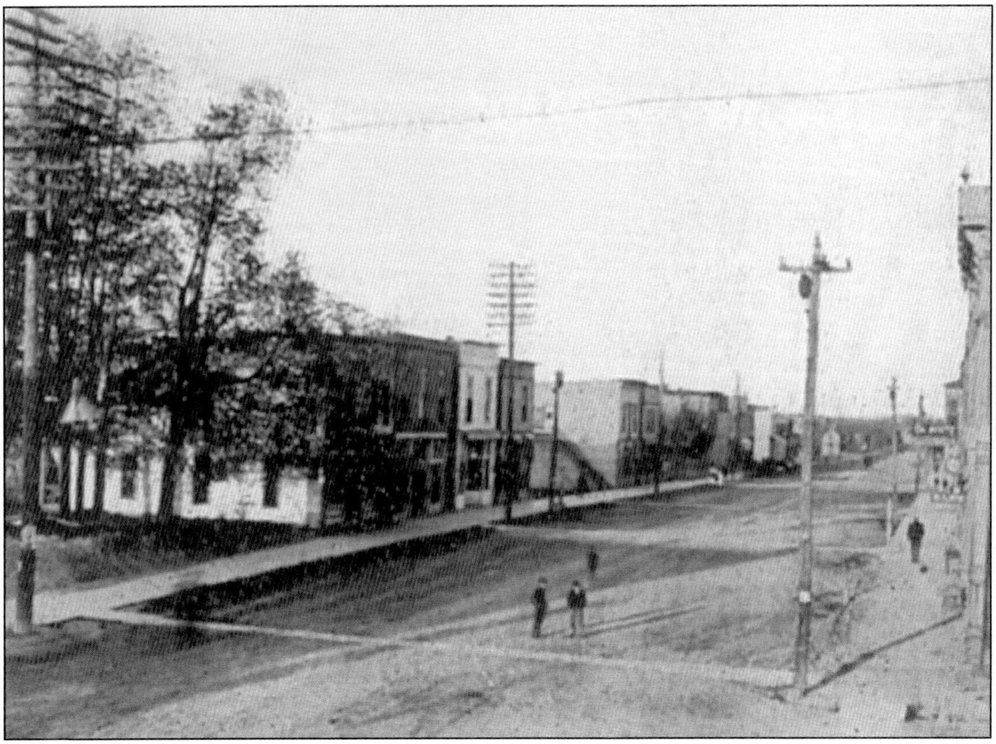

Two

AUBURN

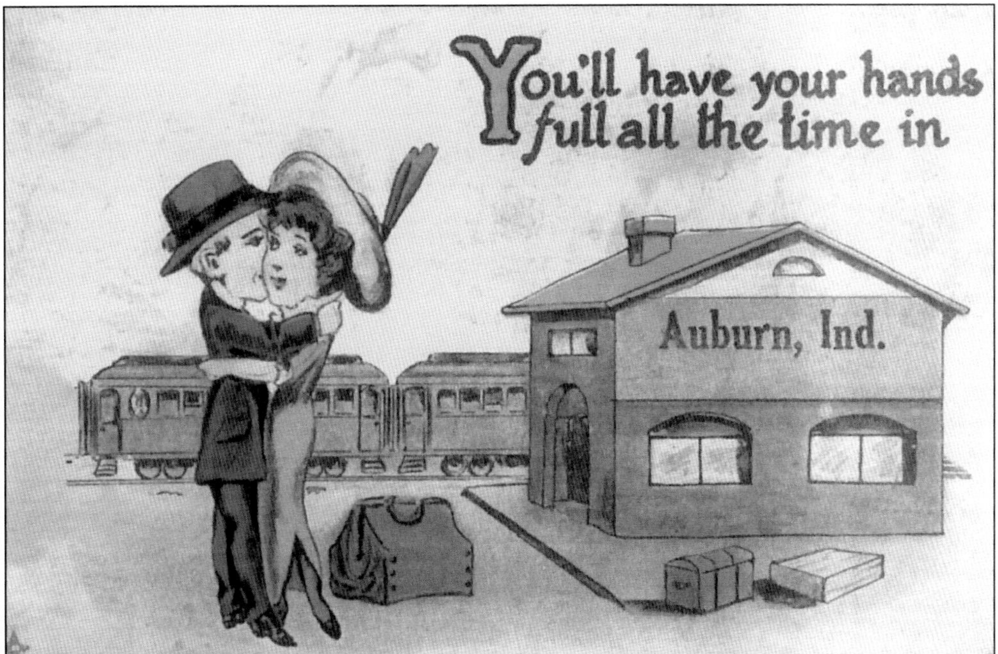

YOU'LL HAVE YOUR HANDS FULL ALL THE TIME IN AUBURN, INDIANA.

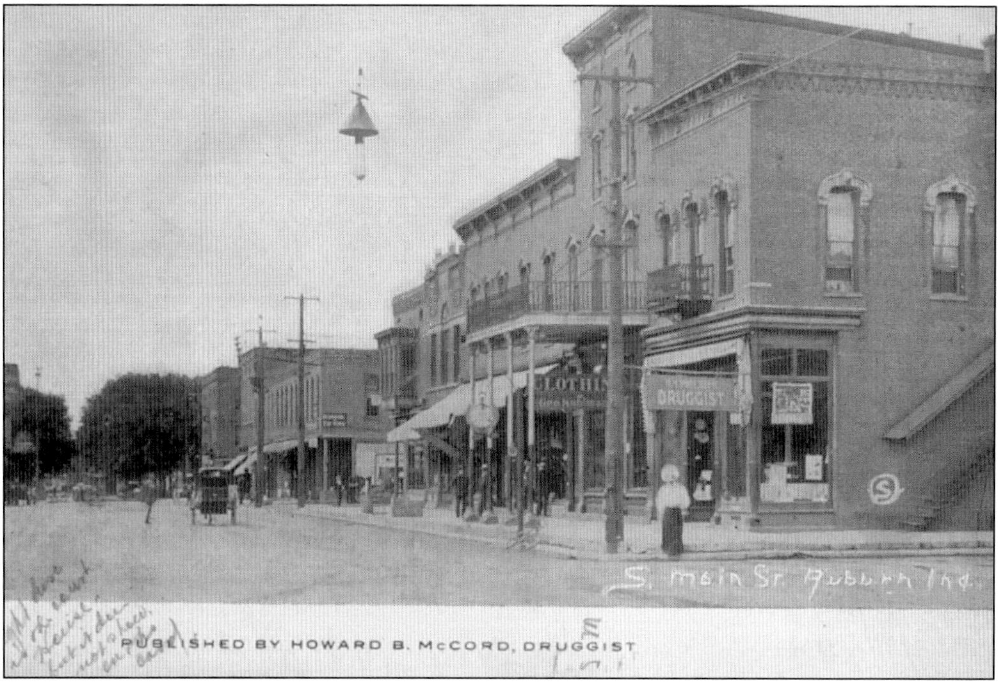

SOUTH MAIN STREET, AUBURN, INDIANA. Shown here is South Main Street looking south from Seventh Street. The signs are "Phillips Druggist" and "Clothing—Geo. Kuhlman."

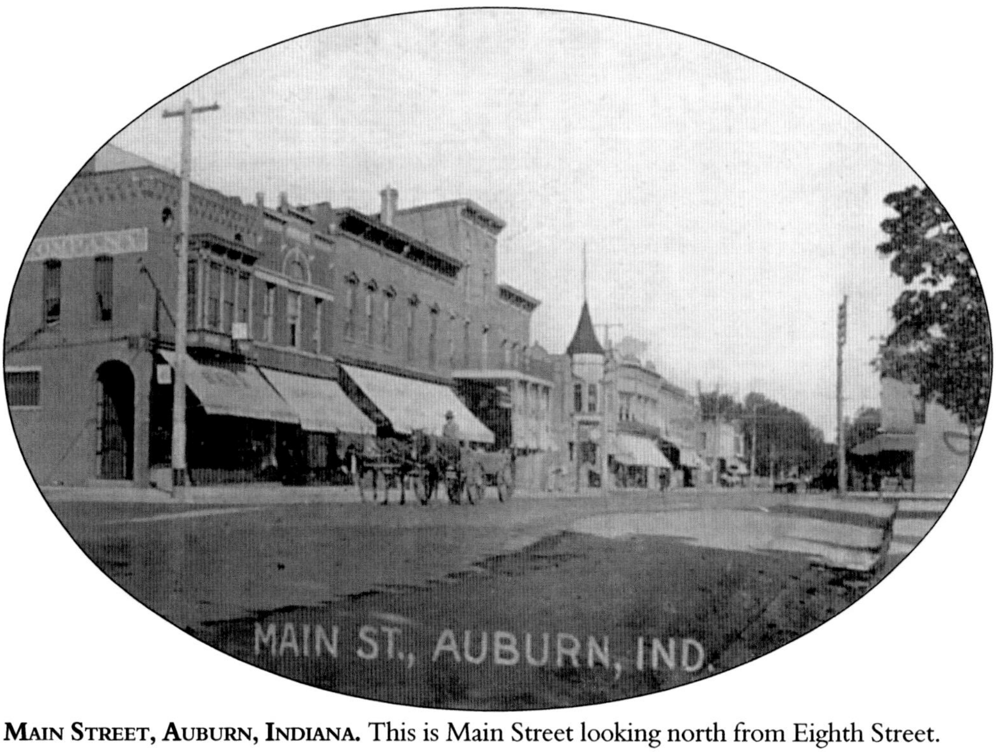

MAIN STREET, AUBURN, INDIANA. This is Main Street looking north from Eighth Street.

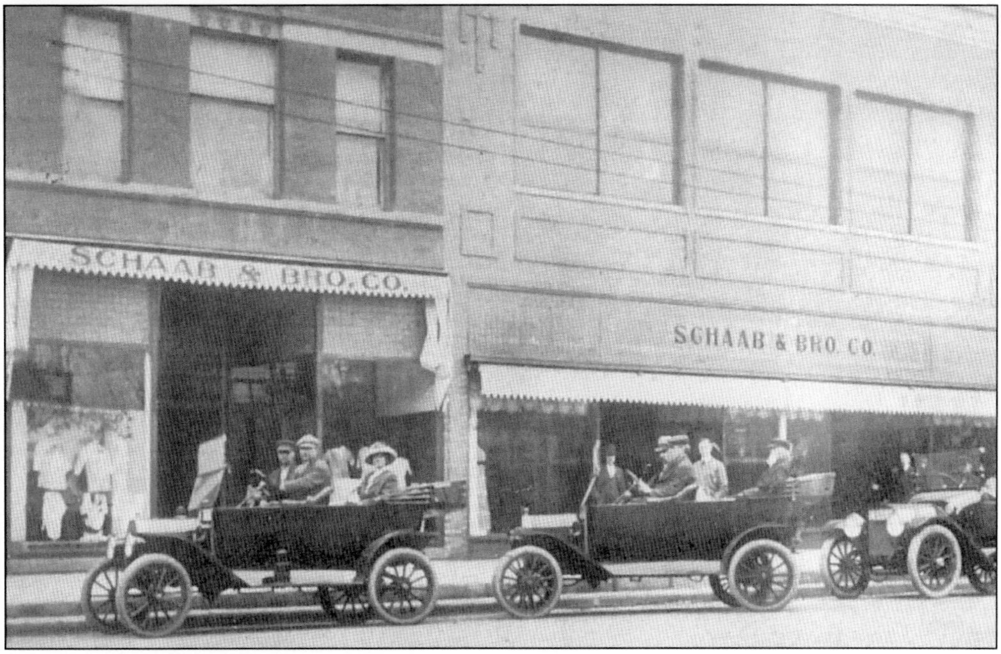

DEPARTMENT STORE, AUBURN, INDIANA. Schaab & Bros. Co. was once Auburn's department store. It would appear that the automobiles are lined up to make a trip together.

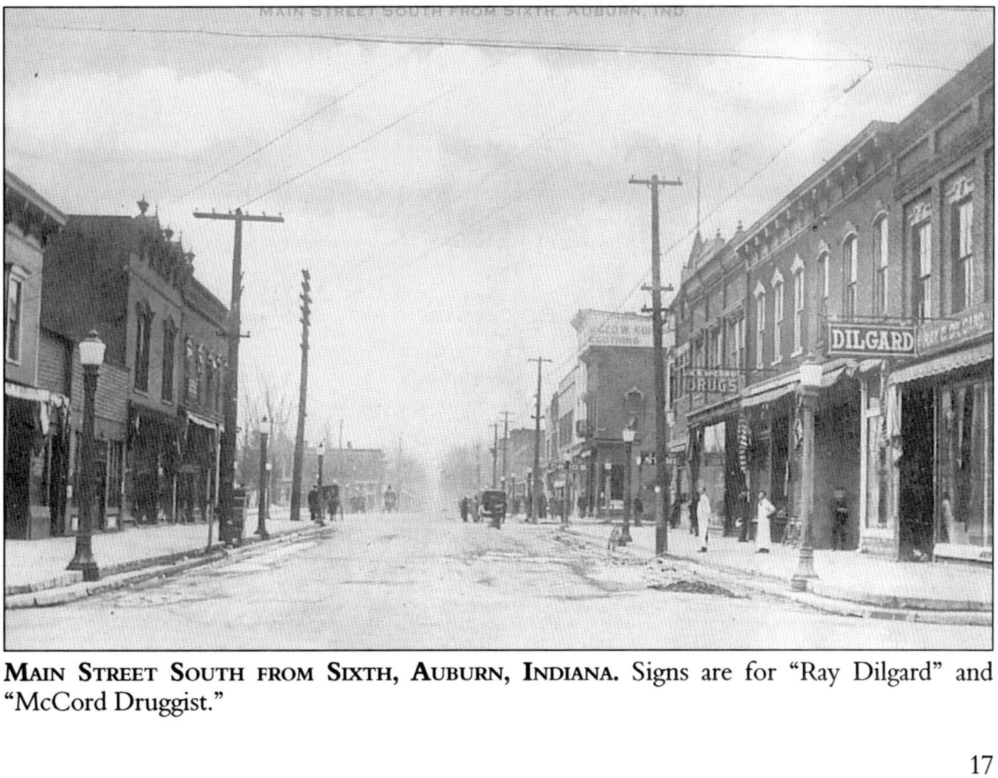

MAIN STREET SOUTH FROM SIXTH, AUBURN, INDIANA. Signs are for "Ray Dilgard" and "McCord Druggist."

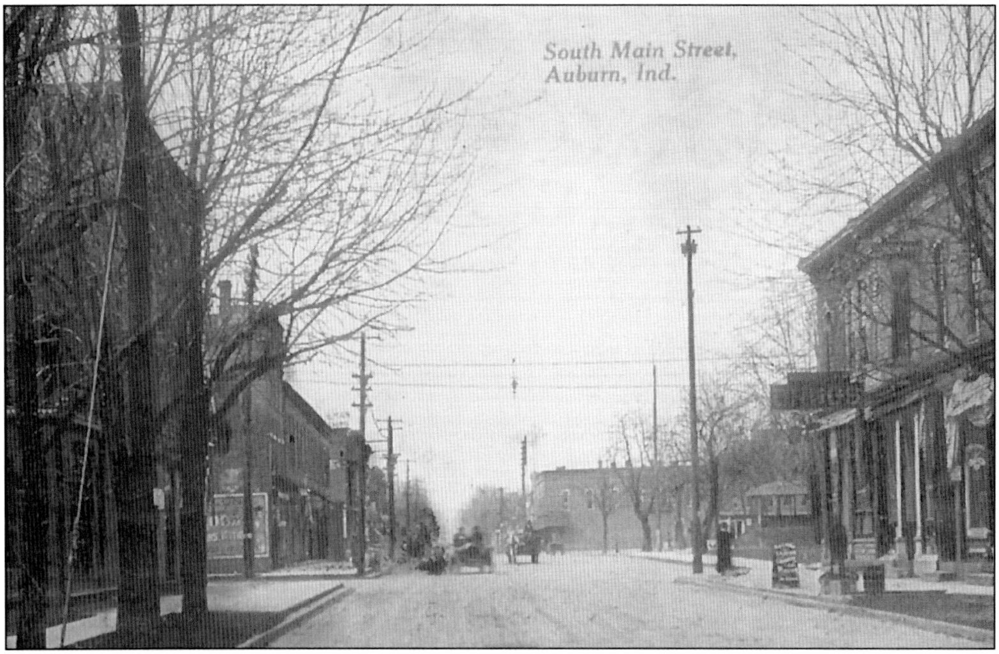

SOUTH MAIN STREET, AUBURN, INDIANA. Shown here is Main Street looking north from Tenth Street. The sign on the right reads, "Drugs."

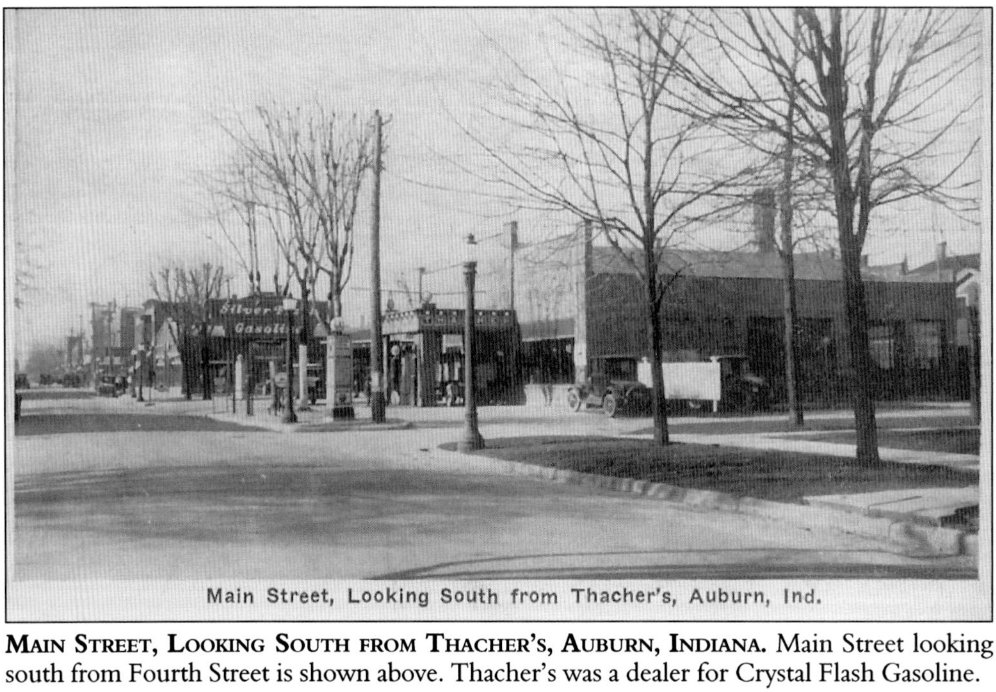

MAIN STREET, LOOKING SOUTH FROM THACHER'S, AUBURN, INDIANA. Main Street looking south from Fourth Street is shown above. Thacher's was a dealer for Crystal Flash Gasoline.

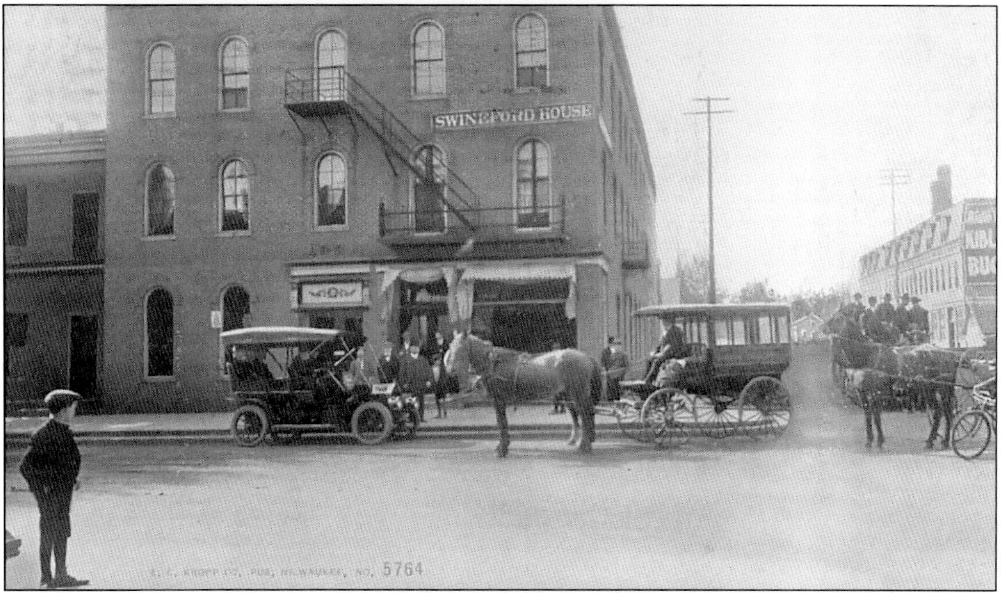

SWINEFORD HOUSE, AUBURN, INDIANA. The Swineford House was at the southwest corner of South Main and Ninth Streets. It was later remodeled and became the Auburn Hotel. The horse-drawn hack brought railroad passengers from the railroad depots at Auburn Junction and West Seventh Street to the hotel. An Auburn Touring car is on the left, and a Kiblinger/McIntyre nine-passenger "bus" is heading east on Ninth Street. A horse and buggy complete the scene. The factory on the right was the Kiblinger/McIntyre buggy and automobile company.

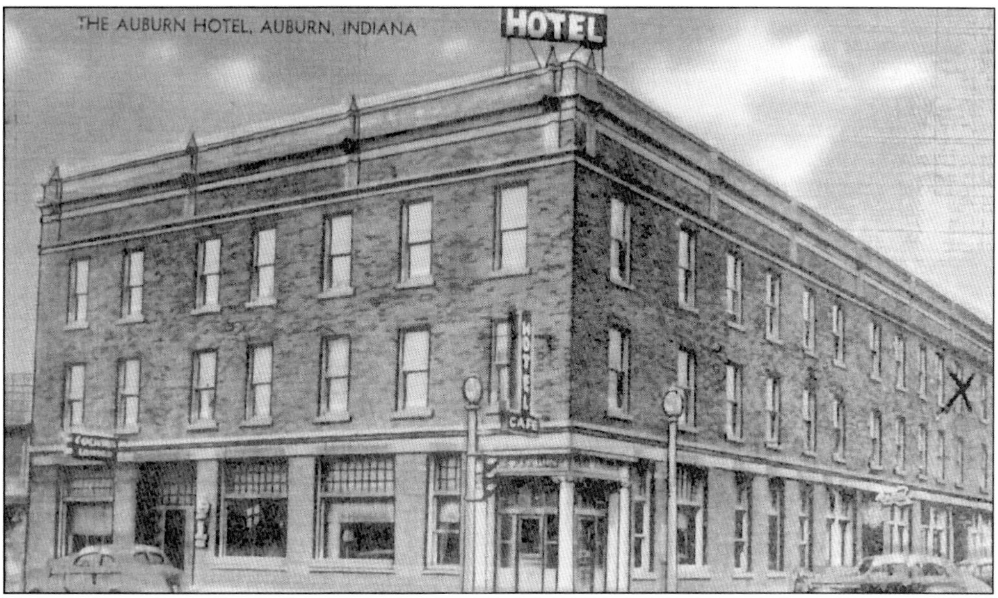

THE AUBURN HOTEL, AUBURN, INDIANA. After remodeling in the 1920s, the Auburn Hotel was one of the finest. This message states: "Hello Sweetheart—how is my little girl. I said I would send you a card so here it is. I will be home this weekend. X is window in my room. Love Daddy."

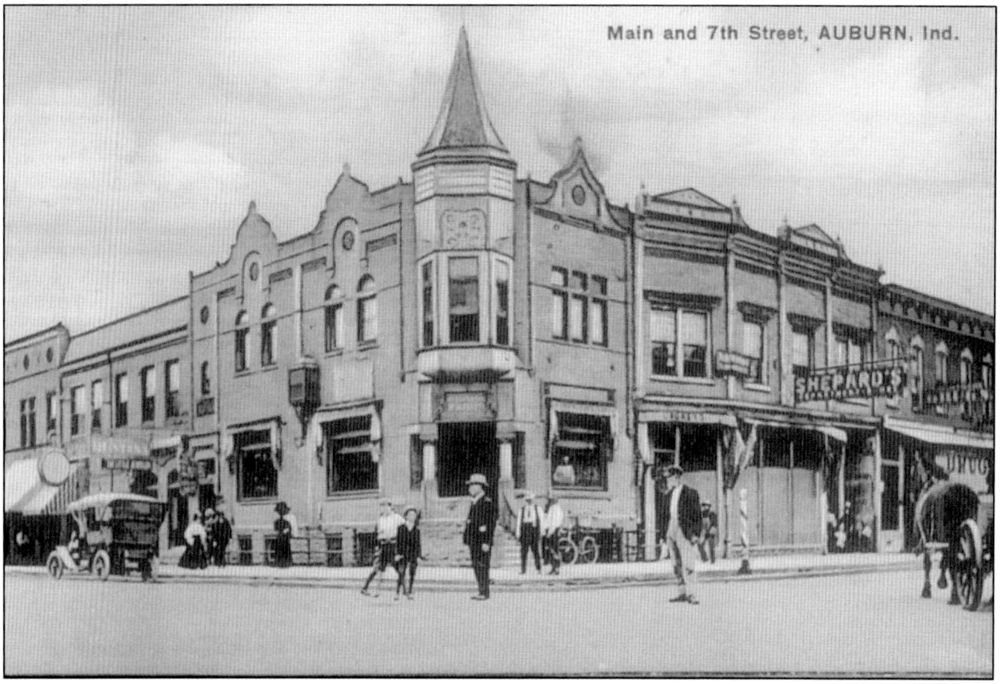

Main and Seventh Street, Auburn, Indiana. This is the northwest corner of Main and Seventh Streets. The ornate bank was the focal point of the principal intersection in Auburn. Shepard's Department Store is on the right. The box between the bank windows on the left was an alarm that could be sounded in the event of a robbery.

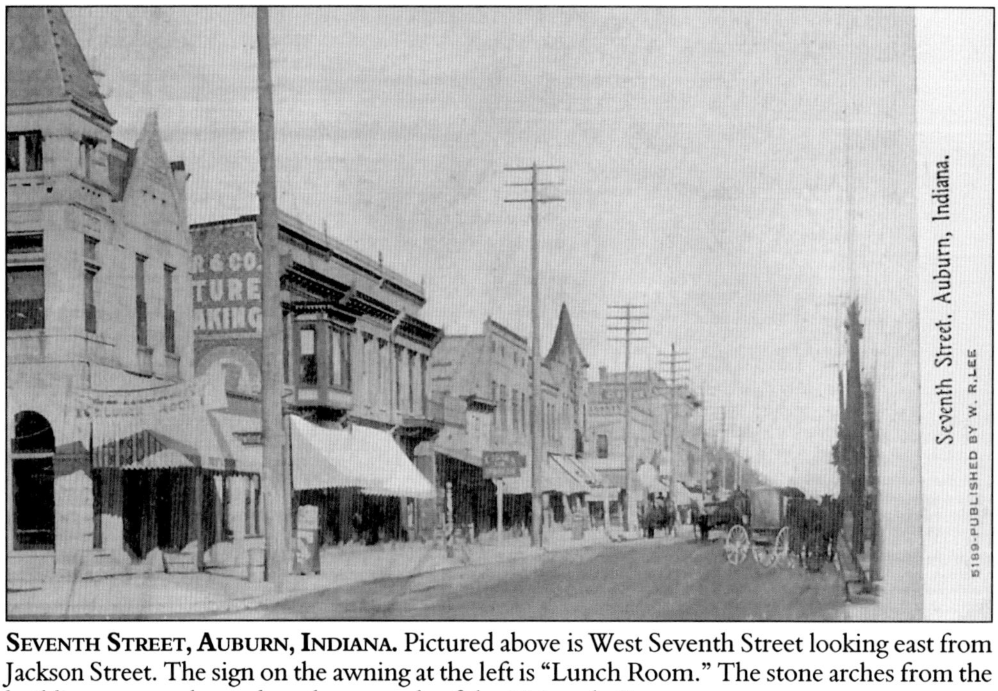

Seventh Street, Auburn, Indiana. Pictured above is West Seventh Street looking east from Jackson Street. The sign on the awning at the left is "Lunch Room." The stone arches from the building are now located on the grounds of the Heimach Center.

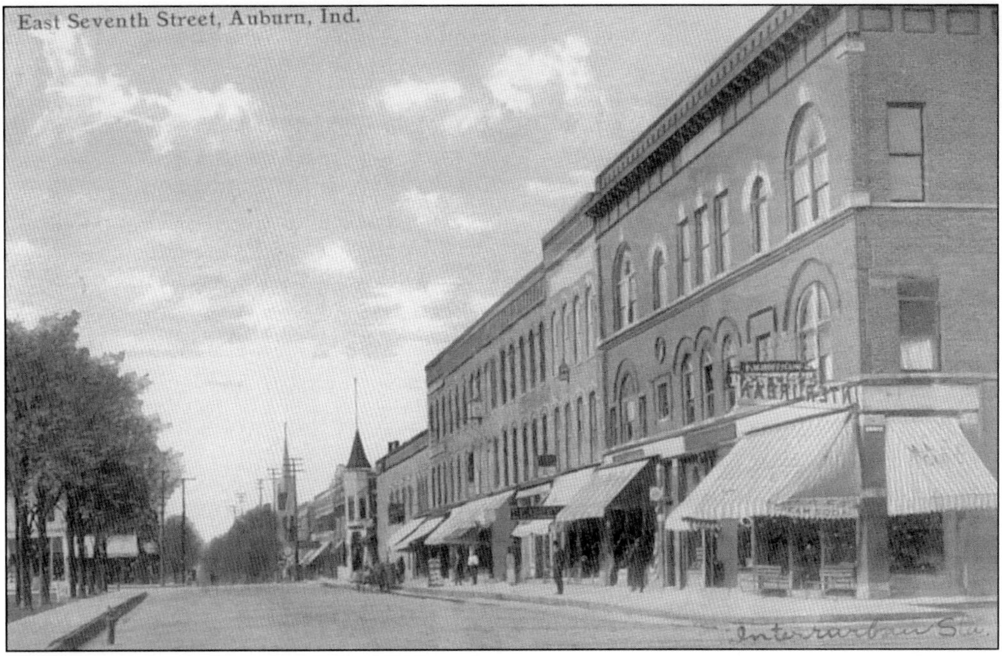

East Seventh Street, Auburn, Indiana. This is a view of East Seventh Street looking west from Cedar Street.

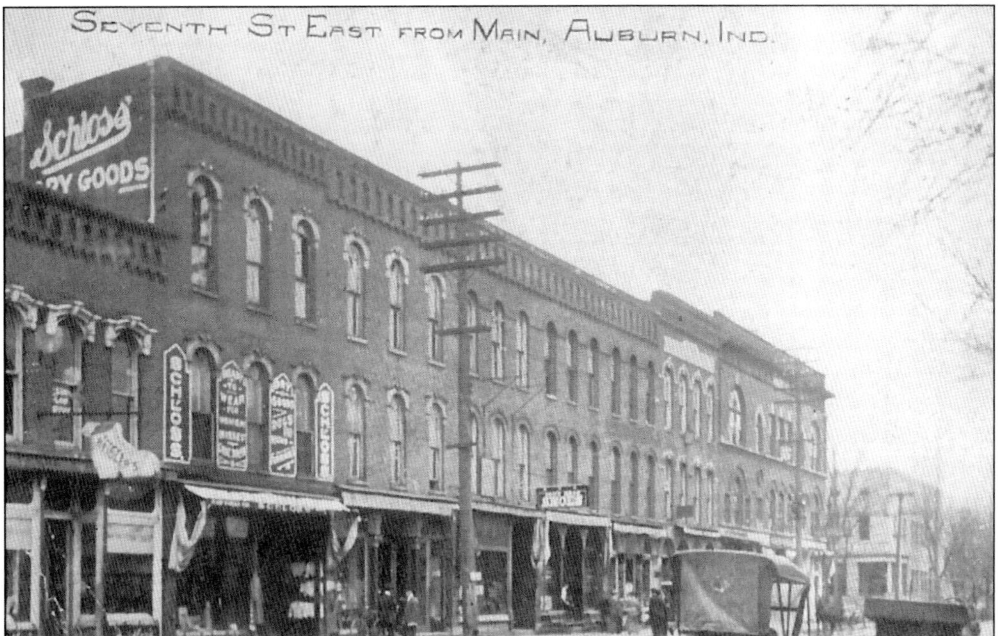

Seventh Street East from Main, Auburn, Indiana. This is East Seventh Street looking east from Main Street. The signs are on Schlos's Dry Goods Store.

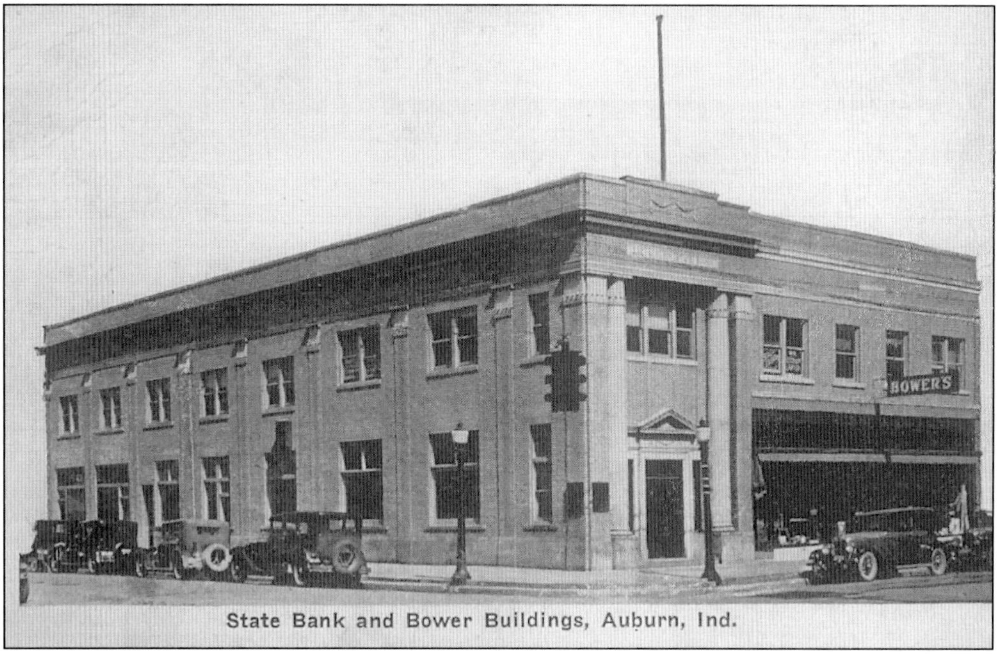

STATE BANK AND BOWER BUILDINGS, AUBURN, INDIANA. The Auburn State Bank replaced the former building. Bower's was a five and dime store.

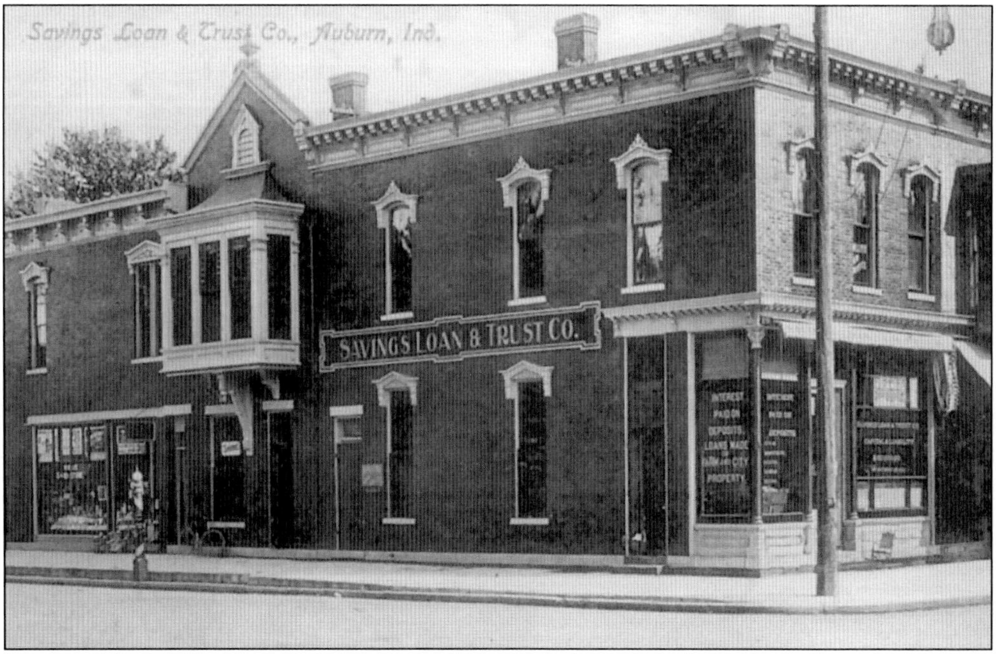

SAVINGS LOAN & TRUST CO., AUBURN, INDIANA. The signs on the windows are "Interest Paid on Deposits—Loans Made on Farm & City Property."

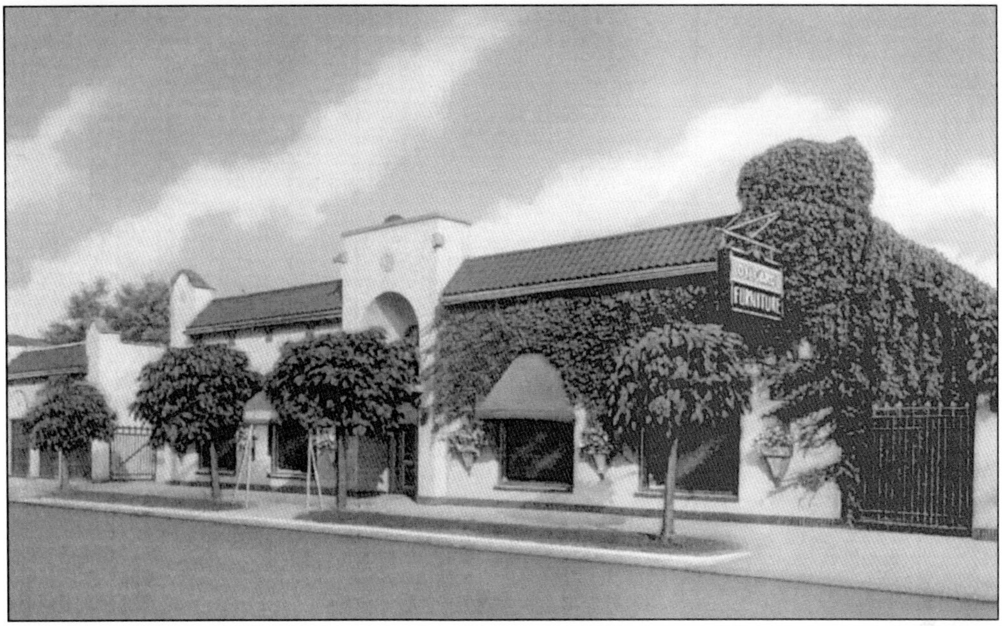

Dilgard & Cline Furniture. They claimed to be the finest furniture store in Indiana. The company was established in 1904. This store was a place where the customer is always right.

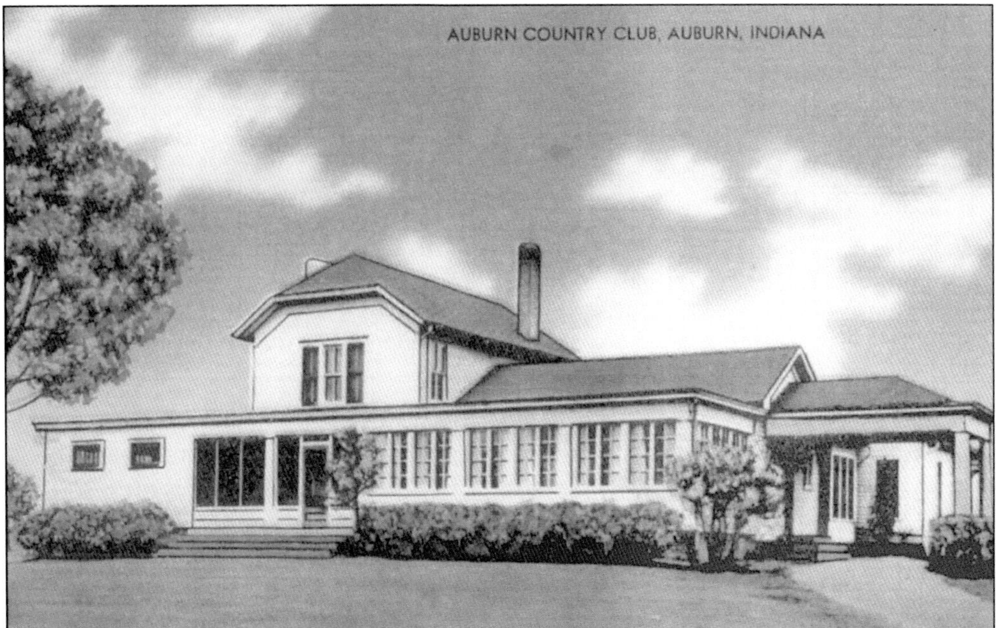

Auburn Country Club, Auburn, Indiana. Also known as Greenhurst Country Club, the golf course was located on the former Greenhurst Farm of Egbert Mott, who was the first judge of the DeKalb Court.

ECKHART PUBLIC LIBRARY, AUBURN, INDIANA. The library was built and endowed by funds provided by Charles Eckhart, who was the founder of the Eckhart Carriage Company.

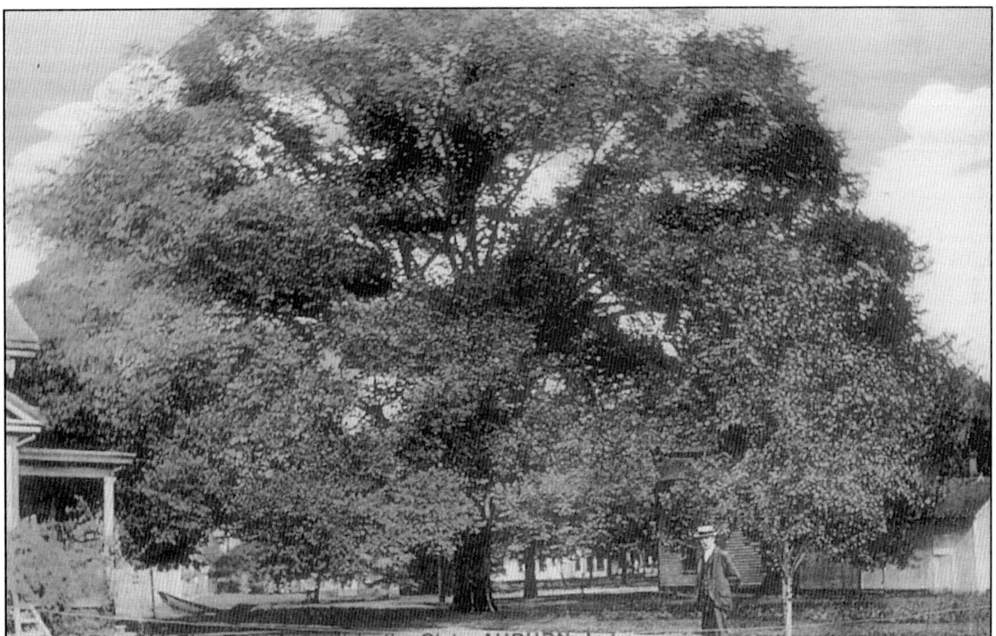

THE OLD ELM TREE, LARGEST IN THE STATE, AUBURN, INDIANA. The large elm tree was located in the middle of Thirteenth Street between South Main and South Jackson Streets.

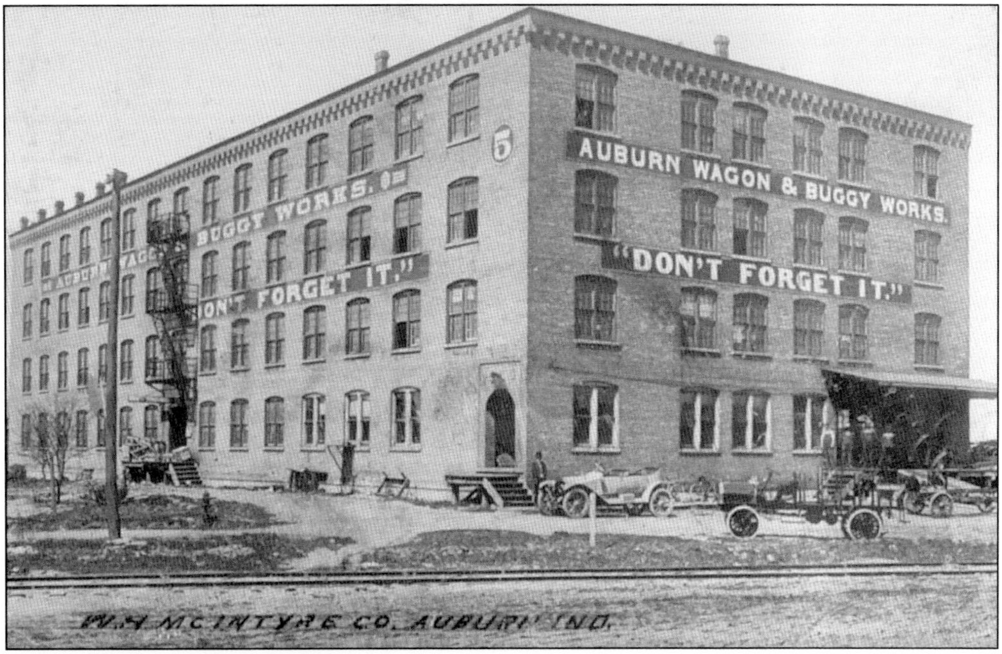

W.H. McIntyre Co., Auburn, Indiana. Located on West Seventh Street west of the Fort Wayne and Jackson Railroad, the W.H. McIntyre Company Building #5 formerly housed the Auburn Wagon & Buggy Works.

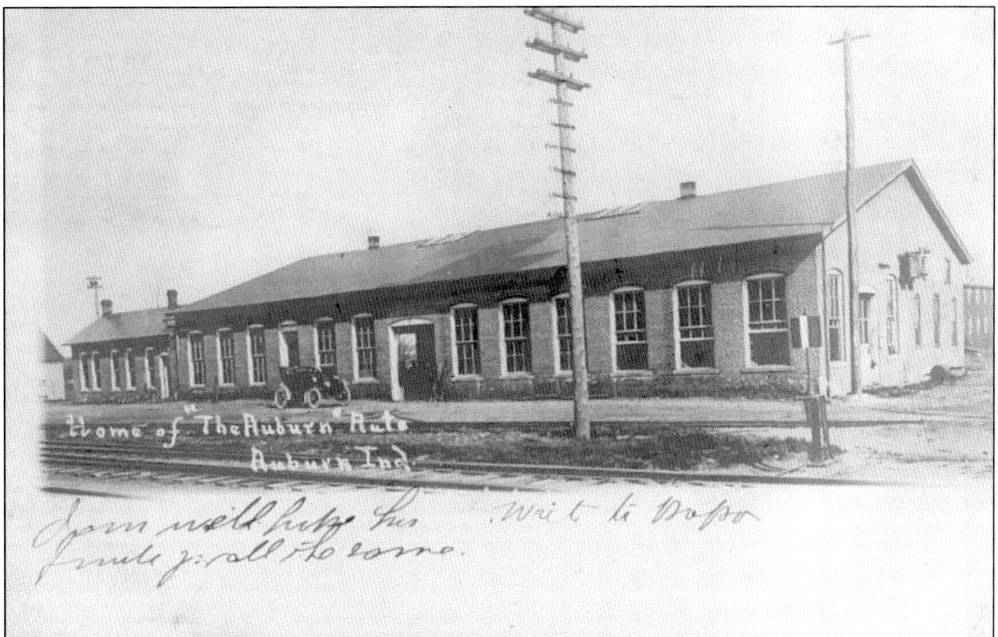

Home of "The Auburn" Auto, Auburn, Indiana. The original building of the Auburn Automobile Company was located along the Vandalia Railroad at the south end of Main Street. An early Auburn car is adjacent to the building.

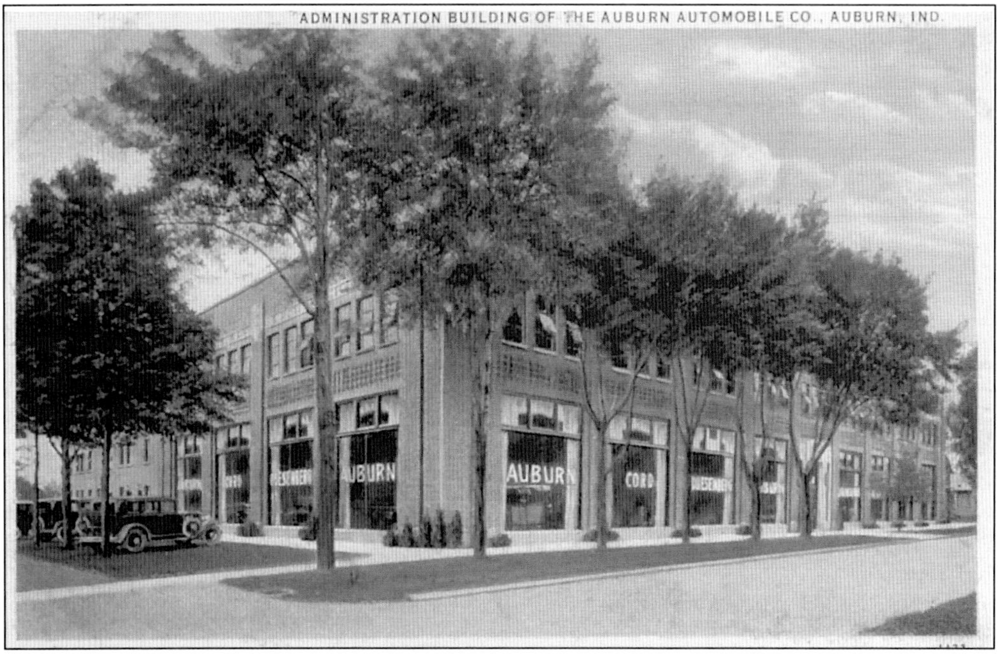

ADMINISTRATION BUILDING OF THE AUBURN AUTOMOBILE CO., AUBURN, IND. Several new Auburns are parked next to the Art Deco building.

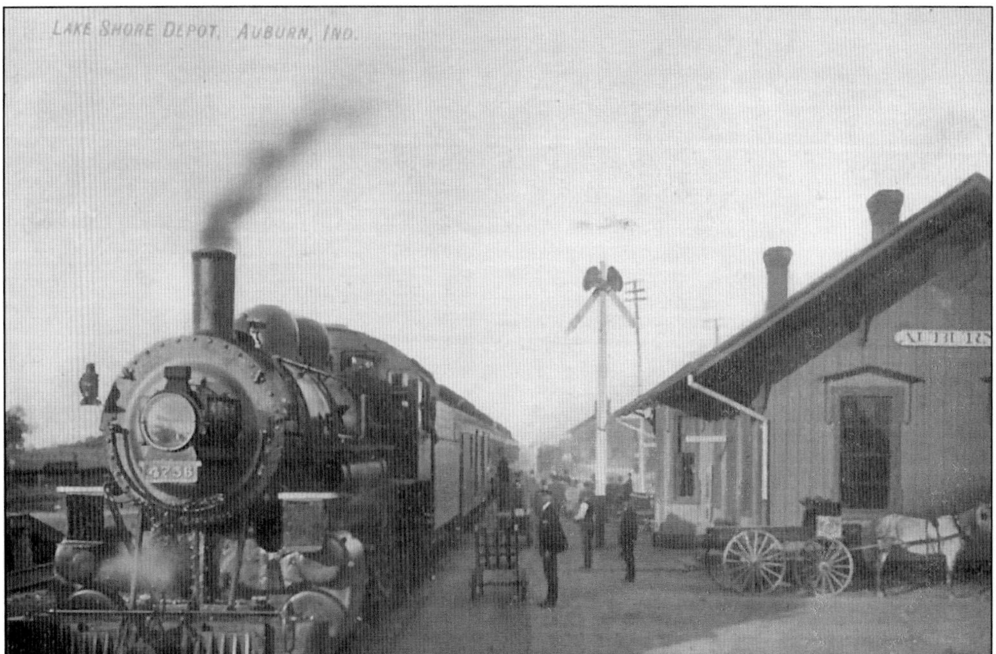

LAKE SHORE DEPOT, AUBURN, INDIANA. The name "Lakeshore" is from the Lakeshore and Michigan Southern Railroad. The depot was located on the north side of West Seventh Street.

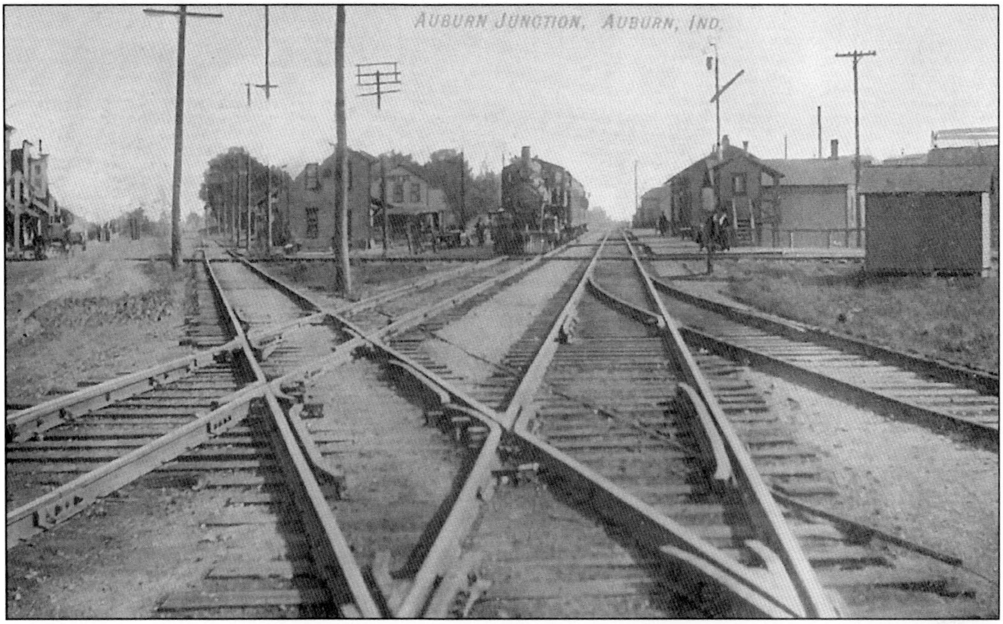

Auburn Junction, Auburn, Indiana. The Baltimore and Ohio, Vandalia and Fort Wayne, and Jackson Railroads intersected at Auburn Junction. The interurban tracks also crossed at this point. There were several stores at Auburn Junction. Rail passengers were taken to downtown Auburn by the horse-drawn hack shown below.

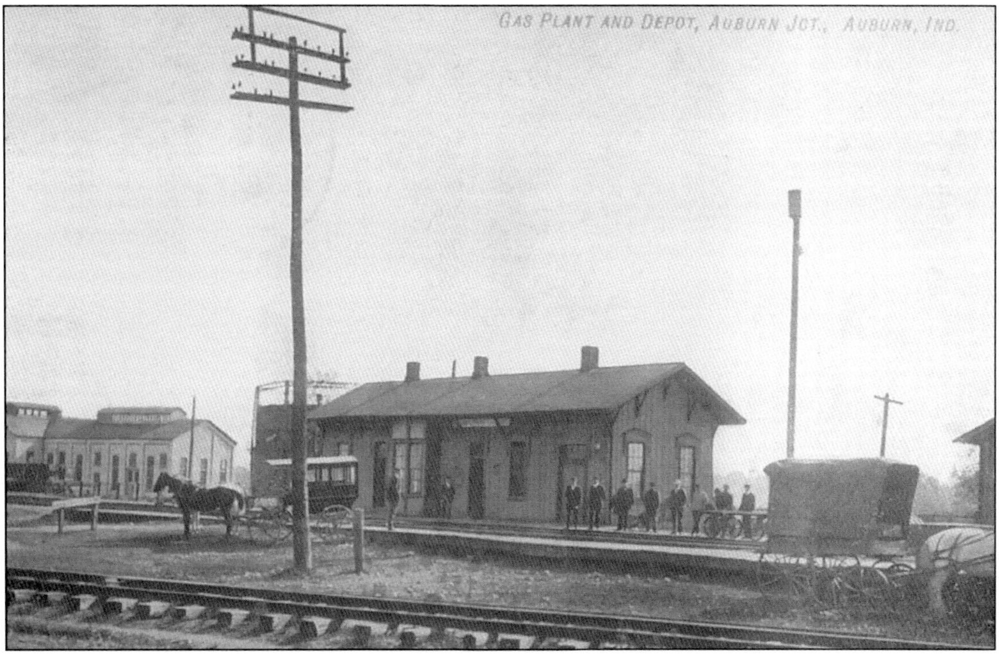

Gas Plant and Depot, Auburn Junction, Auburn, Indiana. The "Union Depot" was built by the B&O Railroad but served all of the railroads. It has been moved several times and is now restored and located at the northwest corner of Fifteenth and Union Streets. The gas company made gas from a coal process.

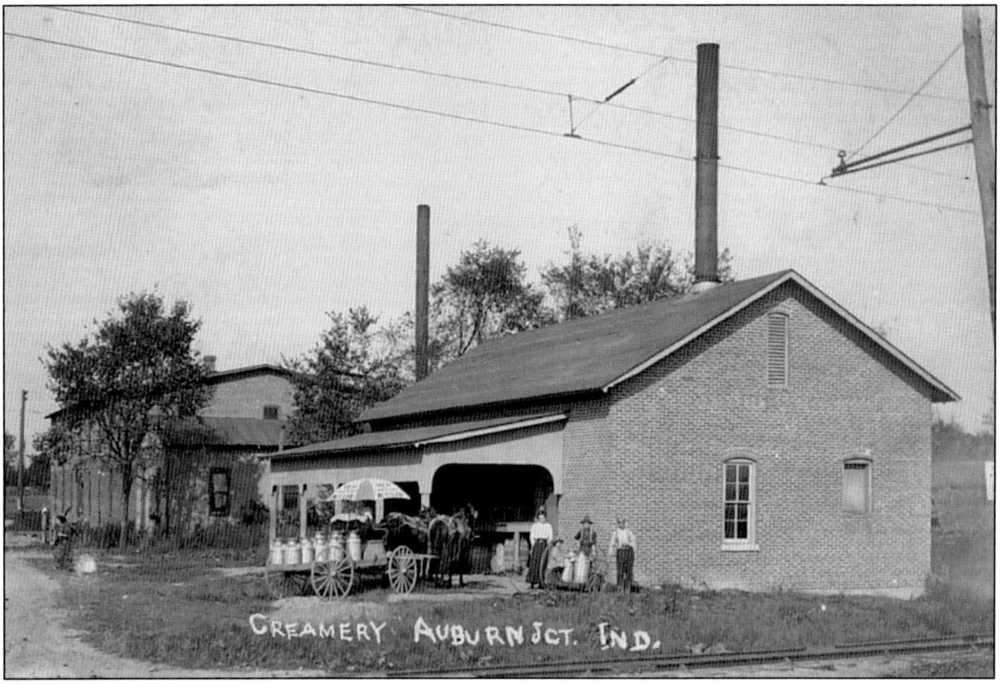

Creamery, Auburn Junction, Indiana. Farmers brought cans of cream to be shipped on the railroads. The sauerkraut factory is on the left.

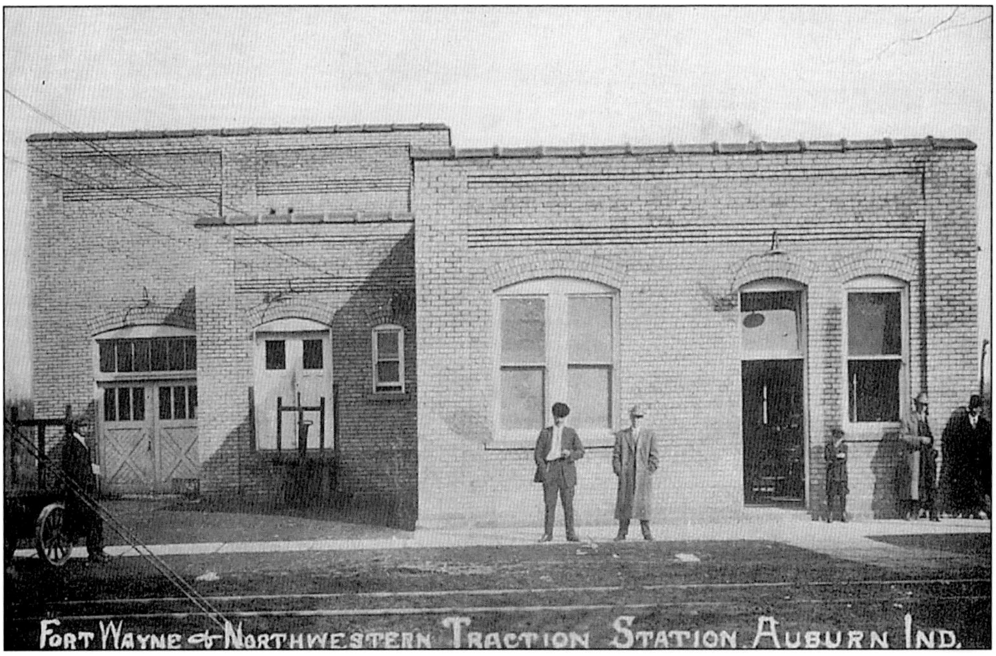

Fort Wayne—Northwestern Traction Station, Auburn, Indiana. This building, located at the northeast corner of South Cedar and East Twelfth Streets, was a station, freight house, and generating station for the interurban line.

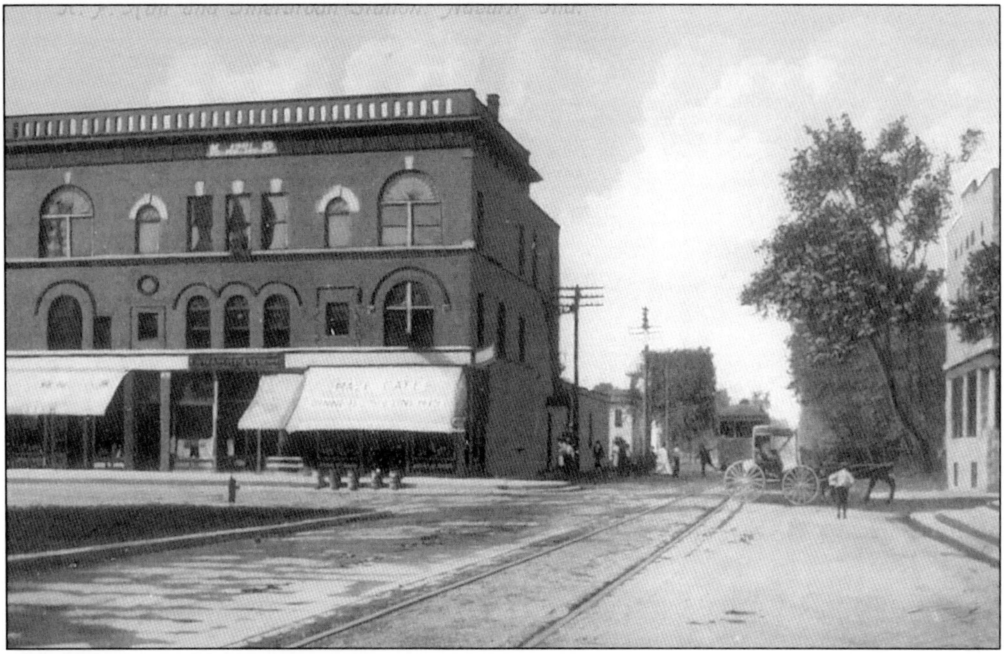

K.P. Hall and Interurban Station, Auburn, Indiana. The interurban tracks were laid down the middle of the dirt Cedar Street at East Seventh Street. The awning sign reads "Maze Café—Dinners & Lunches."

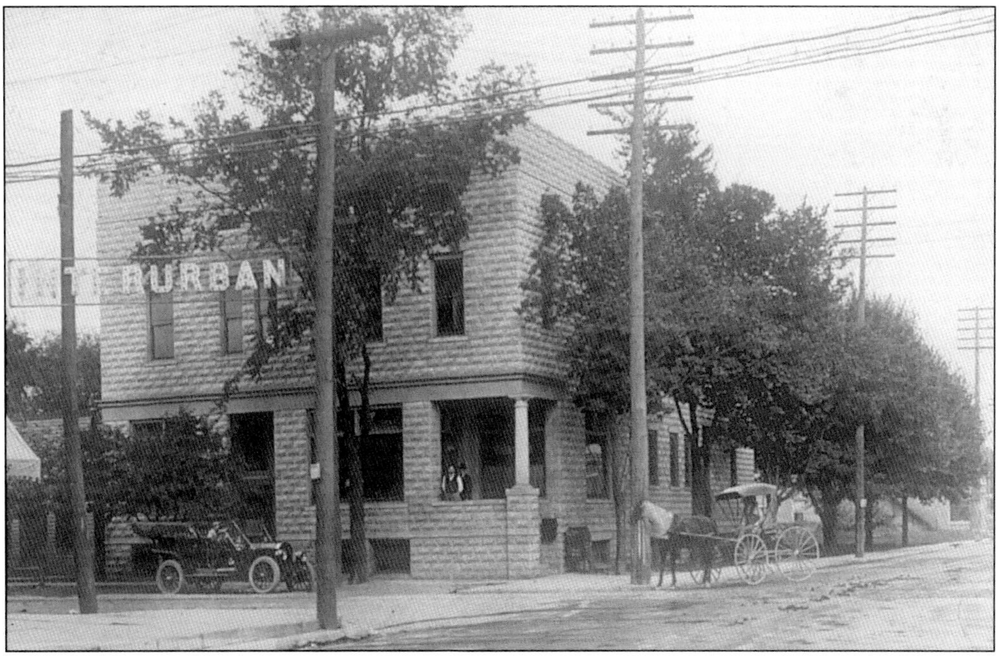

Post Office, Auburn, Indiana. The interurban station was a prominent place. This building is the Auburn Post Office.

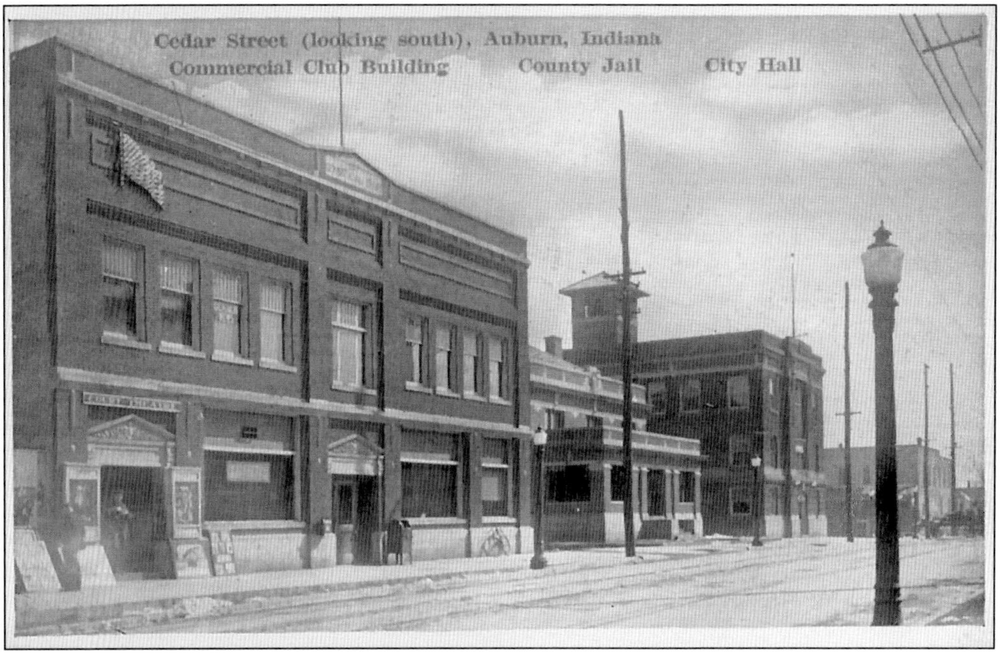

Cedar Street (looking south) Auburn, Indiana. Commercial Club Building, County Jail, City Hall. The east side of the square featured three handsome buildings. The Court Theatre was located in the Commercial Club Building.

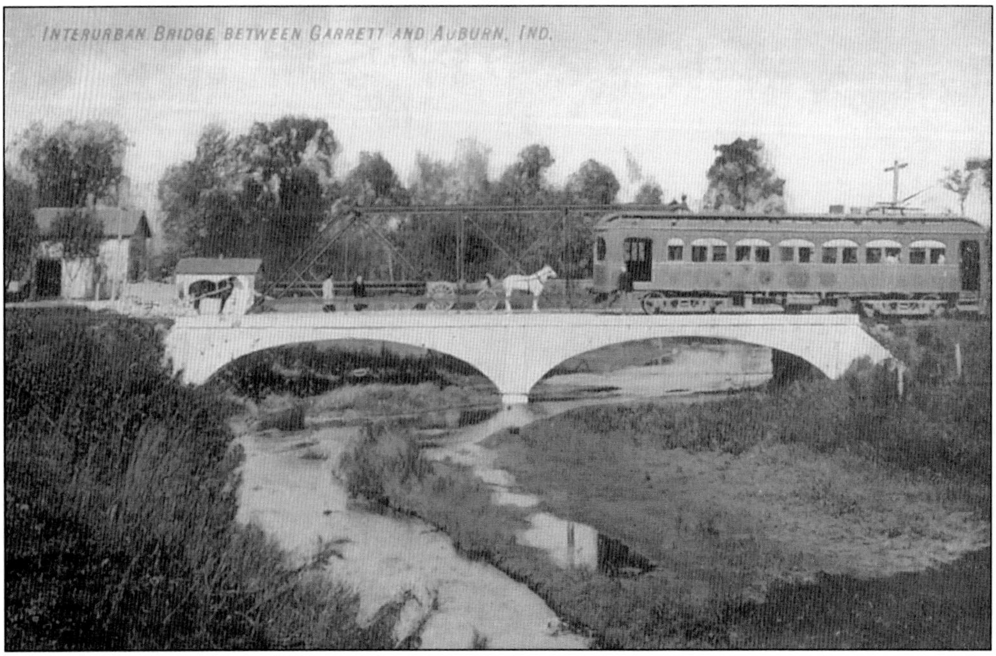

Interurban Bridge Between Garrett and Auburn, Indiana. The interurban was a single electrically powered "car," which hauled passengers and light freight.

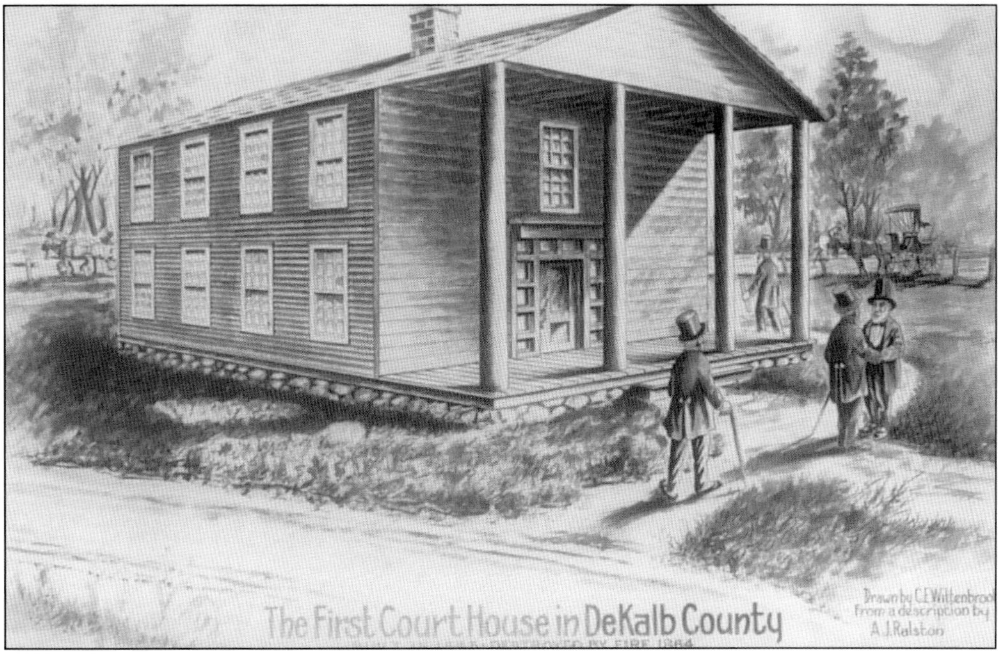

The First Courthouse in DeKalb County; Built in 1843—Destroyed by Fire in 1864. The first courthouse was a classical structure located on the square. The courtroom occupied the entire second story. Other offices were located on the ground floor. As they outgrew the space, small buildings were built along the west side of the square to house the various offices.

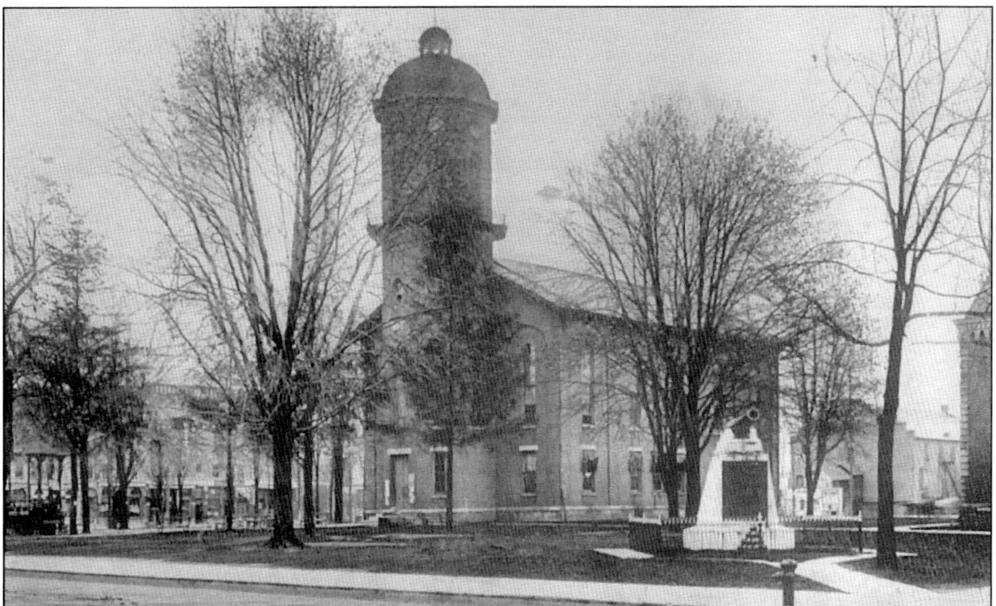

DeKalb County Courthouse, Auburn, Indiana. The second courthouse faces west. The cannon and jail are to the right.

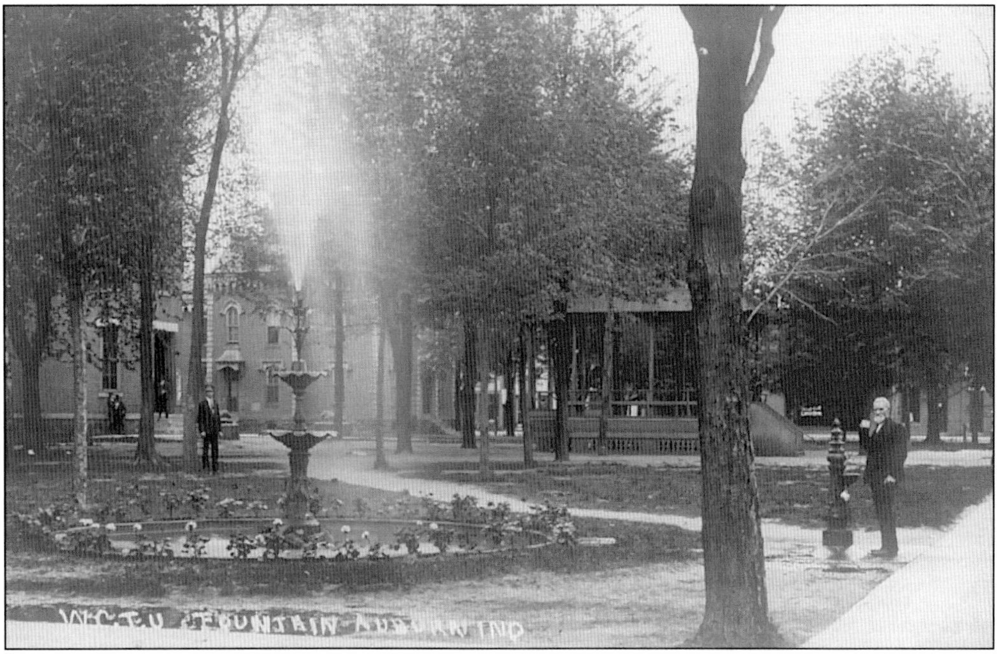

W.C.T.U. WATER FOUNTAIN. "W.C.T.U." stood for "Women's Christian Temperance Union." The fountain is in the foreground. A distinguished gentleman is getting a drink of water from a tin cup at the public drinking fountain. The bandstand is in the background, and the jail and courthouse are in the left background.

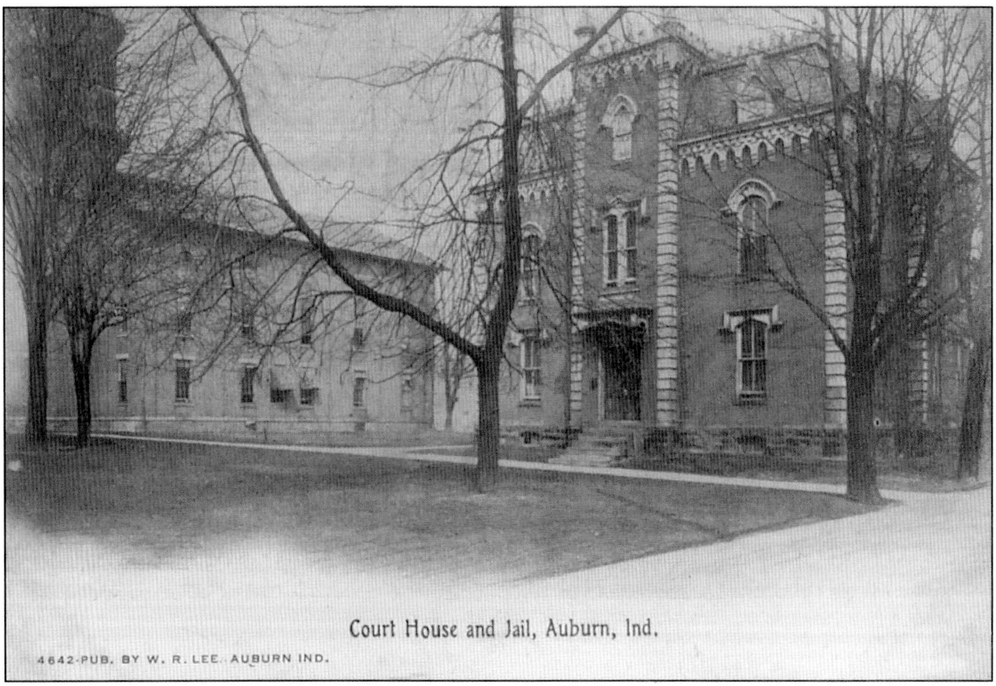

COURTHOUSE AND JAIL, AUBURN, INDIANA. The jail and sheriff's residence was an elaborate Italianate structure. There was a public toilet directly behind the jail.

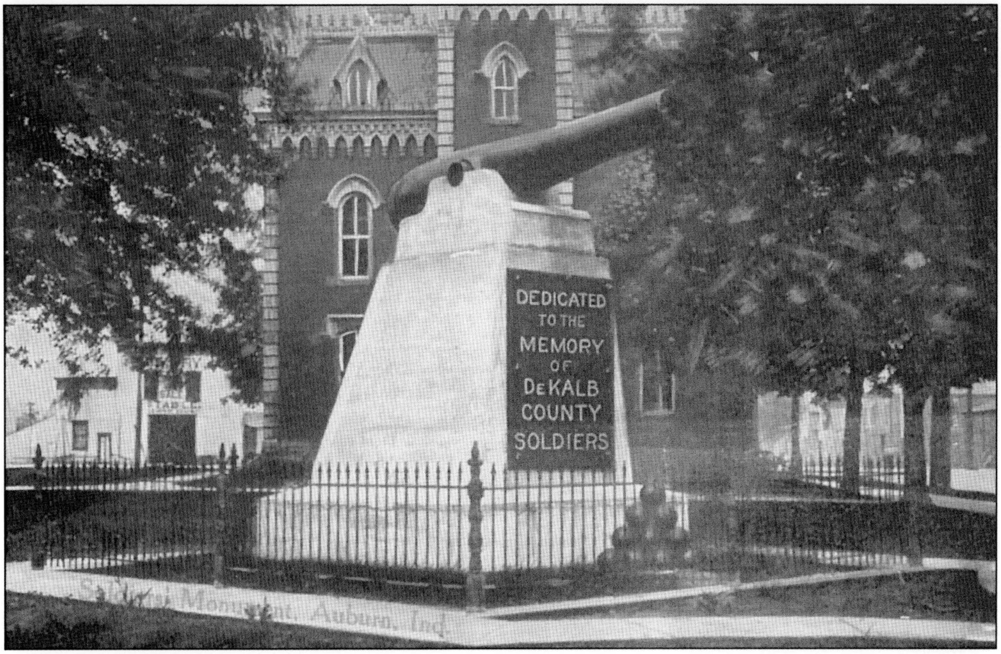

SOLDIER'S MONUMENT, AUBURN, INDIANA. The cannon is a landmark on the southwest corner of the square. An iron fence once surrounded it. Cannonballs are stacked in front of the monument. The jail is in the background, with the livery stable barely visible on Cedar Street.

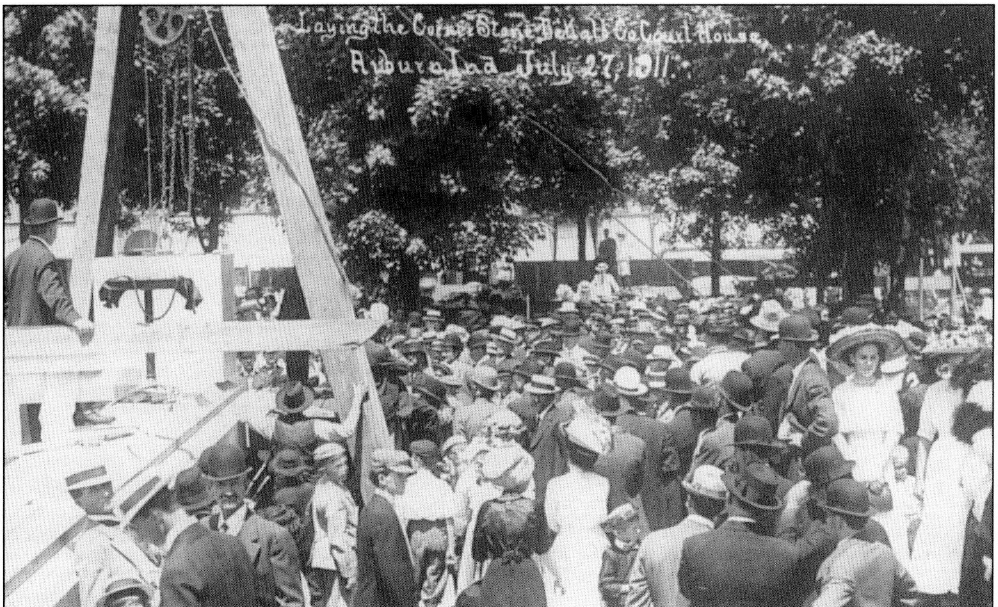

LAYING IN THE CORNERSTONE, DEKALB COUNTY COURTHOUSE. AUBURN, INDIANA, JULY 27, 1911. Members of the Masonic Lodge laid the cornerstone of the third courthouse. The principal speaker was Governor Thomas R. Marshall, who was from Columbia City. He announced his candidacy for President of the United States, and he was later elected Vice President under Woodrow Wilson.

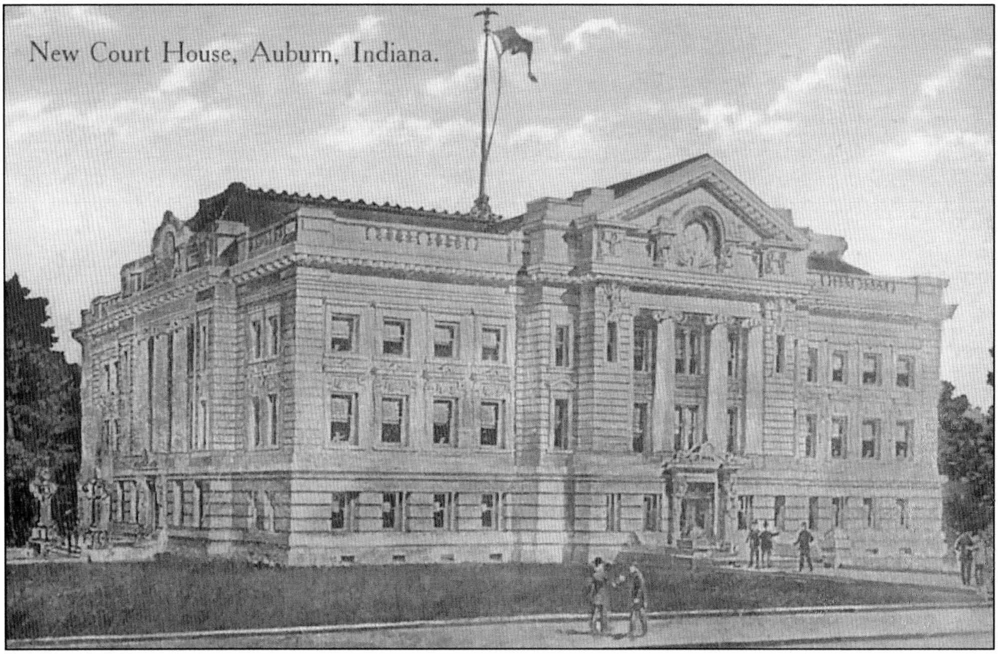

NEW COURTHOUSE, AUBURN, INDIANA. Designed by Mahurin and Mahurin, architects of Fort Wayne, the courthouse has served the county well. This is an artist's conception. There are some slight differences between the drawing and the finished building.

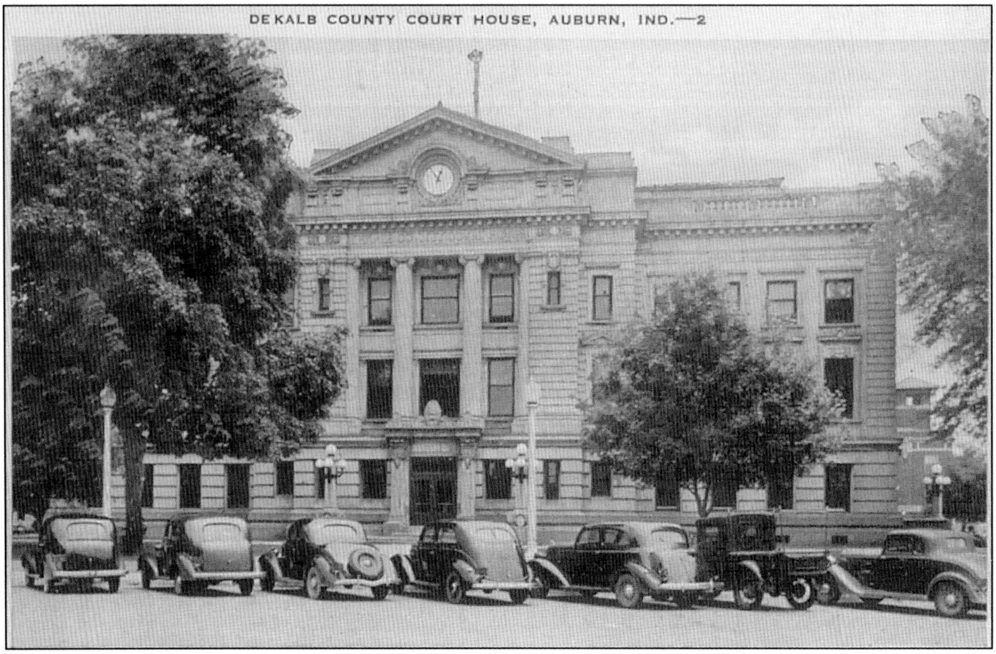

DEKALB COUNTY COURTHOUSE, AUBURN, INDIANA. The finished building was photographed from the west, with 1930s cars and trucks parked on South Main Street.

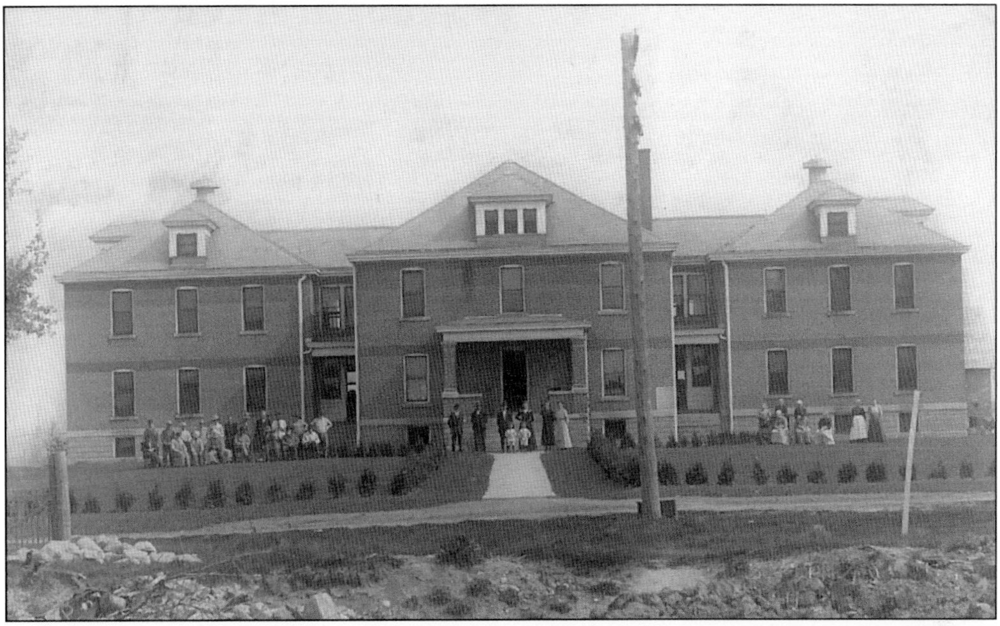

DeKalb County Farm. The County Farm housed those who were unable to support or care for themselves. It was and is a working farm where those who were able to work were required to do so.

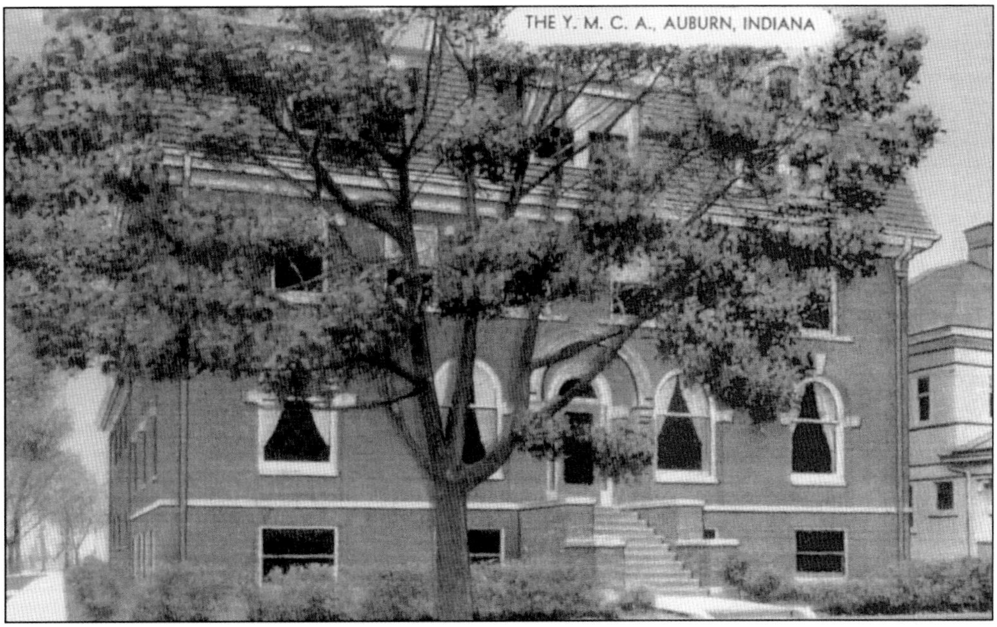

The YMCA, Auburn, Indiana. The Young Men's Christian Association provided rooms for students and workers and recreation, including a pool, bowling alley, gymnasium, and "canteen" for light meals.

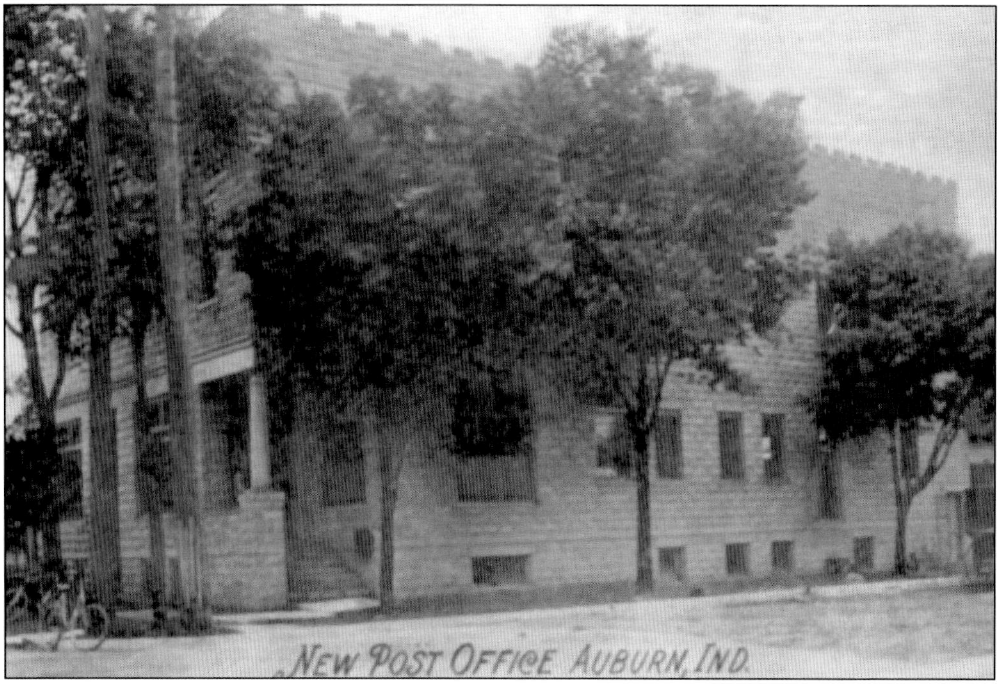

New Post Office, Auburn, Indiana. The post office and armory was at the northeast corner of North Cedar and East Seventh Streets. The 44th Indiana Regiment occupied the second floor.

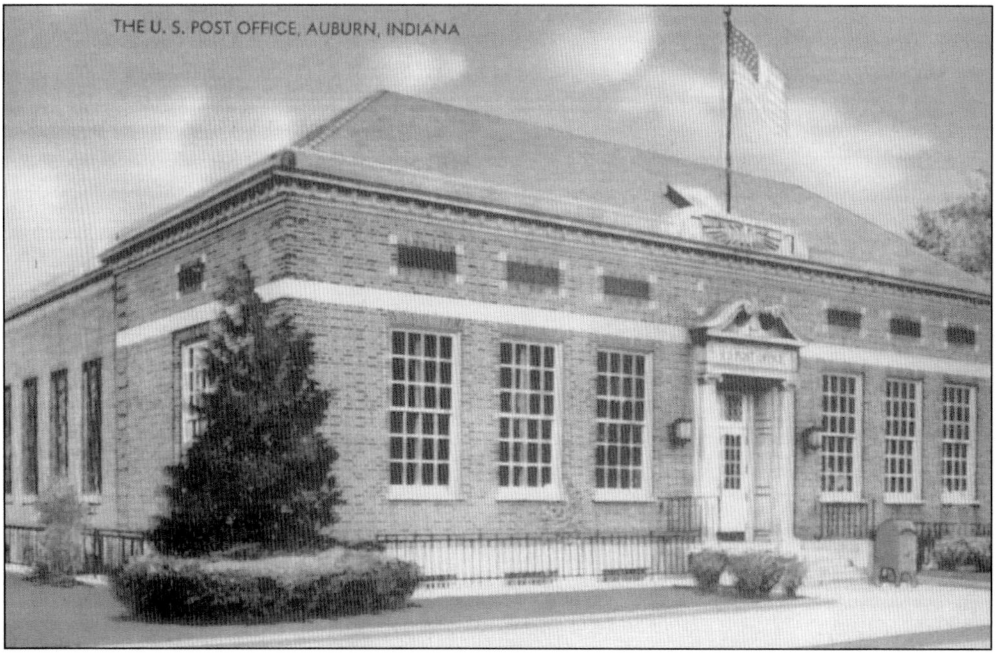

The United States Post Office, Auburn, Indiana. Another "new post office" was built in the 1930s on South Jackson Street between West Eighth and Ninth Streets.

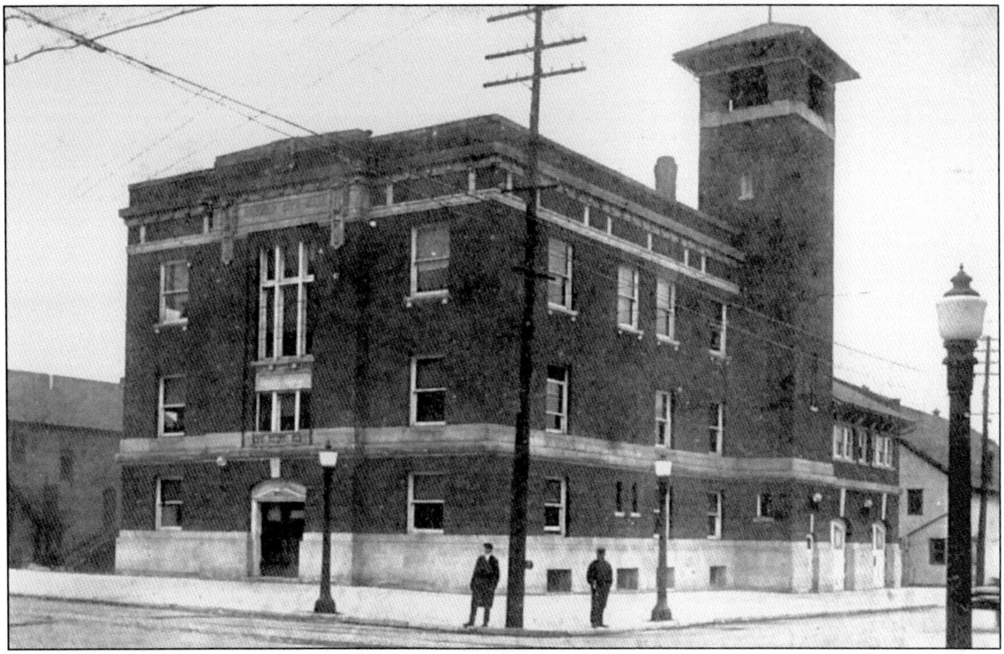

CITY HALL, AUBURN, INDIANA. The Auburn City Hall was built in 1918, to house city offices. The "fire barn" was at the rear, where two teams of horses were kept to pull the steam-fired pumpers to a fire.

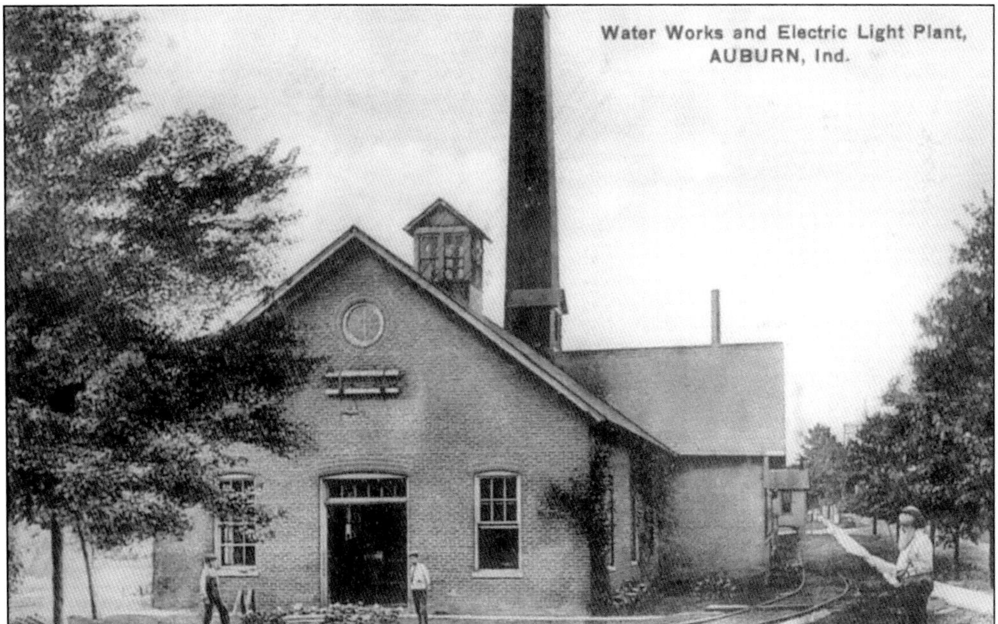

WATER WORKS AND ELECTRIC LIGHT PLANT, AUBURN, INDIANA. The building was located at the southeast corner of Ensley Avenue and Wayne Street. It was extensively remodeled in 1934. Note the rail siding, which curves around the west side of the building.

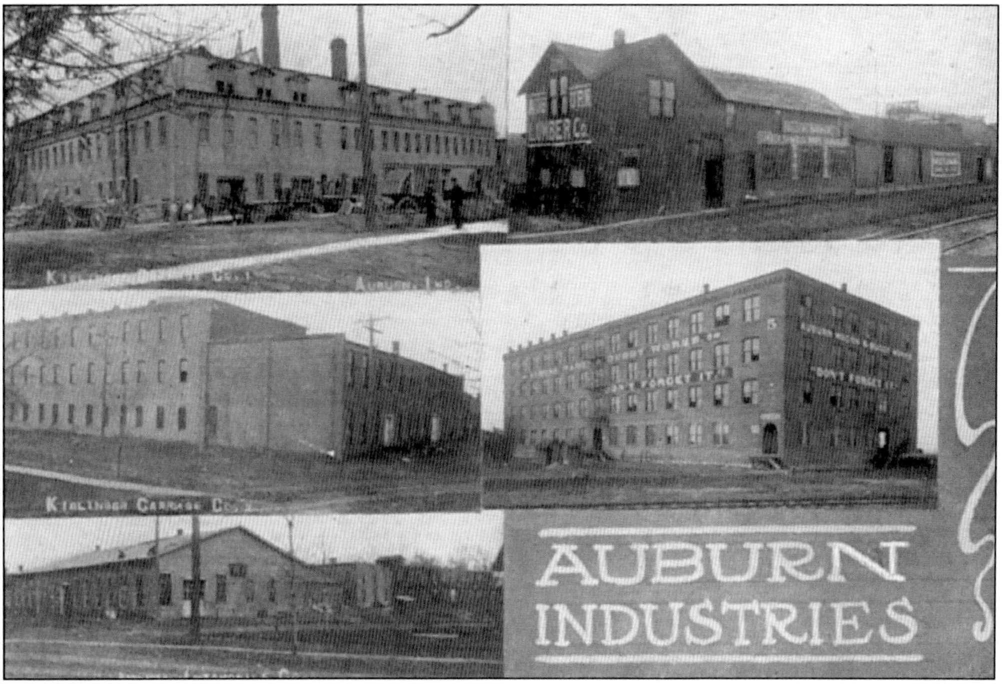

Auburn Industries. The buildings include Kiblinger Carriage Co. (upper left and middle left), Auburn Automobile Co. (lower left), Auburn Lumber Co. (upper right), and Auburn Wagon and Buggy Works (middle right).

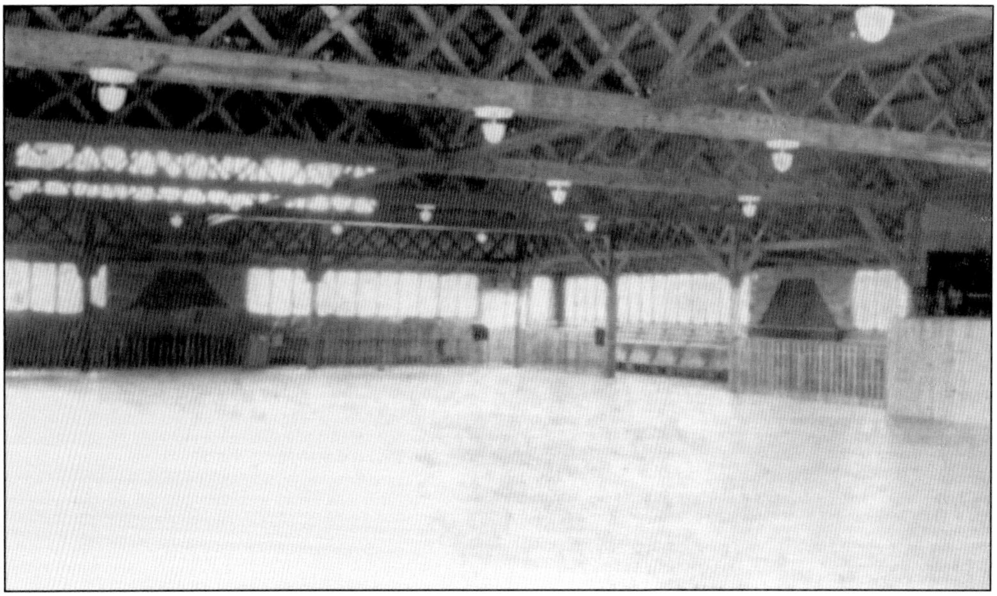

Interior of Silver Moon Dance Hall on Route 13, North of Auburn, Indiana. The Silver Moon later became a roller skating rink.

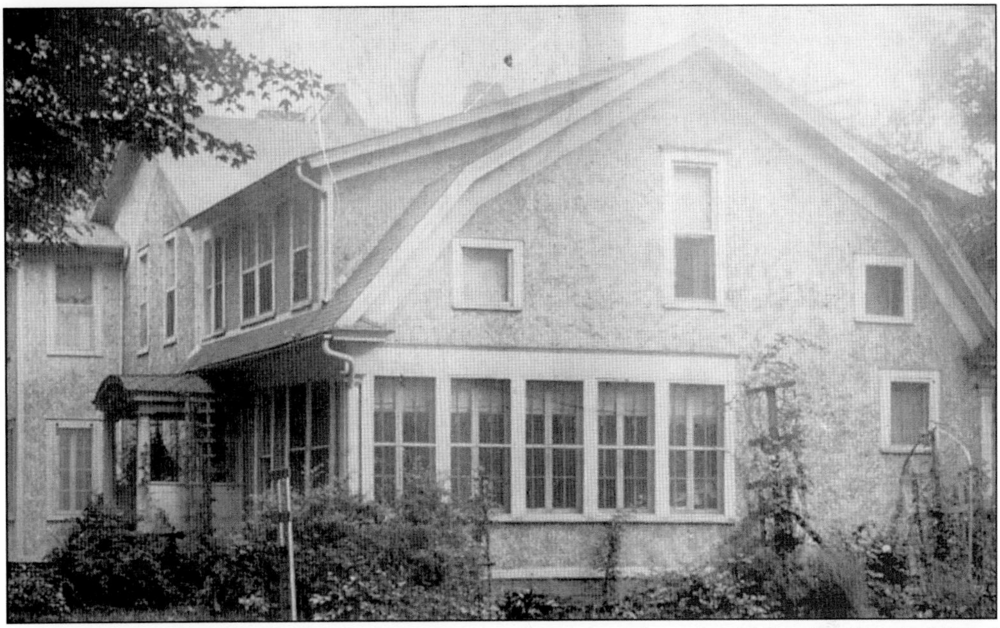

Dr. Bonnell M. Souder Hospital, Auburn, Indiana. The original Souder Hospital faced West Seventh Street.

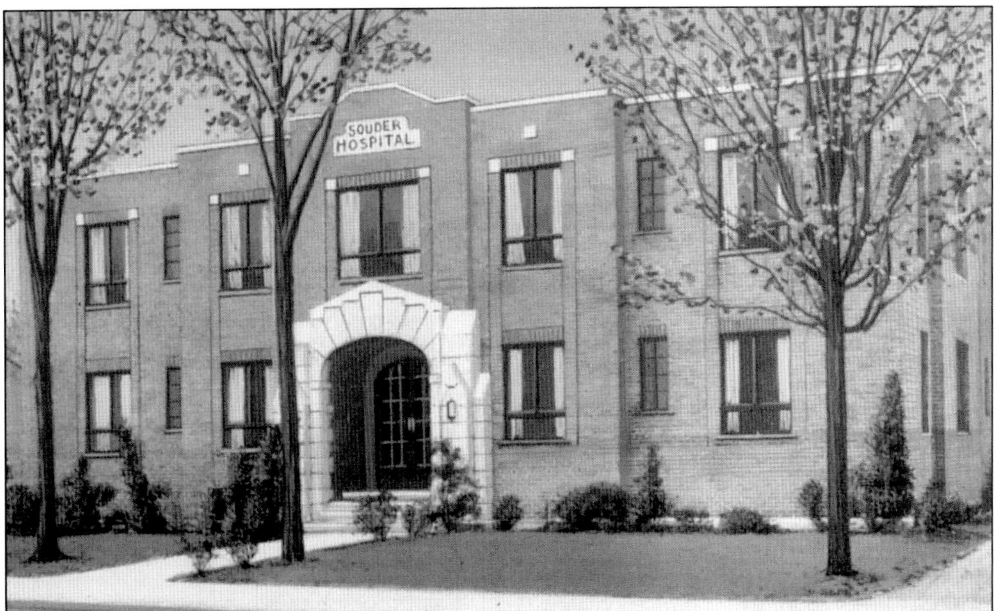

Dr. Bonnell M. Souder Hospital, Auburn, Indiana. The "new" hospital faced West Sixth Street but incorporated the "old" buildings on the south side.

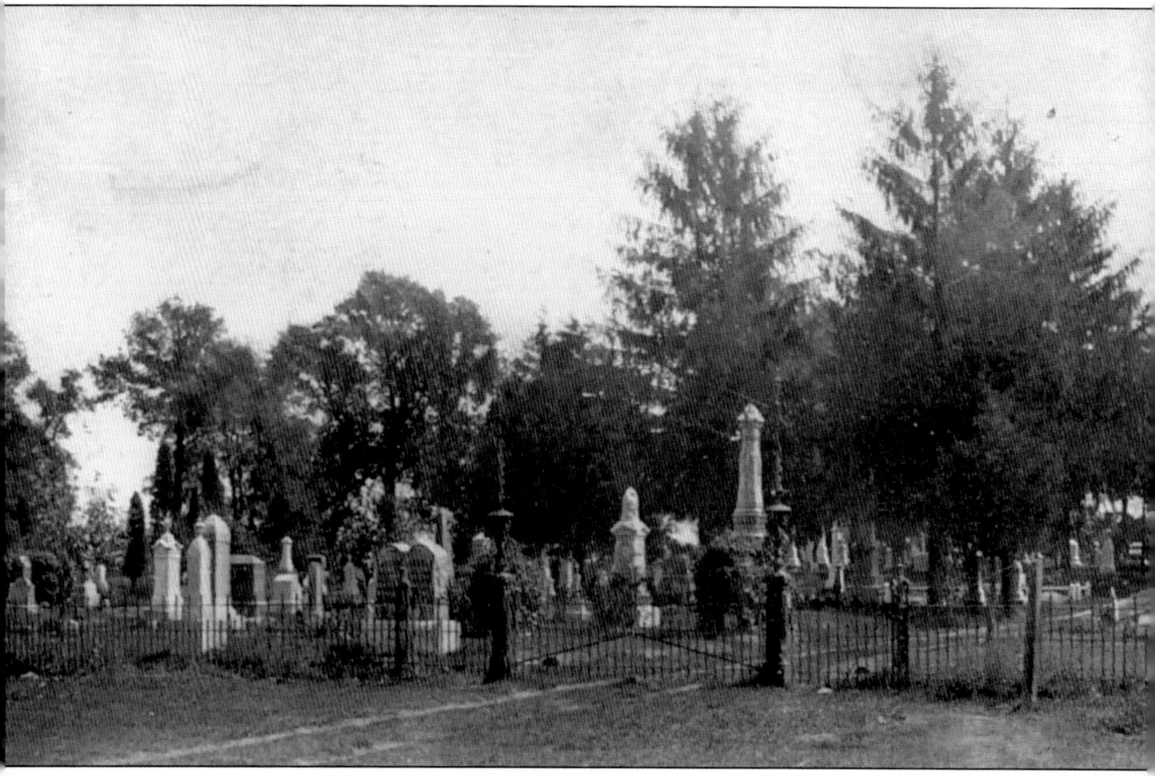

EVERGREEN CEMETERY, AUBURN, INDIANA. Most pioneer citizens of Auburn were buried at the Evergreen Cemetery on South Union Street.

Three

BUTLER

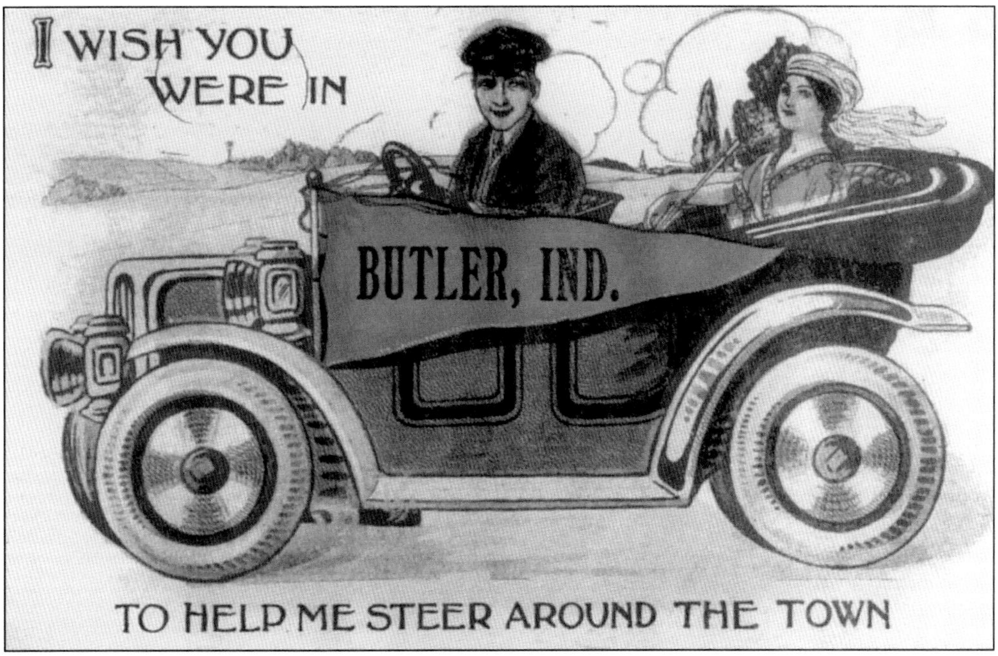

I WISH YOU WERE IN BUTLER, INDIANA, TO HELP ME STEER AROUND THE TOWN. Butler was originally known as Norristown, then Jarvis, and finally Butler.

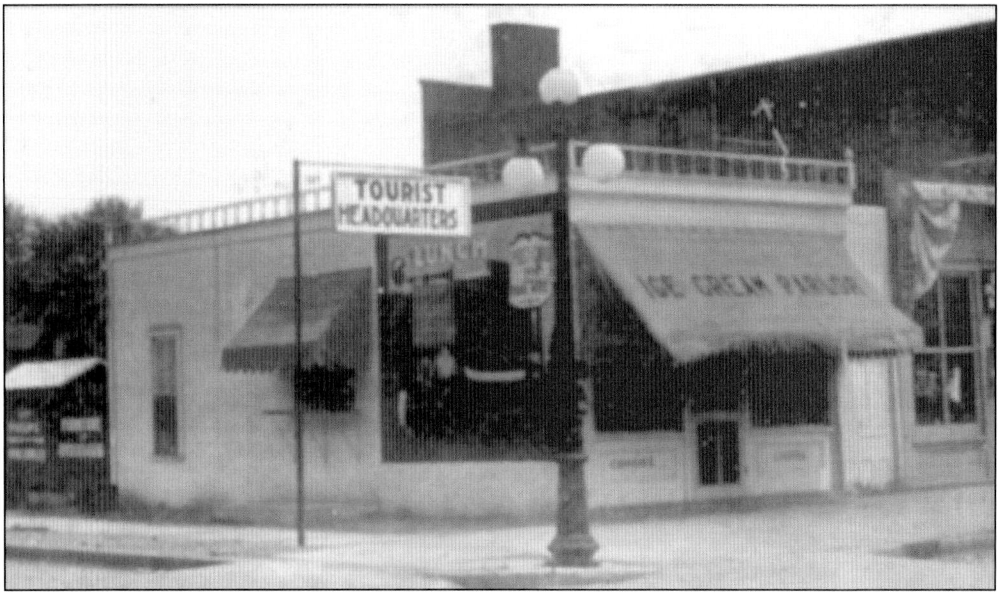

Keefer's Luncheonette, Butler, Indiana. Mr. and Mrs. Henry Keefer owned Keefer's Luncheonette. It was at the southeast corner of Main and Broadway and on the Toledo Chicago Pike, later U.S. Six. Note that postcards and road maps were available. Henry Keefer also operated a bus between Butler and Bryan, Ohio.

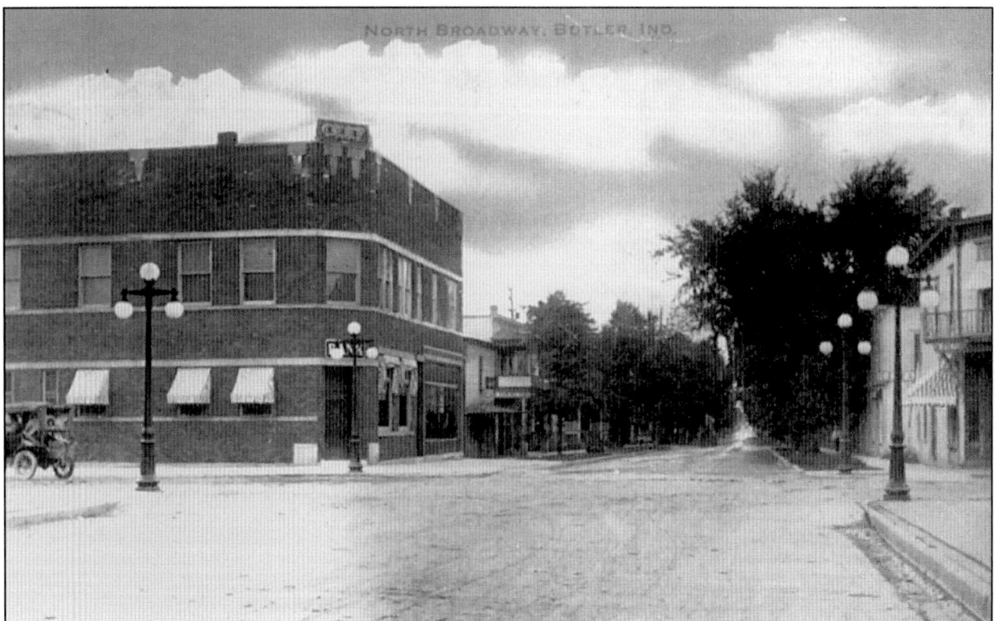

North Broadway, Butler, Indiana. The building on the left is the First National Bank. The east-west road was the Toledo Chicago Pike, now U.S. Six.

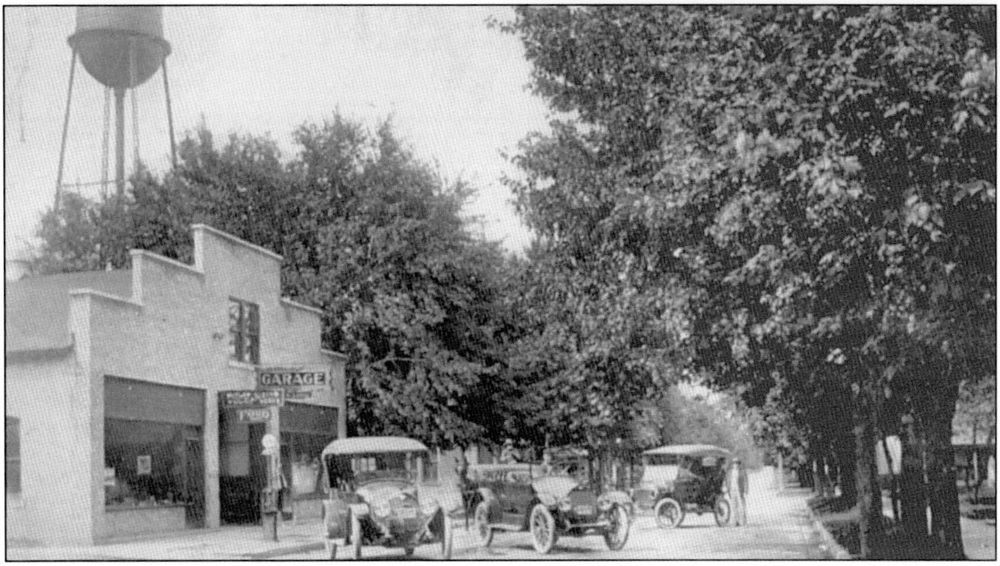

MAIN STREET WEST FROM BROADWAY, BUTLER, INDIANA. Now the location of Maxton Motors, this was then the Ford Garage.

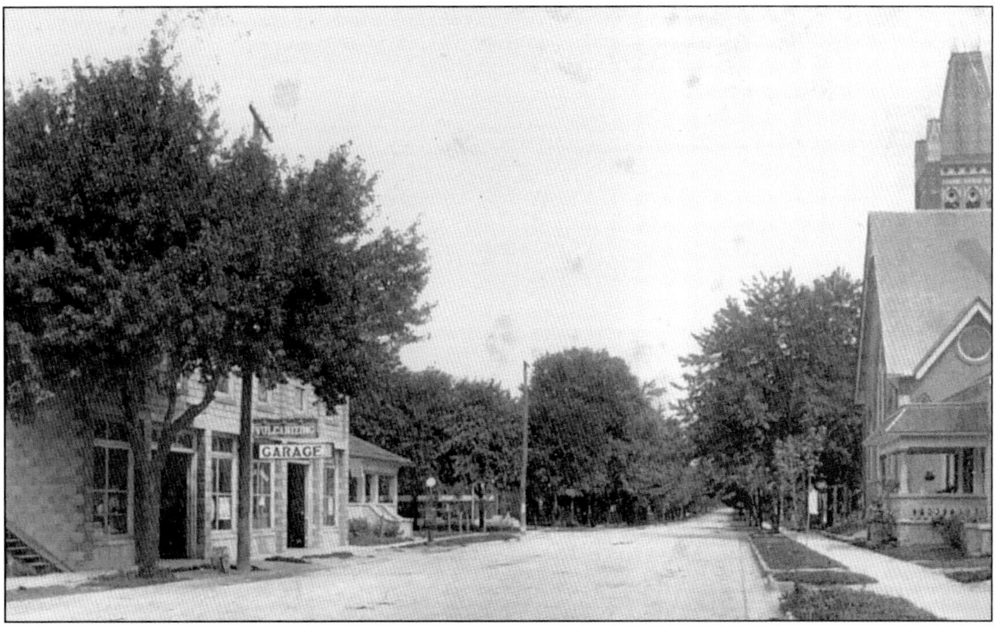

EAST MAIN STREET, BUTLER, INDIANA. John H. Creager and Walter Creager, the author's great-grandfather and grandfather operated Creager Garage on the left. The Methodist church is on the right.

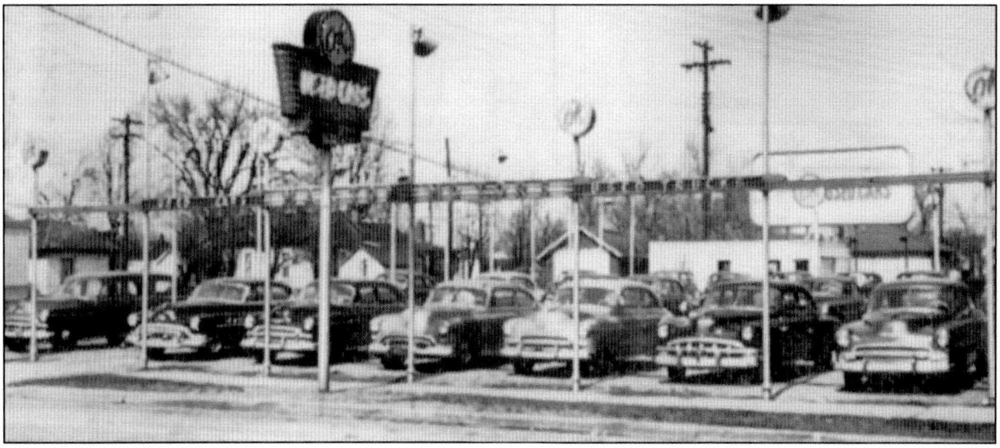

MAXTON MOTORS, INC. BUTLER, INDIANA. "WHERE YOUR DOLLARS GO FARTHER." The Maxton Motors Used Car Lot features many 1949–1952 Chevrolets, Buicks, and Oldsmobiles.

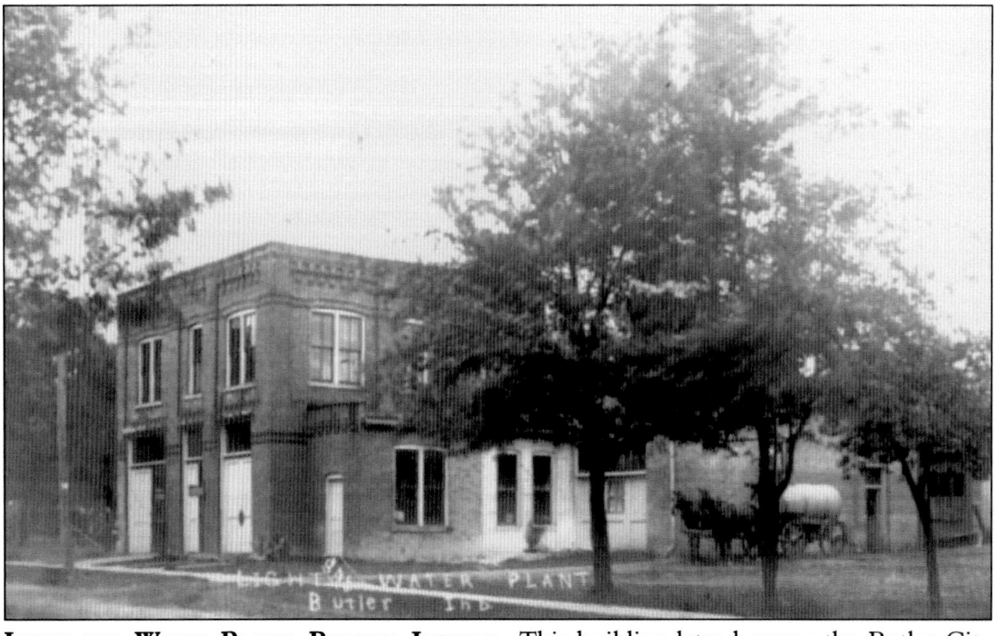

LIGHT AND WATER PLANT, BUTLER, INDIANA. This building later became the Butler City Hall. Note the horse-drawn water wagon on the right. These were used to wet dusty streets during summer dry periods.

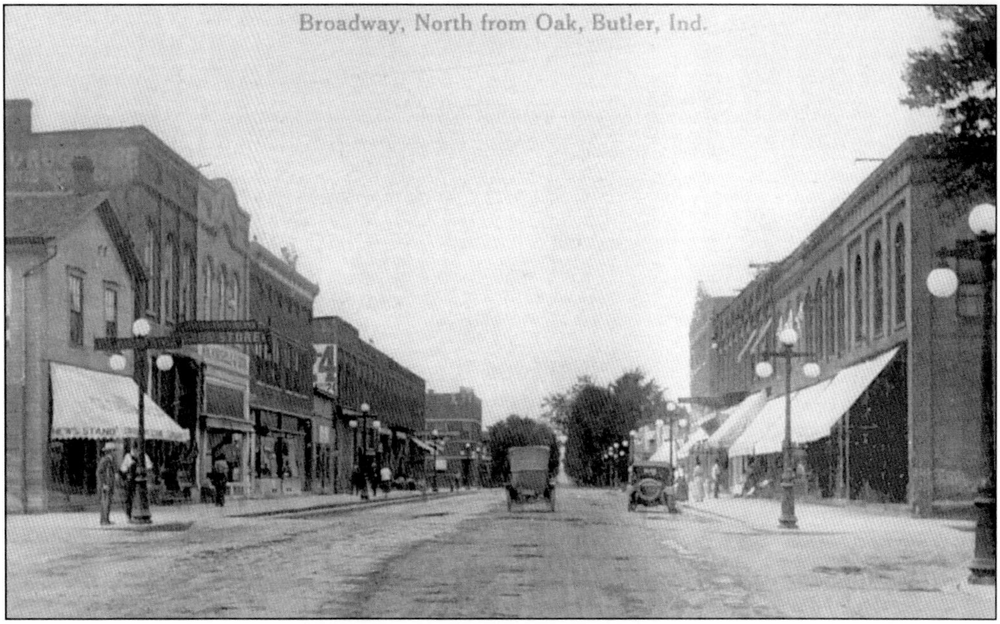

Broadway, North from Oak, Butler, Indiana. The frame building on the left was the newsstand. A bandstand later occupied this site. The next building is a drugstore. The third building is H.W. Knisely & Sons.

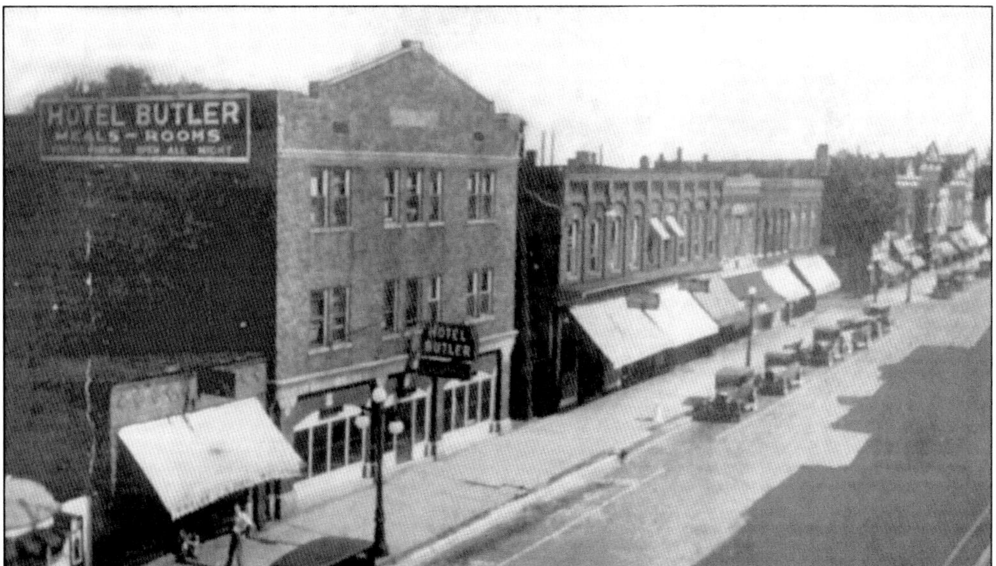

Business Section Looking South, Butler, Indiana. The Hotel Butler sign states: "Meals—Rooms—Strictly Modern—Open All Night." The small building on the left was Dovey's Diner.

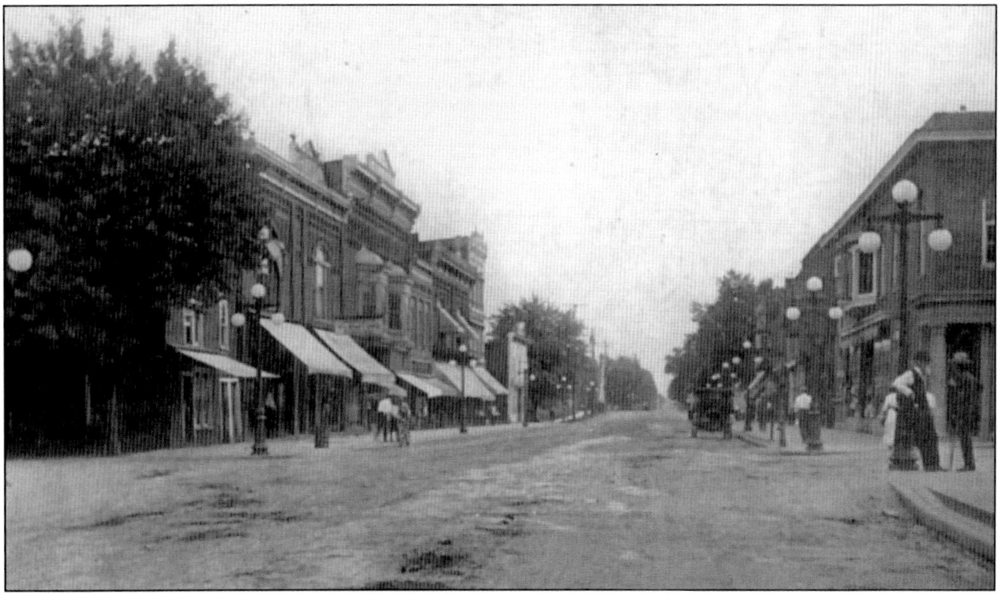

BROADWAY SOUTH FROM OAK, BUTLER, INDIANA. The Thompson Opera House is the tallest building on the left..

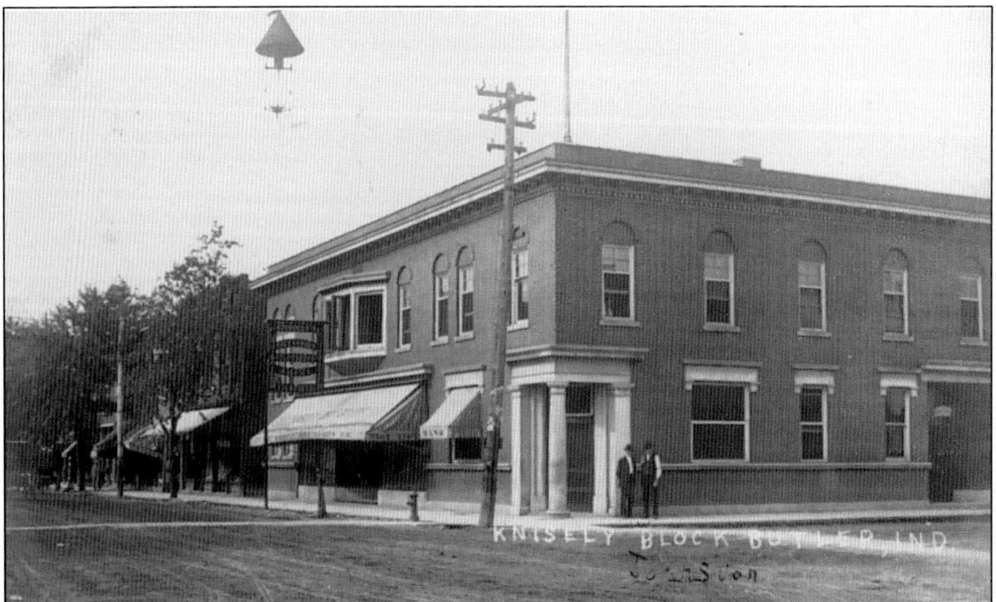

KNISELY BLOCK, BUTLER, INDIANA. The Knisely Block is on the right. The sign states: "Knisely's—Dry Goods—Clothing—Shoes—Carpets—Furnishings." The Knisely National Bank occupied the corner space. The postcard is dated July 2, 1908.

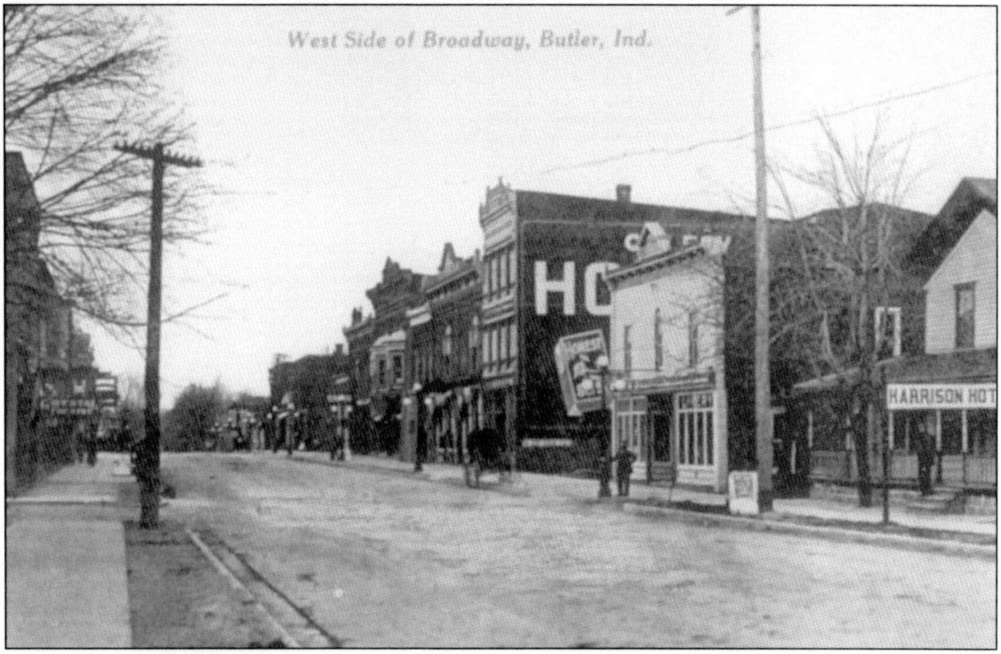

WEST SIDE OF BROADWAY, BUTLER, INDIANA. Actually, the view is of the east side, looking north from Depot Street. Ed Groff's Livery Stable and Garage is the second building on the right. The Crystal Theatre is on the left.

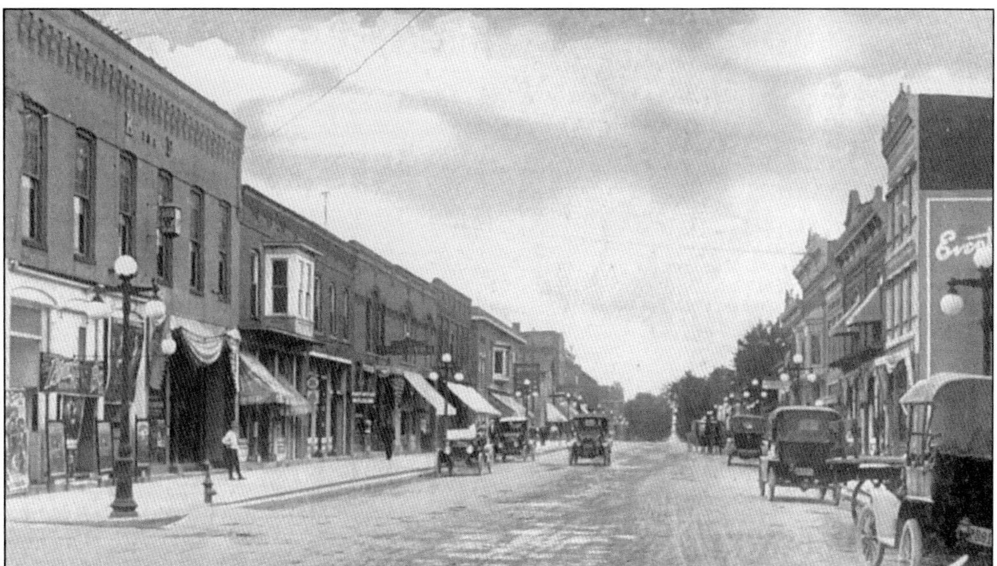

BROADWAY, NORTH FROM R.R., BUTLER, INDIANA. This is the west side of Broadway looking north from Depot Street. The Crystal Theatre is on the left in the lower part of the K of P (Knights of Pythias) Building.

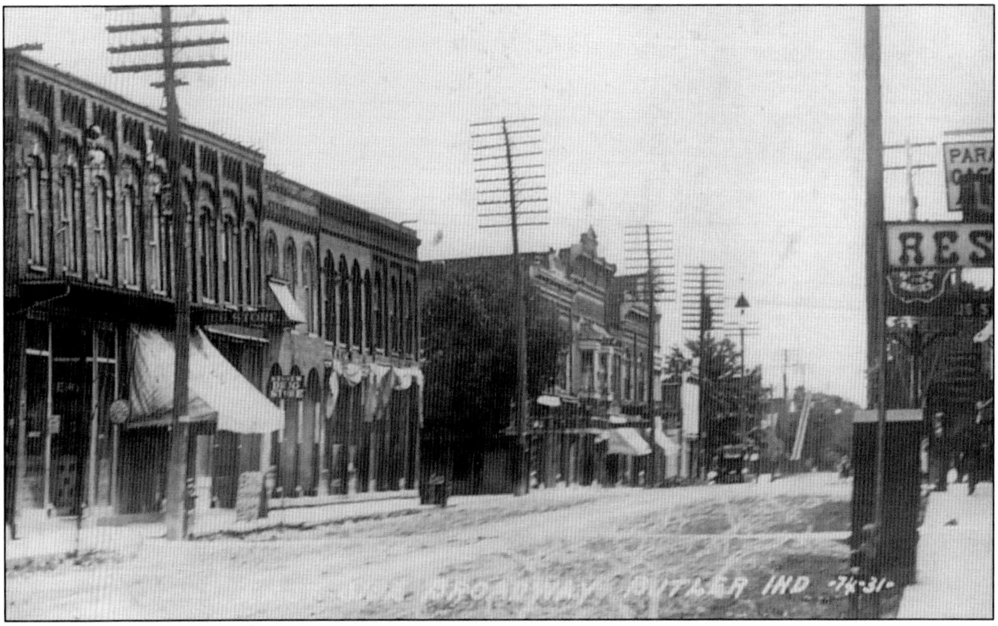

EAST SIDE OF BROADWAY, BUTLER, INDIANA. Note the dirt streets. Stone's Drug Store is on the left.

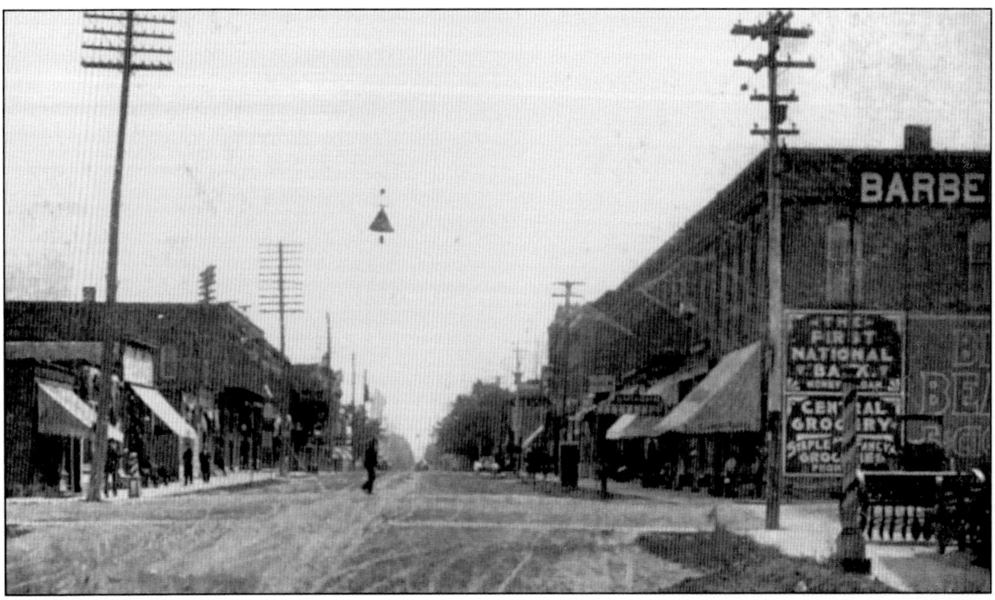

BROADWAY, BUTLER, INDIANA. This view is looking south from Main Street. The sign on the building states: "The First National Bank—Money to Loan," and "Central Grocery—Simple & Fancy Groceries."

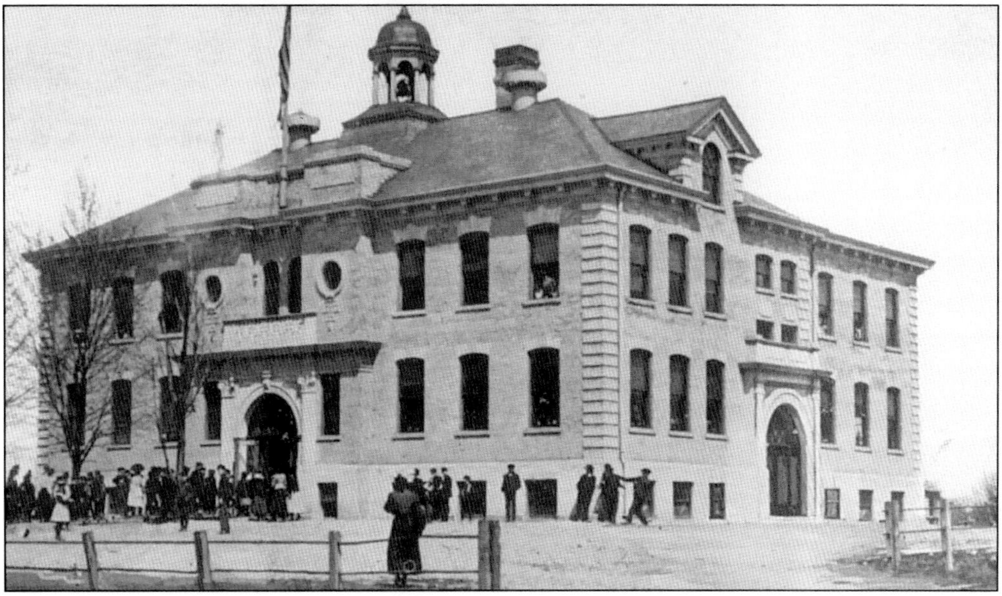

High School, Butler, Indiana. This was later the Butler Elementary School, where the author attended grades one through eight. There was a large tube on the right side of the building, which was a fire escape from the second floor. Fire drills were fun in that students got to slide down the tube. The biggest boys were "catchers" to catch the kids as they came out of the chute.

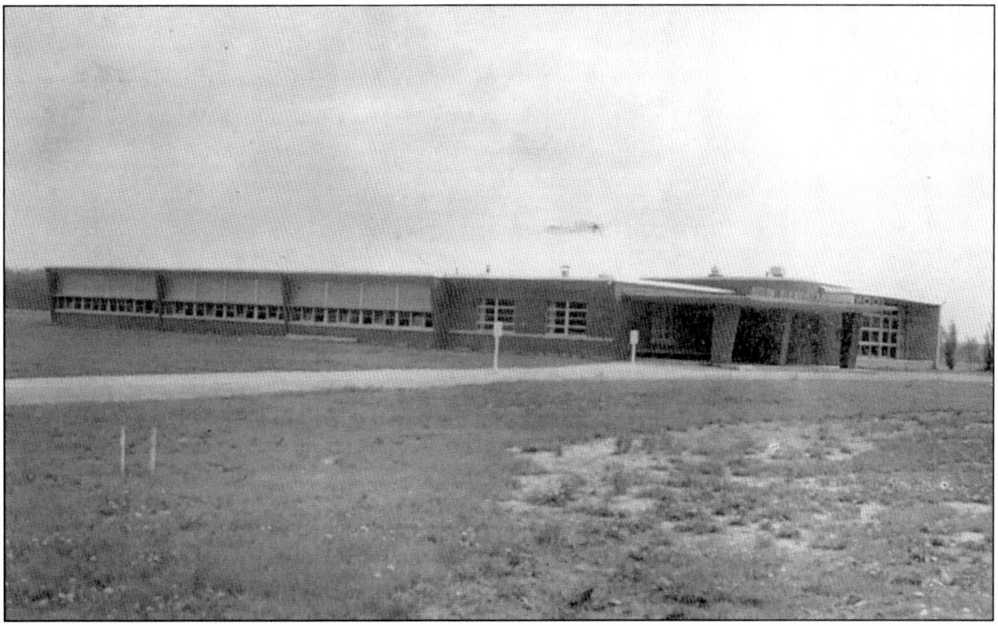

Butler Elementary School, East Green Street, Butler, Indiana. The "new" school now encompasses a campus for the Eastside School District.

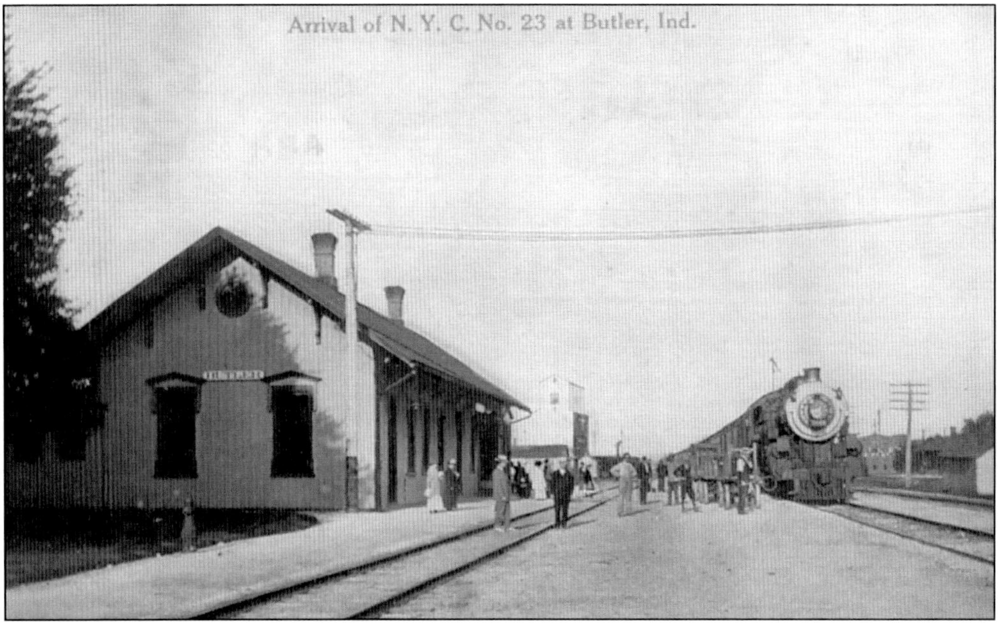

ARRIVAL OF N.Y.C. NO. 23 AT BUTLER, INDIANA. This depot was a very busy place. In the 1920s, 26 trains stopped each day.

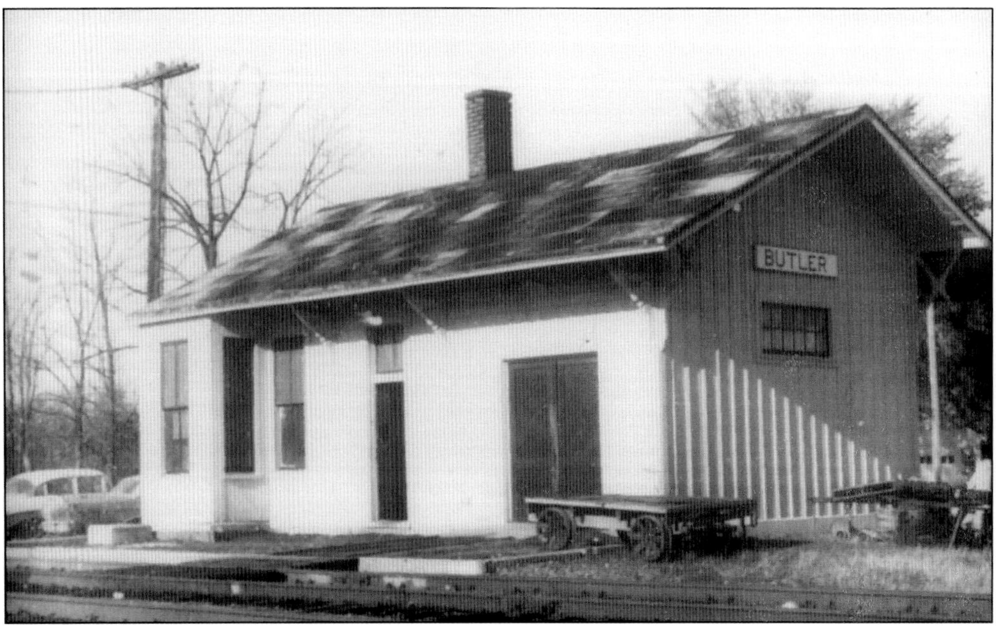

WABASH DEPOT, BUTLER, INDIANA. The Wabash Depot was on South Broadway. The famous Wabash Cannonball train stopped here.

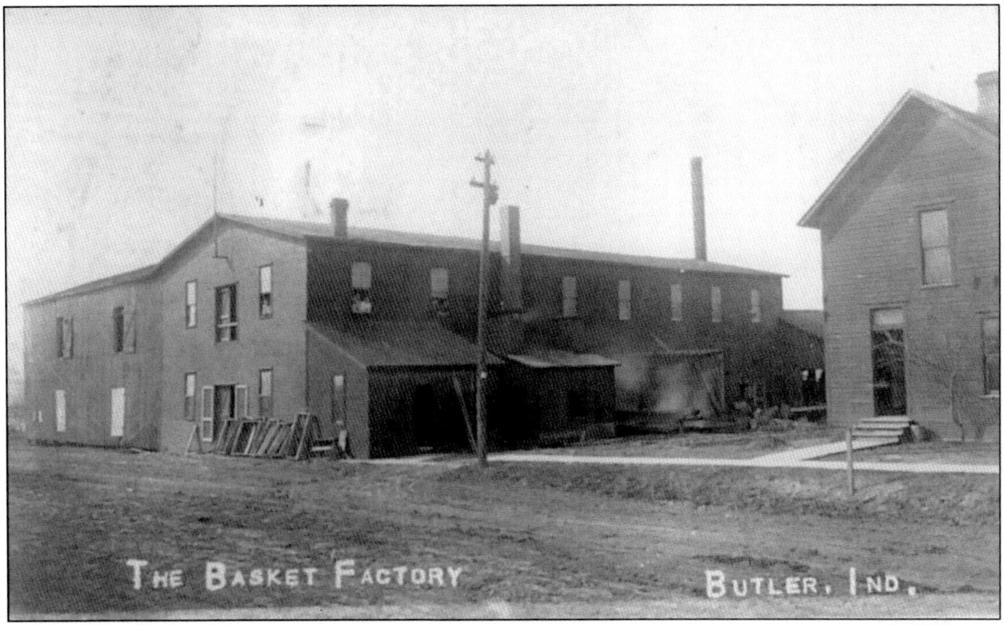

THE BASKET FACTORY, BUTLER, INDIANA. The Butler Basket Factory was located on the west edge of Butler and manufactured all kinds of wooden baskets.

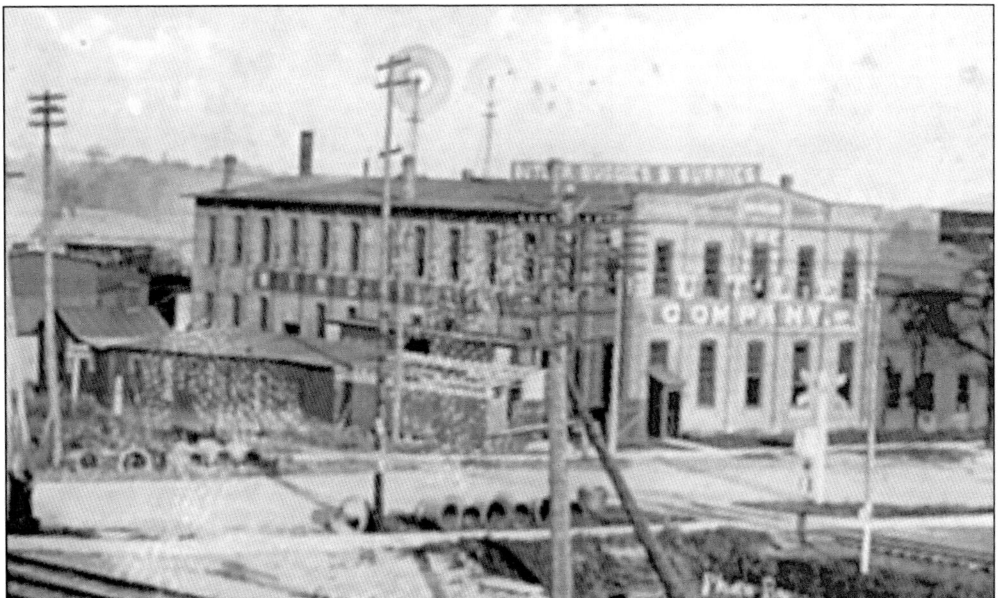

THE BUTLER COMPANY. The sign states "Butler Buggies and Surries," and "Windmills." This was Butler's principal industry, which manufactured windmills in later years. Note the windmill on top of the building.

PUBLIC LIBRARY, BUTLER, INDIANA. The Butler Carnagie Library was located on East Main Street. It is now the DeKalb County Historical Society.

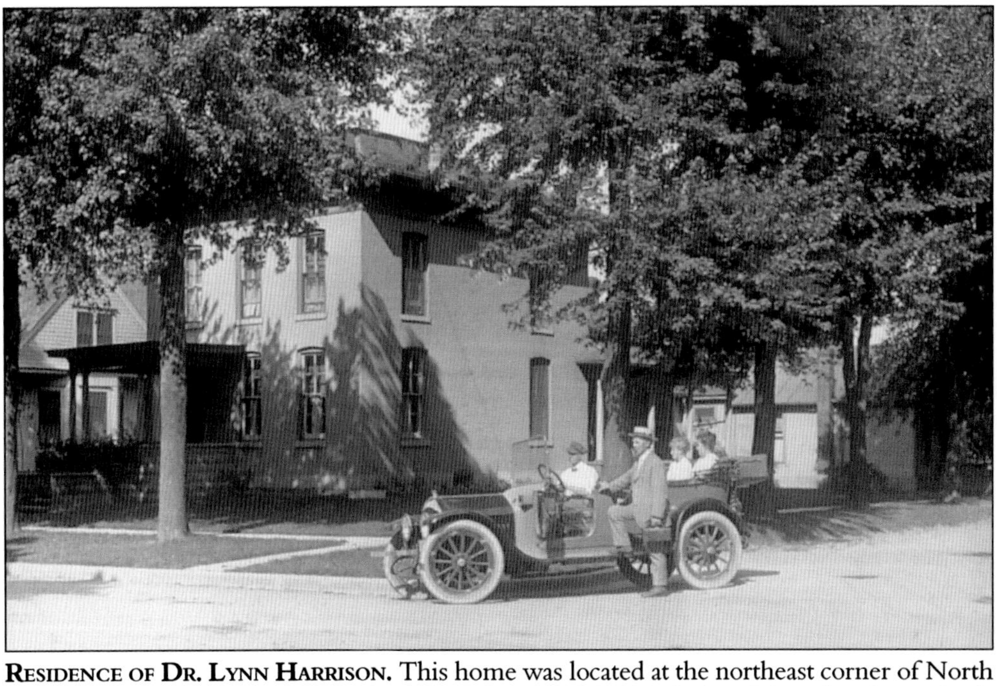

RESIDENCE OF DR. LYNN HARRISON. This home was located at the northeast corner of North Broadway and East Green Streets. The car is a 1912 Buick, being driven by the author's grandfather, Walter Creager. The ladies in the back are Exie Creager and Effie Harrison. Dr. Harrison was a very popular physician who always wore a fresh flower on his lapel.

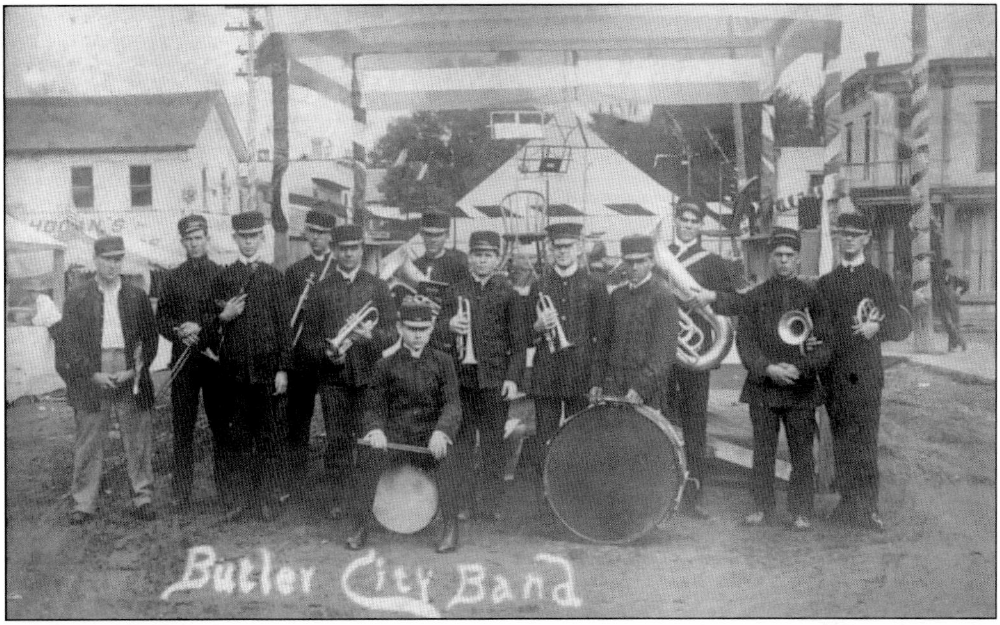

Butler City Band. Every town had at least one city band. They are posed in front of a temporary bandstand.

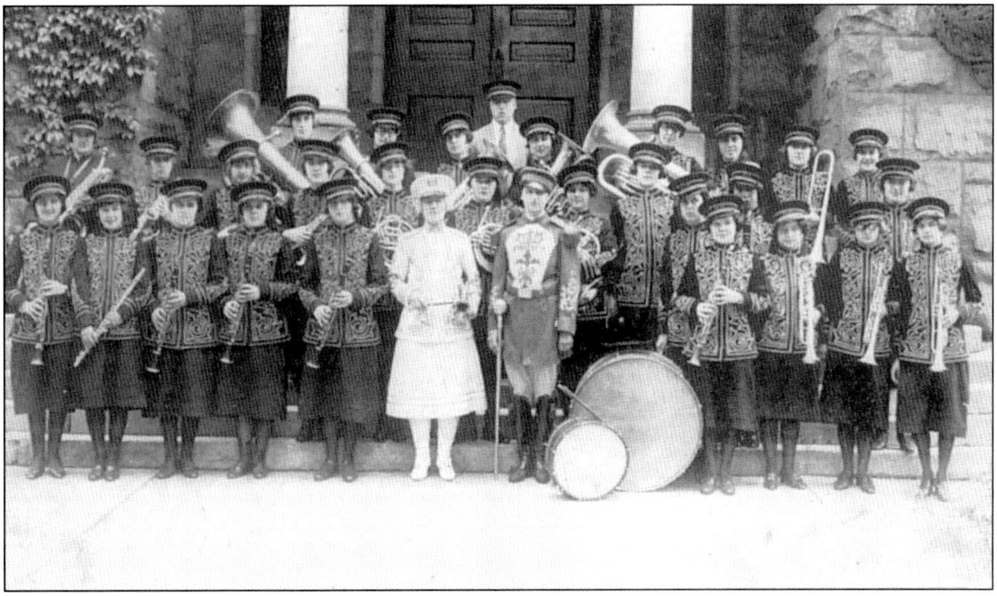

Butler Ladies' Band, Butler, Indiana. Lida Stage, who is in the white uniform, conducted the band.

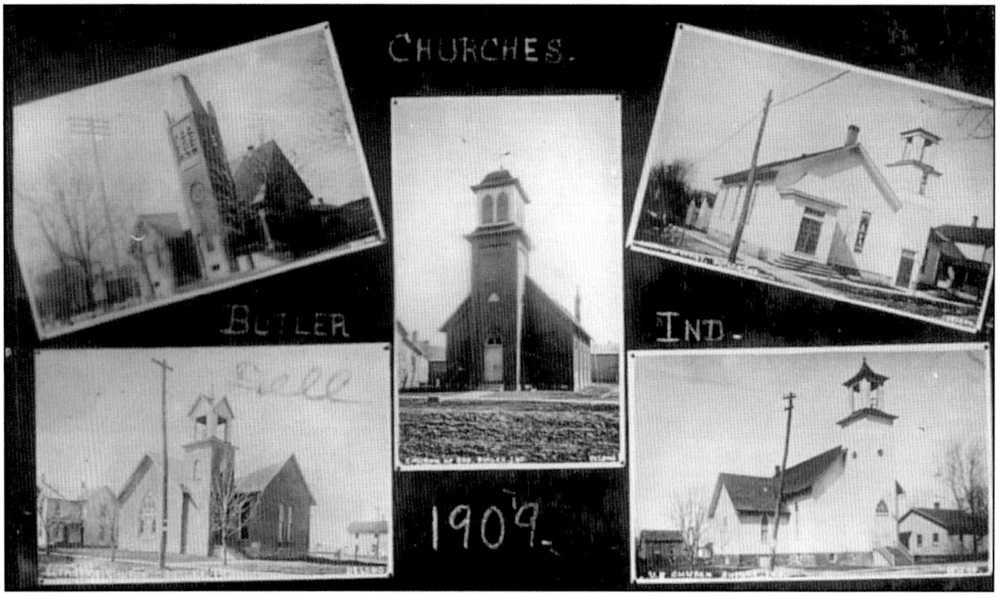

Churches, Butler, Indiana, 1909. Message states: "April 24, 1910. Dear Cousin got your all O.K. which found us all but it has been cold out here for a few days it snowed last night it froze quite hard I hope it done no harm freeze my the fruit. A good many people have not got a bit of garden made so you are a way ahead good by Write Soon. Dell."

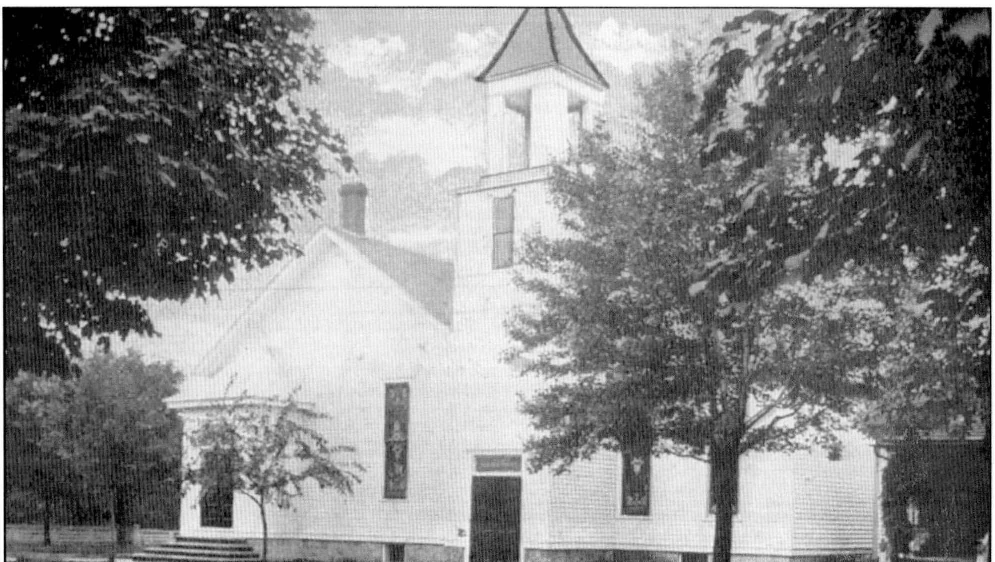

Church of Christ, Butler, Indiana.

M.E. Church, Butler, Indiana. The brick building of the Butler Methodist Church was one of the finest in town.

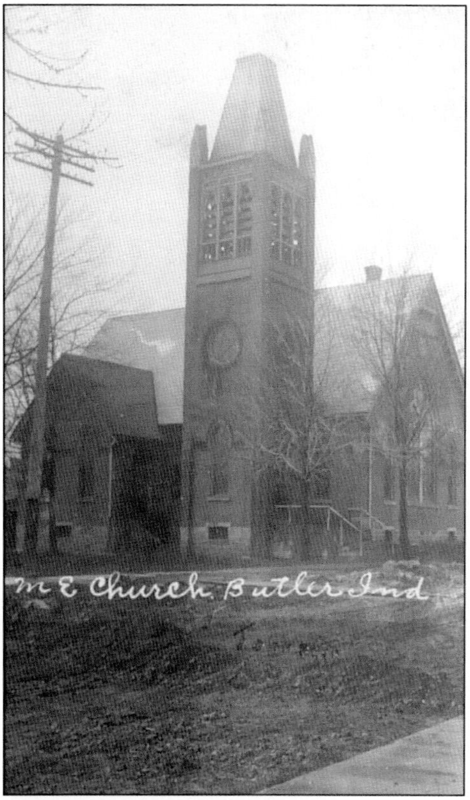

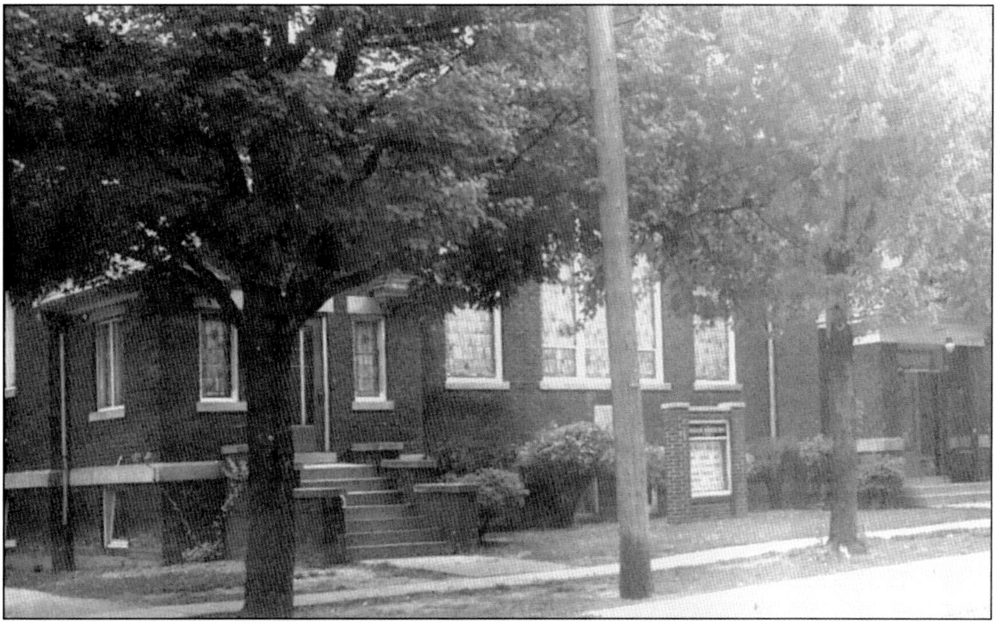

First U.B Church, West Main Street, Butler, Indiana. This church was later known as the Evangelical United Brethren Church. The church was noted for its orchestra, which even included a gentleman who played the musical saw.

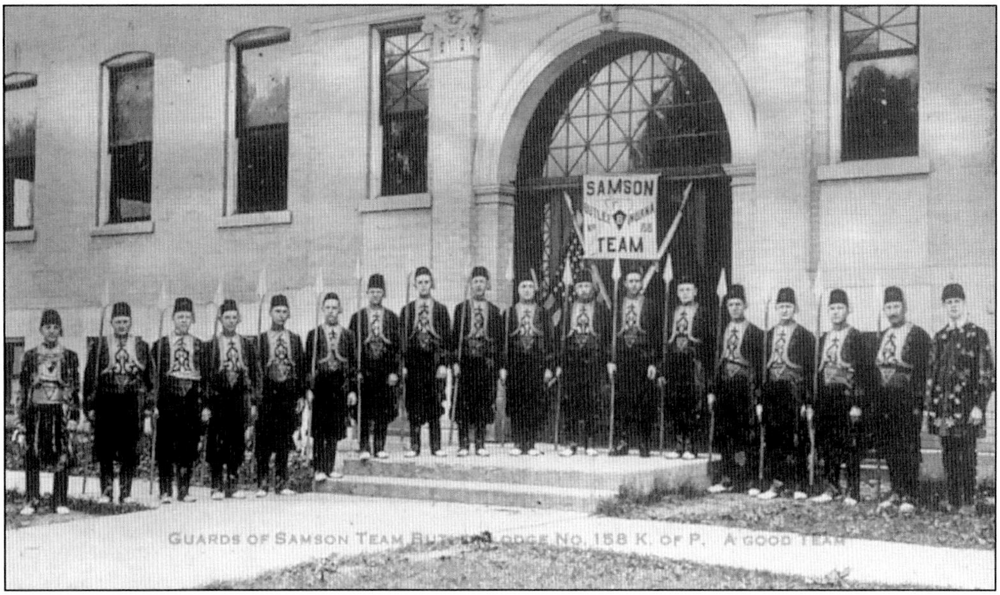

GUARDS OF SAMSON TEAM BUTLER LODGE NO. 158 K OF P, A GOOD TEAM. The drill team of Butler Knights of Pythias Lodge was well known for its precision marching and drill routine.

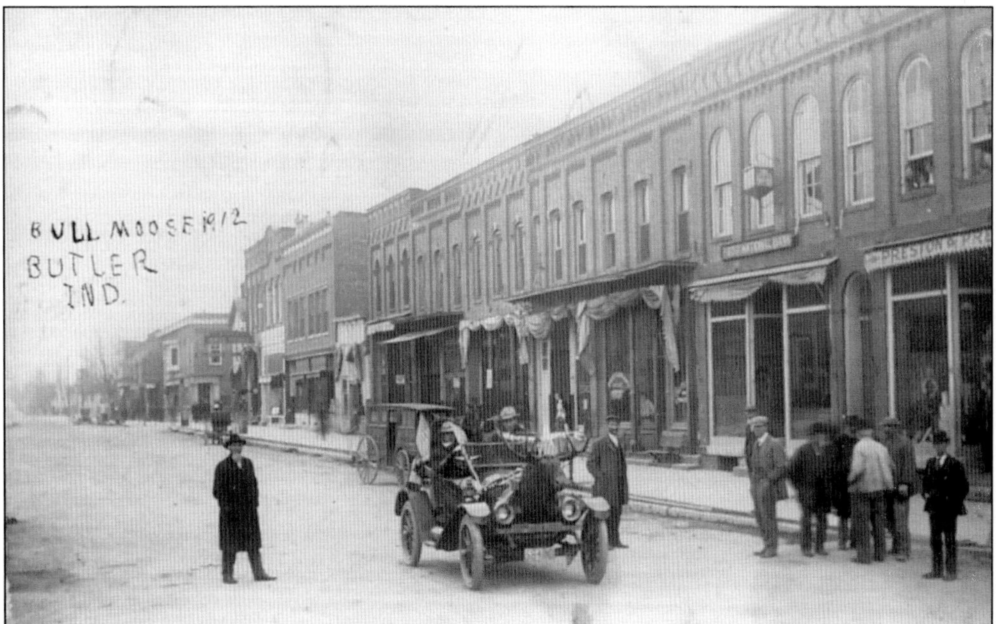

BULL MOOSE, BUTLER, INDIANA. The Bull Moose Party of Teddy Roosevelt was well represented in Butler by this automobile with a stuffed moose head mounted on its radiator.

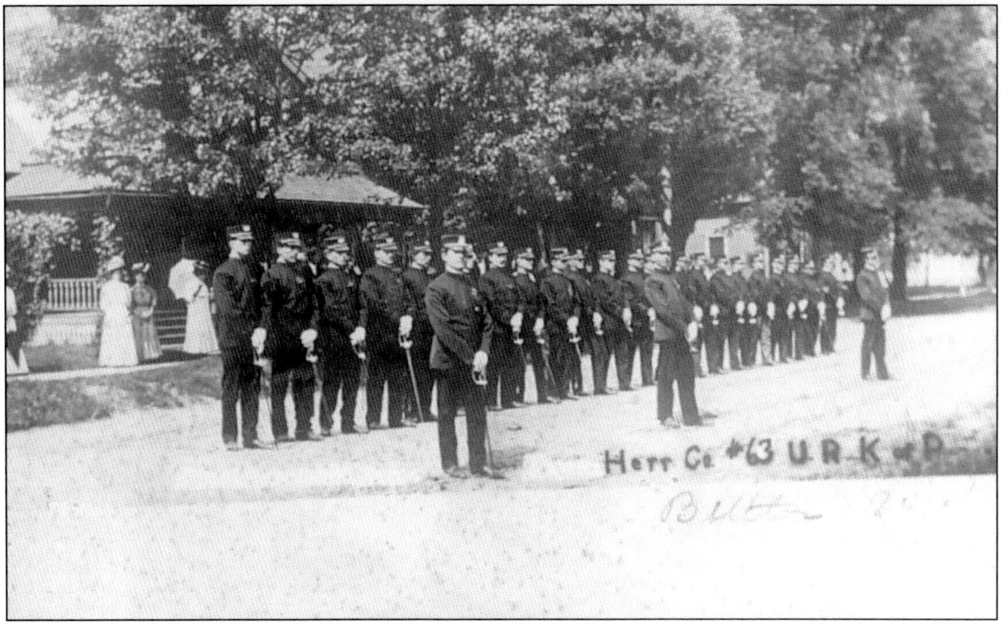

HERR CO. #63 U.R.K., BUTLER, INDIANA. The Herr Drill Team of the Butler Knights of Pythias represented a different facet of the lodge. Note the ladies in long dresses in the background.

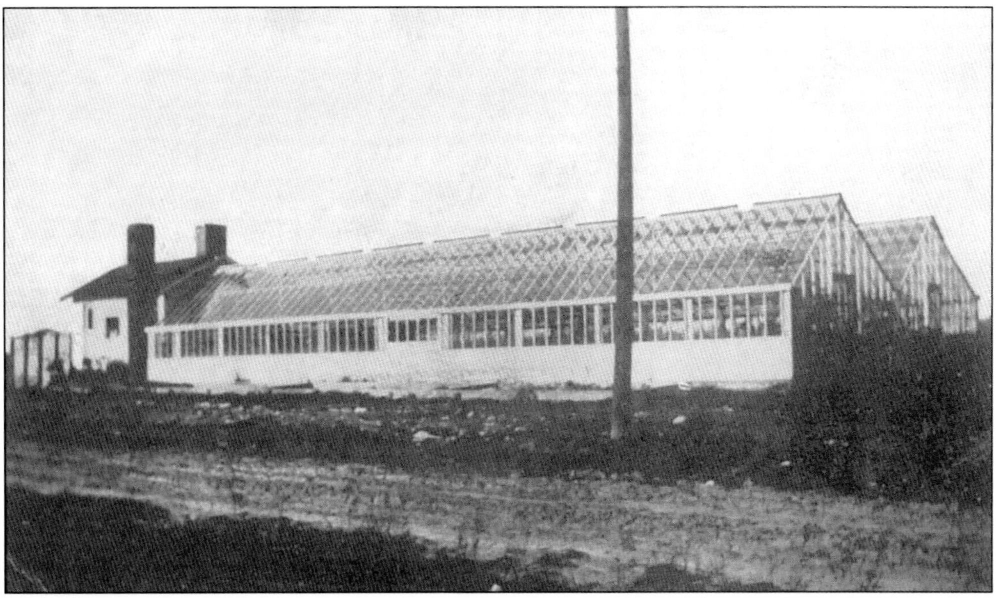

THE TOMBOW FLORAL CO., BUTLER, INDIANA. A source of fresh flowers throughout the year, the Tombow Floral Co. was owned by Leighton and Ola Tombow.

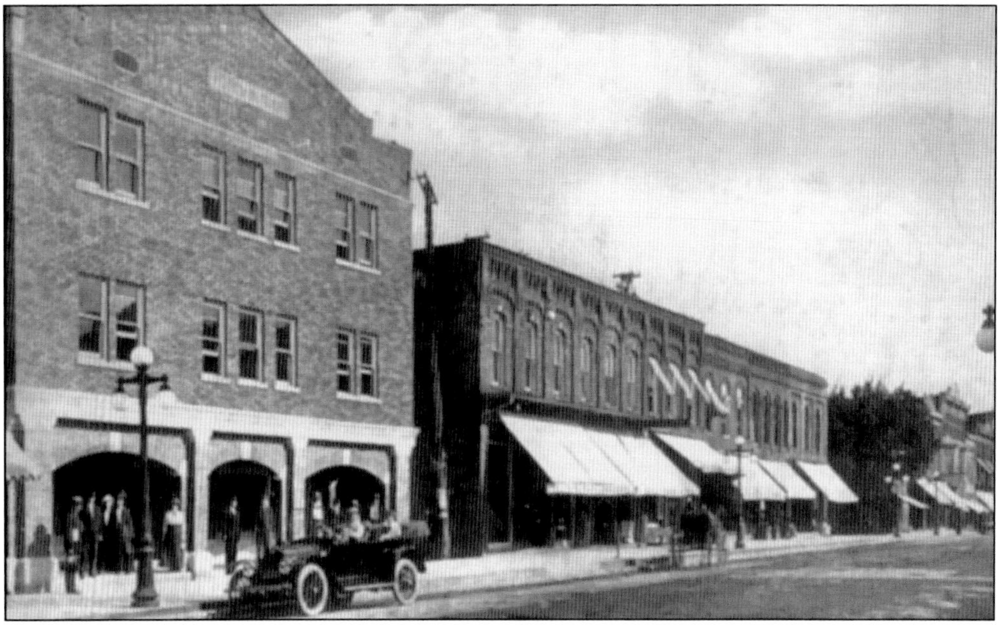

Hotel Butler, Butler, Indiana. The Hotel Butler was a popular stop for business travelers and tourists.

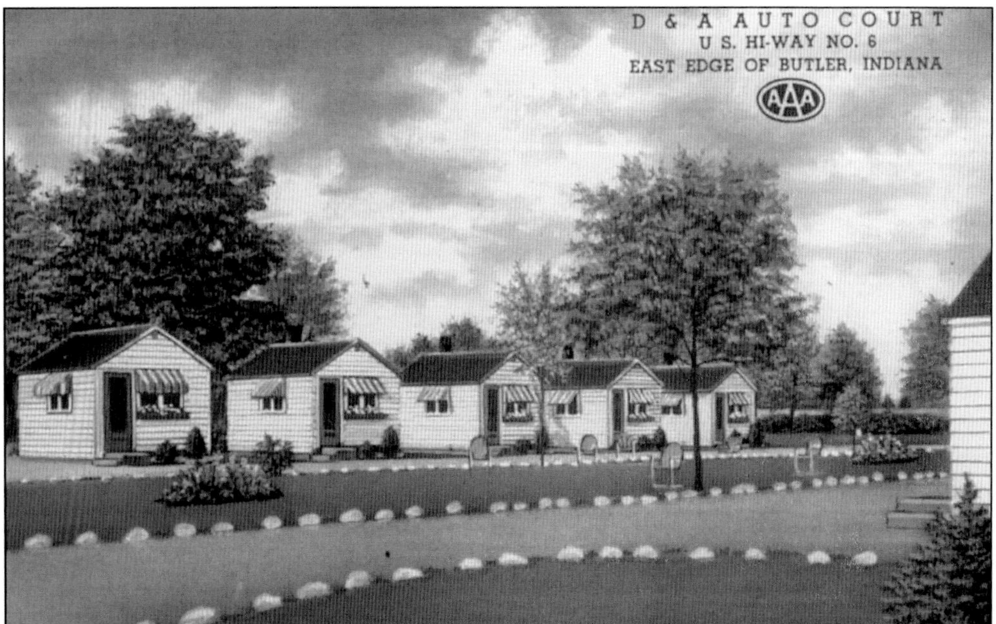

D & A Auto Court, U.S. Highway No. Six, East Edge of Butler, Indiana. The D & A Auto Court was owned by Dayton and Alta Wand. It provided state of the art cabins for travelers in the 1950s.

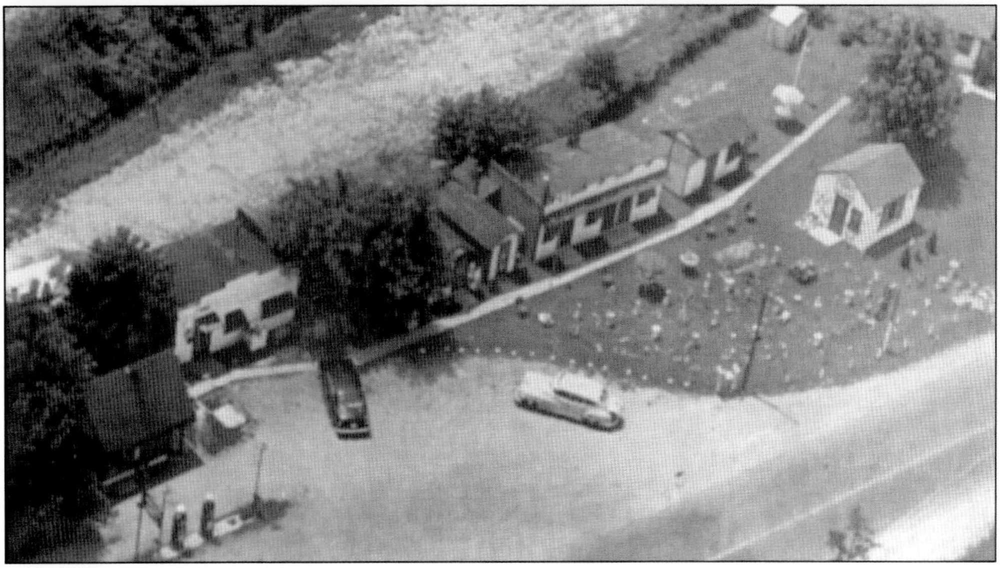

Butler Cabins and Gift Shop—U.S. Route Six—East Butler, Indiana. This complex was located on the east edge of Butler. The items in the yard are lawn ornaments, which were sold to tourists.

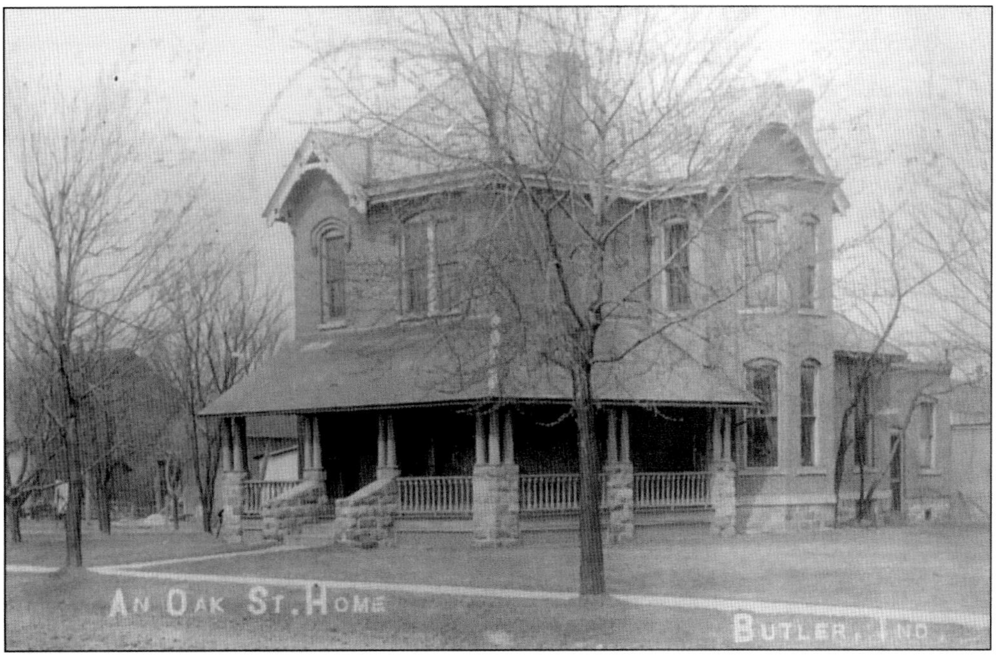

An Oak Street Home, Butler, Indiana. Butler had many fine homes, such as this example located on West Oak Street.

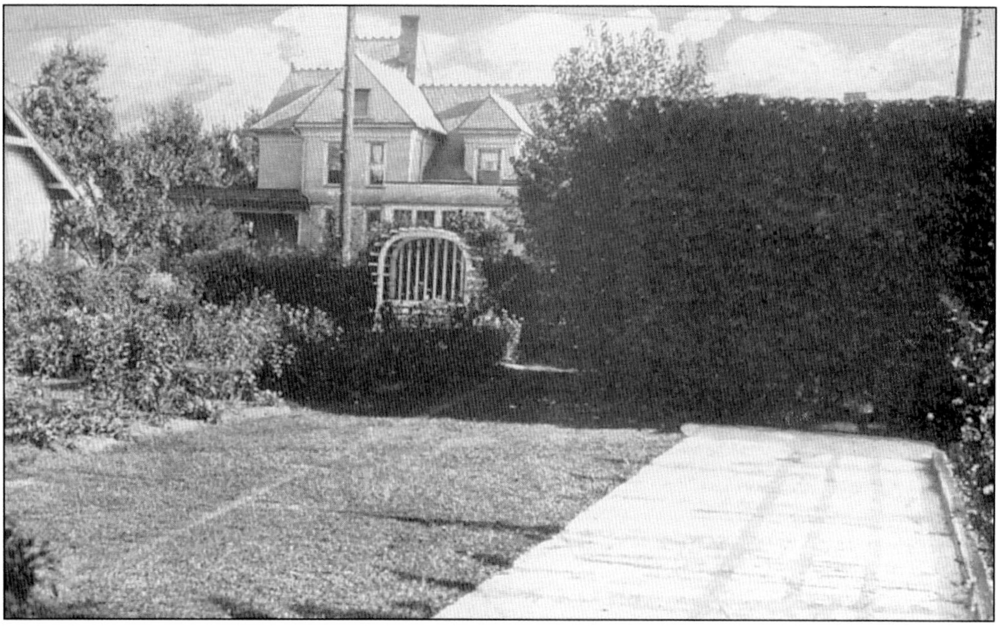

West Oak Street, Floral Scene, Butler, Indiana. The Mason House is in the background.

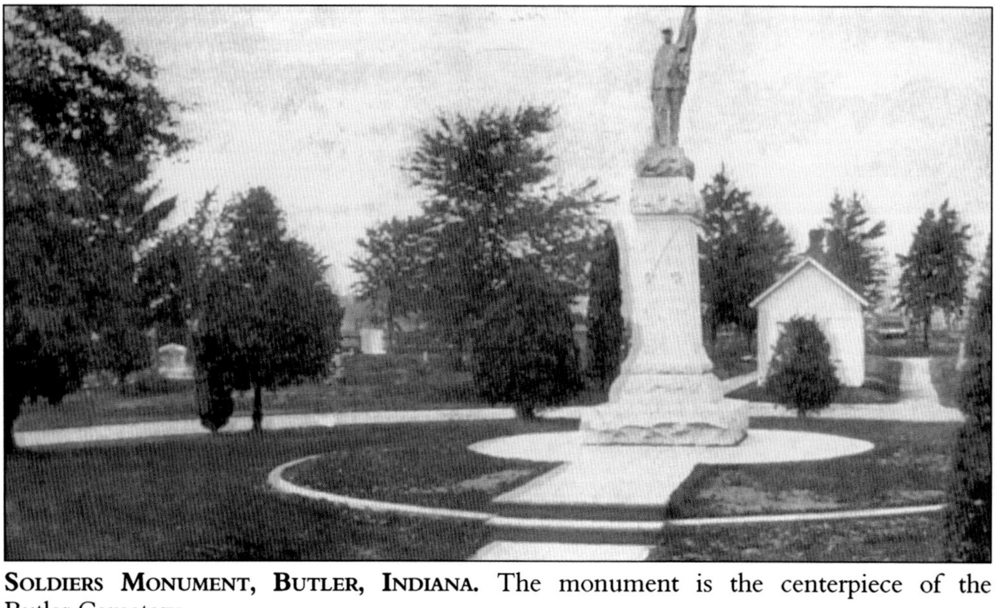

Soldiers Monument, Butler, Indiana. The monument is the centerpiece of the Butler Cemetery.

Four

Corunna

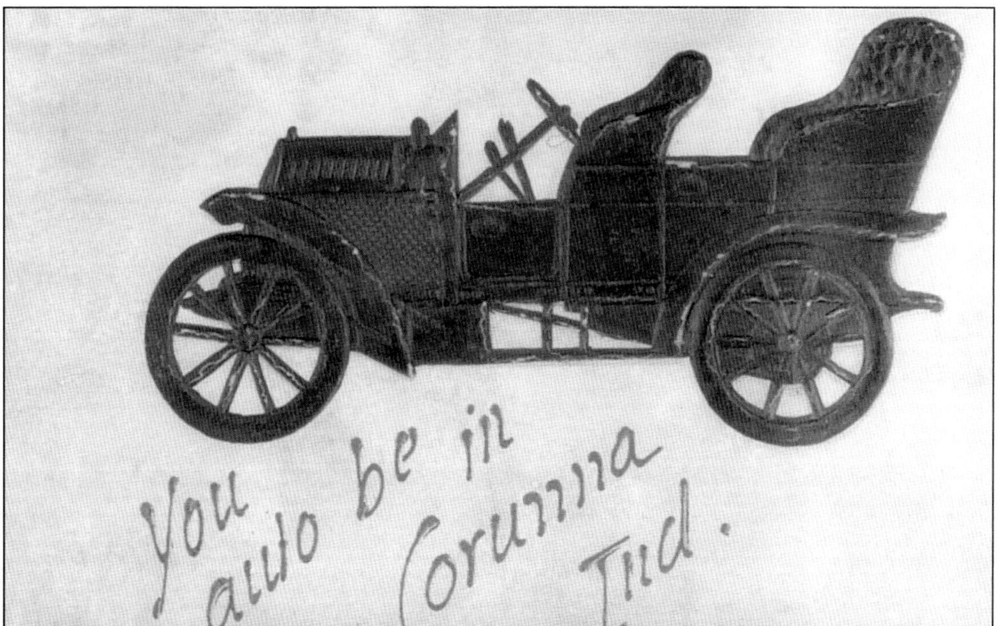

You Auto be in Corunna, Indiana. This is a stock image postcard with the wording applied by hand in gold ink.

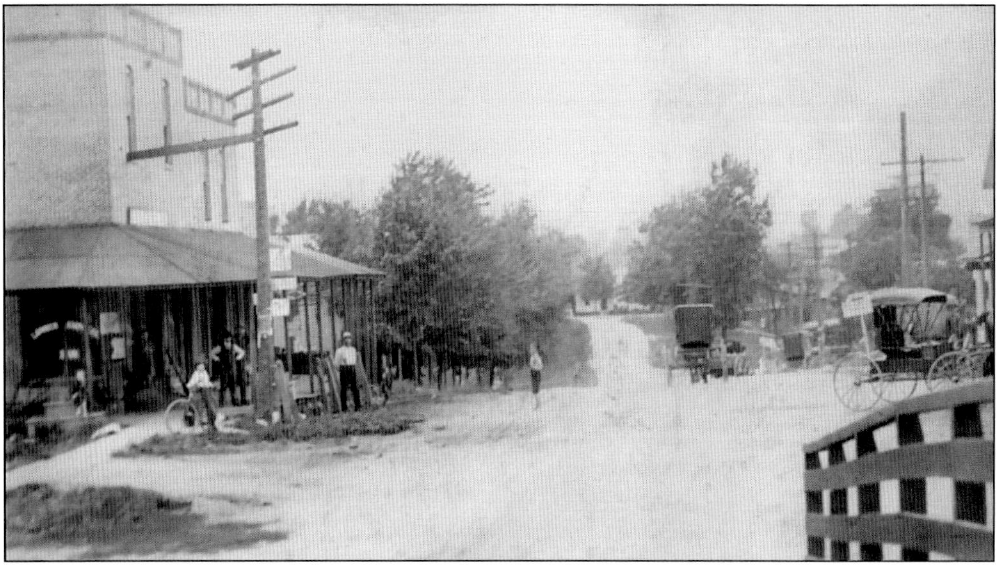

MAIN STREET OF CORUNNA LOOKING NORTH FROM THE BRIDGE. The Milo J. Thomas Store is on the left. It housed a hardware, bank, and telephone exchange. This postcard is postmarked 1903. The only space for a message was below the image.

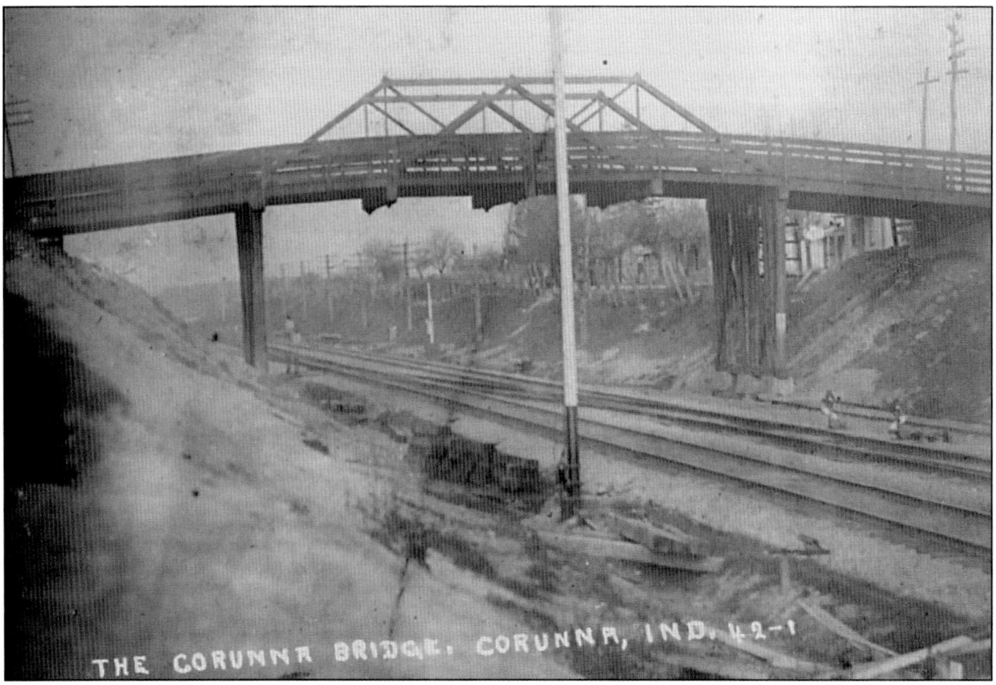

THE CORUNNA BRIDGE, CORUNNA, INDIANA. The bridge carried vehicular traffic over the railroad.

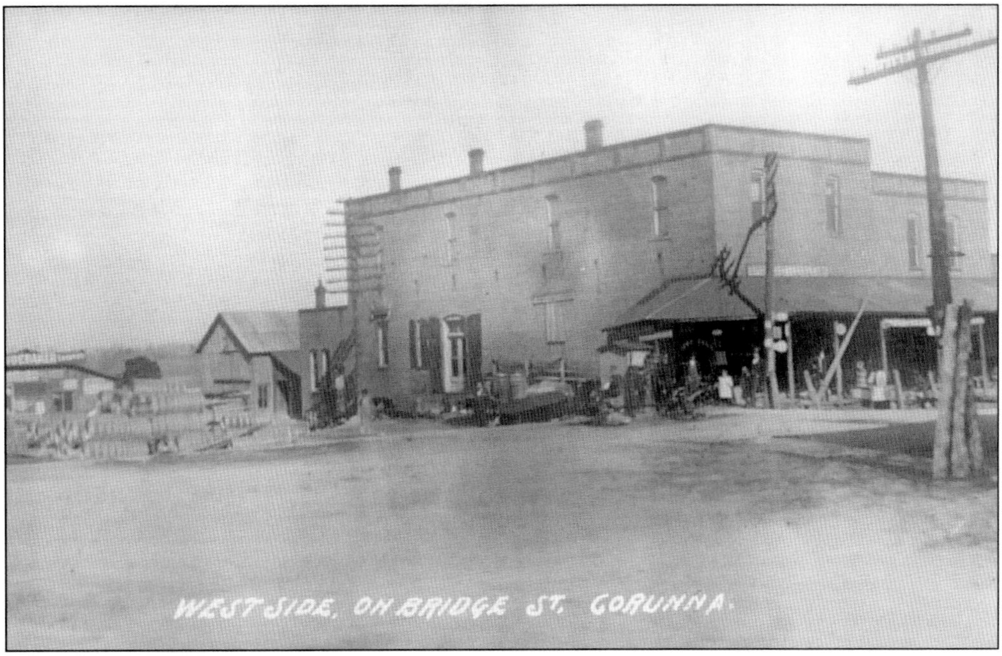

WEST SIDE ON BRIDGE STREET, CORUNNA, INDIANA. Shown here is another view of the Milo J. Thomas Store.

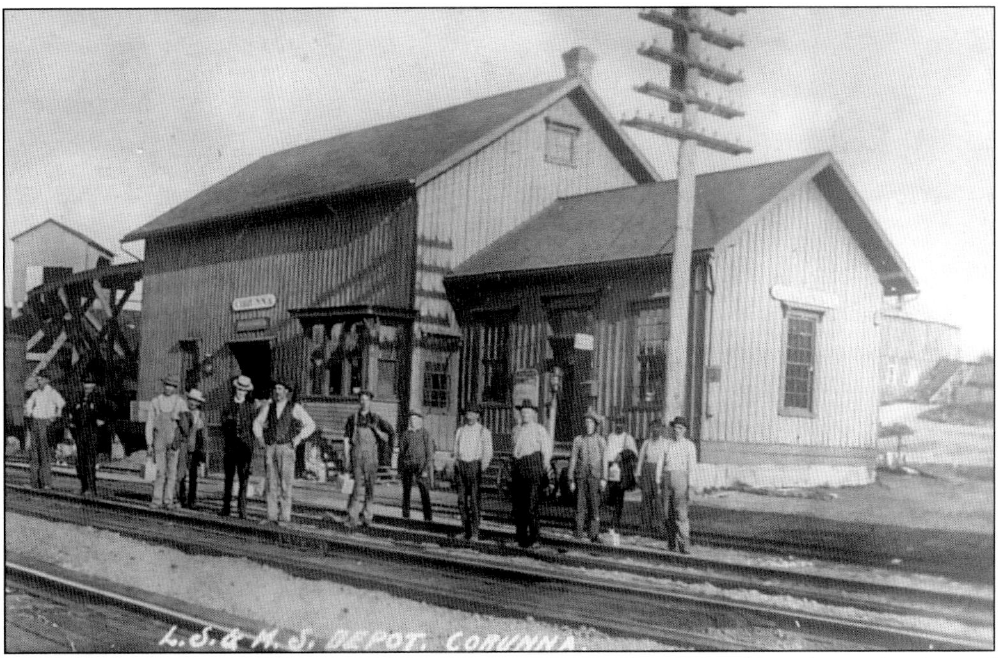

L.S. & M.S. DEPOT, CORUNNA. The Lake Shore & Michigan Southern Depot is pictured here. The men probably worked for the railroad at Corunna.

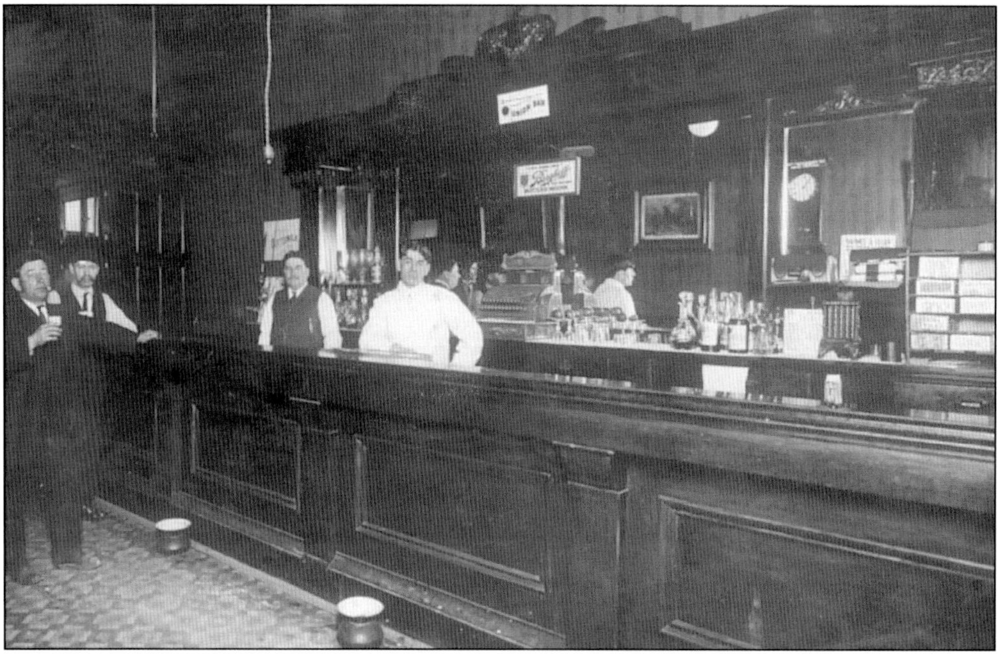

TAVERN AT CORUNNA. The brands of beer advertised on the back bar are Centlivre and Berghoff. Note the spittoons on the floor for those who chewed tobacco.

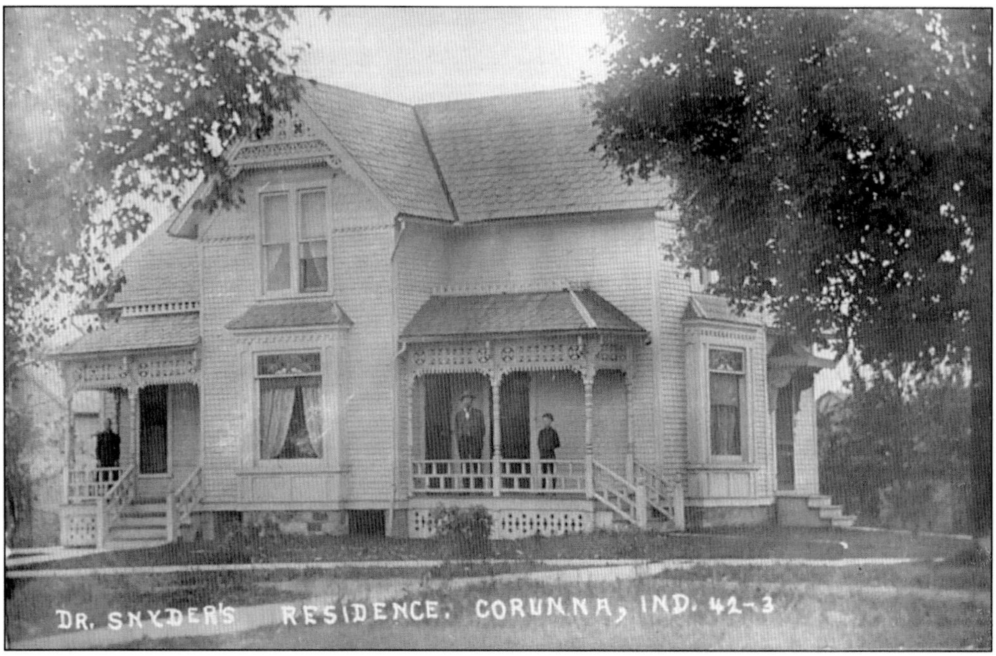

DR. SNYDER'S RESIDENCE, CORUNNA, INDIANA. The doctor's office was at the back.

Five

DEKALB COUNTY FREE FALL FAIR

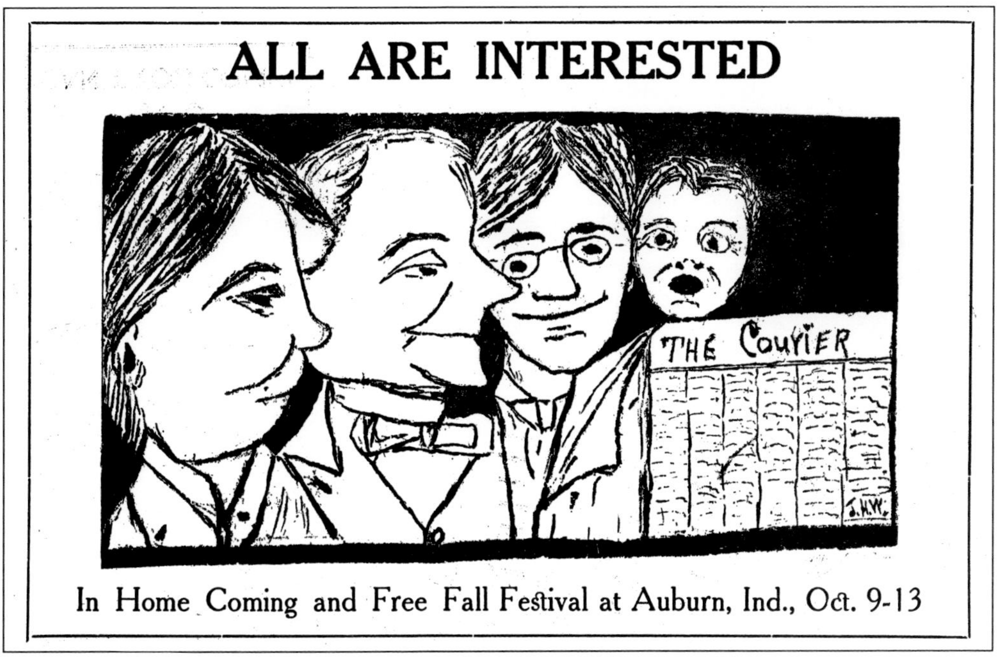

ALL ARE INTERESTED IN HOMECOMING AND FREE FALL FESTIVAL AT AUBURN, INDIANA, OCTOBER 9–13. This postcard was printed by the *Auburn Courier* newspaper to advertise the fair. It was variously called a "homecoming, festival, or fair," but has always been on the streets of Auburn and therefore "free," as opposed to the admission charged to fairgrounds in other counties.

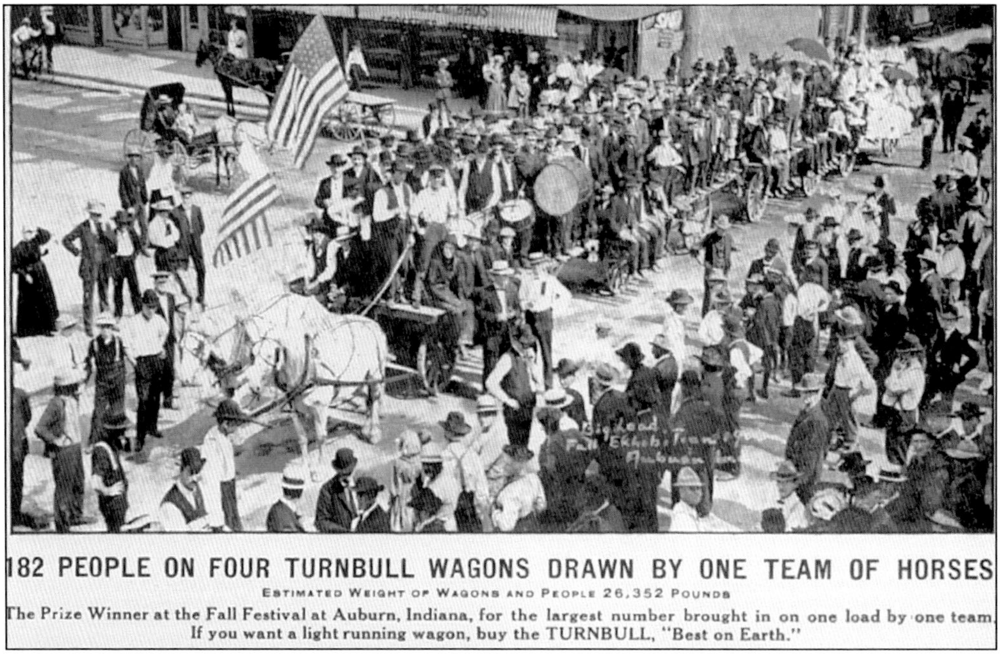

182 People on Four Turnbull Wagons Drawn By One Team Of Horses. The estimated weight of the wagons and people was 26,352 pounds. The prizewinner at the Fall Festival at Auburn, Indiana, was the person with the largest number brought in on one load by one team. If you want a light running wagon, buy the TURNBULL, "Best on Earth." This photograph was taken at the 1907 DeKalb County Free Fall Festival and was used extensively by the Turnbull Wagon Company to advertise their wagons.

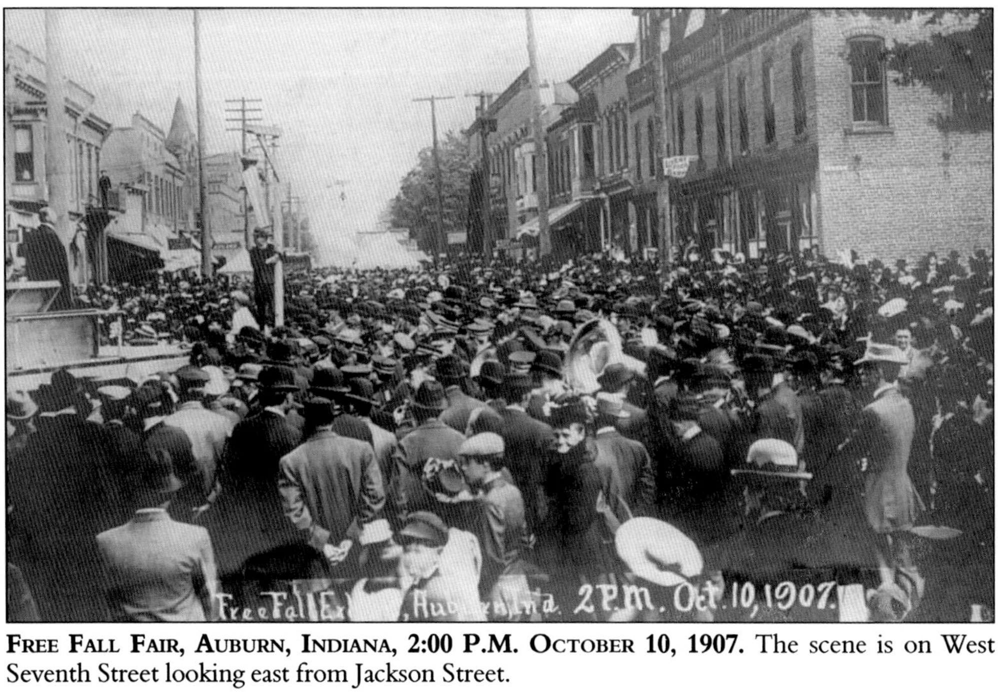

Free Fall Fair, Auburn, Indiana, 2:00 P.M. October 10, 1907. The scene is on West Seventh Street looking east from Jackson Street.

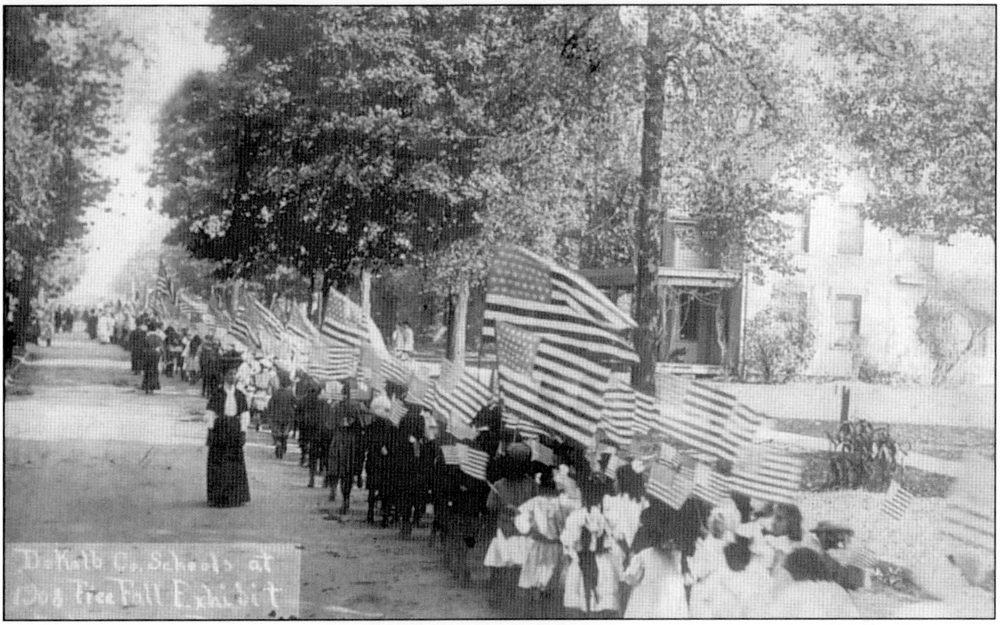

DEKALB COUNTY SCHOOL AT 1908 FREE FALL FAIR EXHIBIT, AUBURN, INDIANA. School children paraded the streets of Auburn waving their flags.

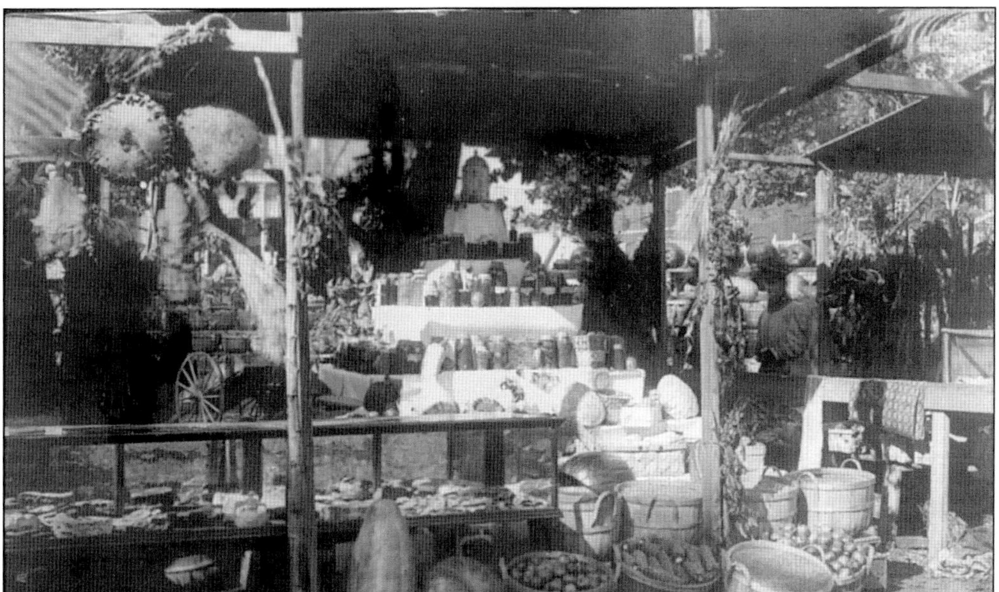

1908 FREE FALL EXHIBIT, AUBURN, INDIANA. The principal purpose of the fair or festival was to exhibit the harvest of crops, vegetables, and flowers. Note the huge sunflowers in the upper left.

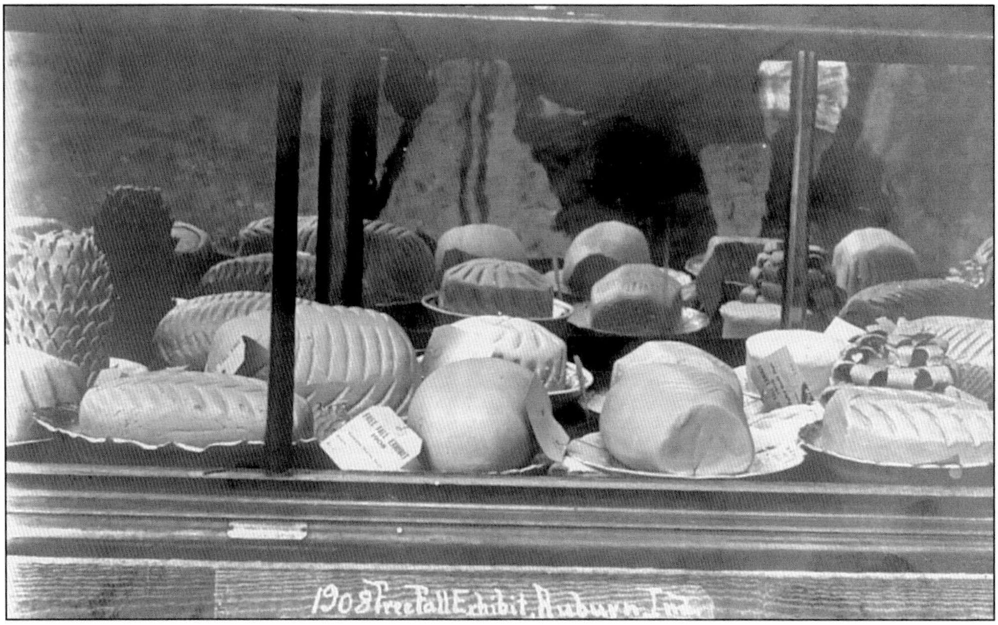

1908 FREE FALL EXHIBIT, AUBURN, INDIANA. Ladies exhibited their breads and other baked goods.

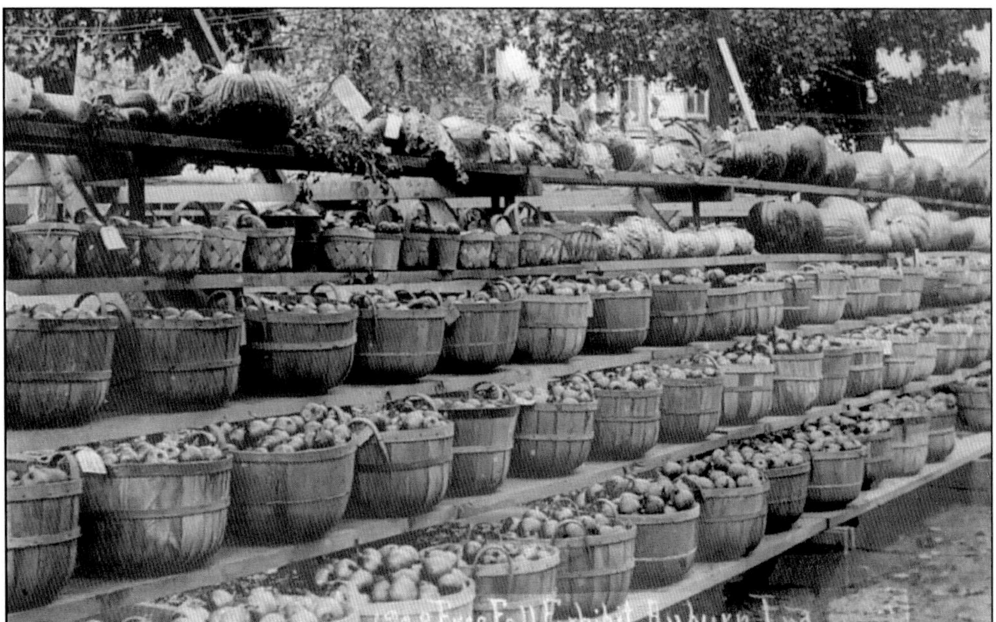

1908 FREE FALL EXHIBIT, AUBURN, INDIANA. Virtually every item that could be grown in DeKalb County was exhibited in quantity.

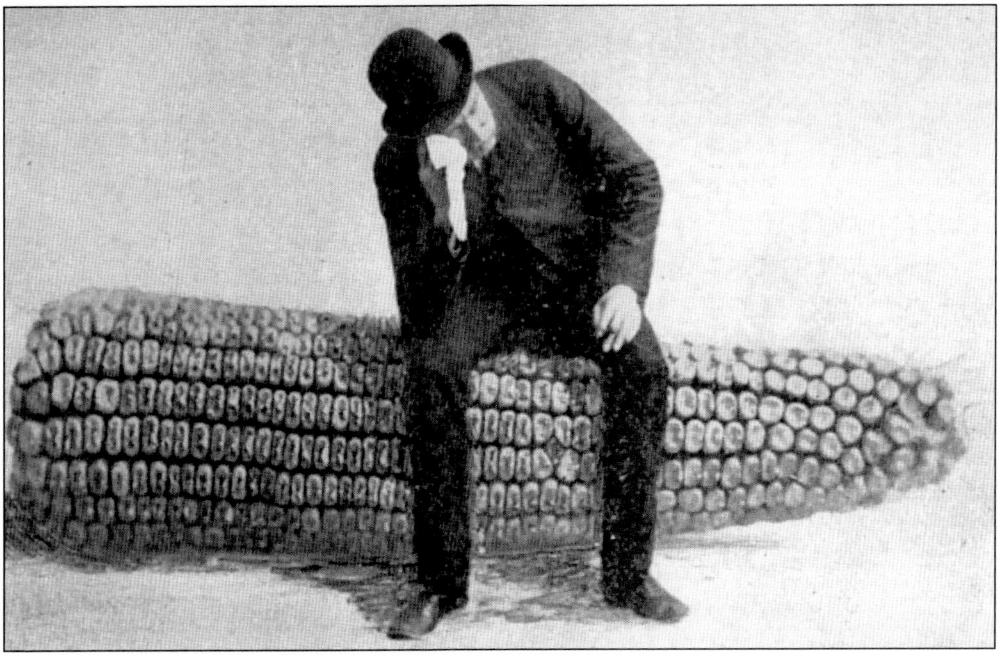

Some Remarkable Corn Dreams. The printed message on the back of this postcard states: "After this picture was shown for the first time, at the Third Annual Free Fall Exhibit at Auburn, Indiana, October 7–8–9, 1908, an investigation was made and not a drop of corn whiskey could be found in the grower's town. Some overly suspicious person accused the grower of having drunk it all up before he saw the vision but, of course, this was malicious slander."

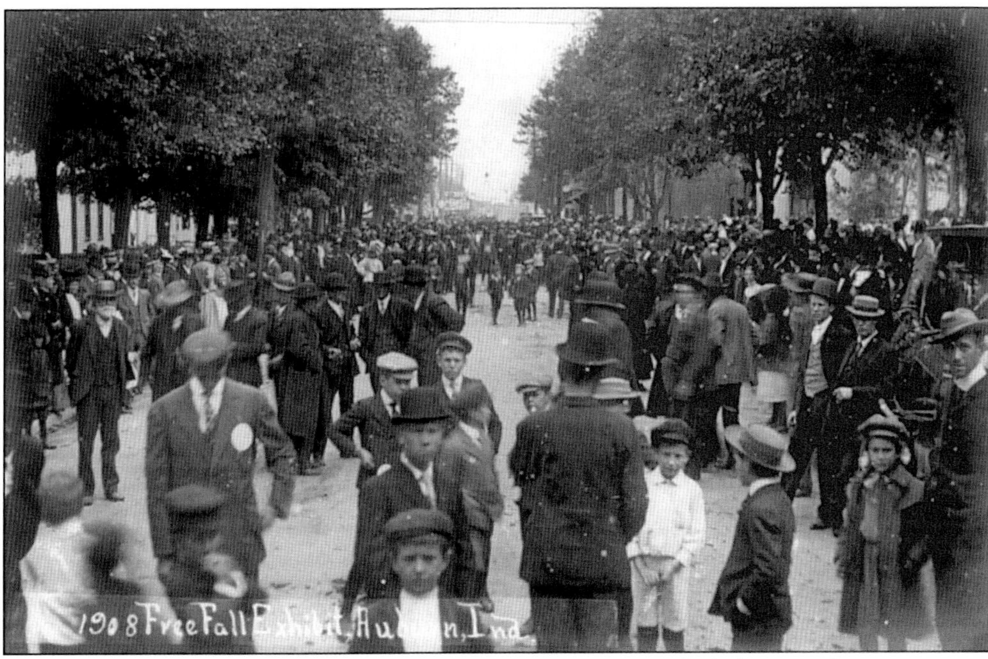

1908 Free Fall Exhibit, Auburn, Indiana. Men and boys milled about on the streets.

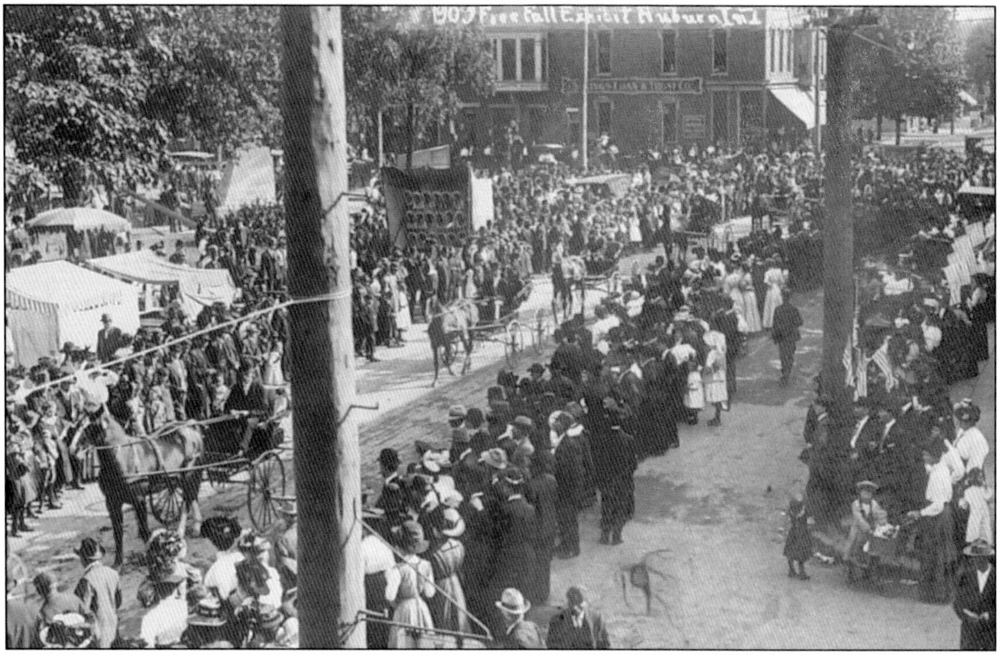

1908 Free Fall Exhibit, Auburn, Indiana. The parade heads north on Main Street along the west side of the square. The cannon can be seen in the upper left.

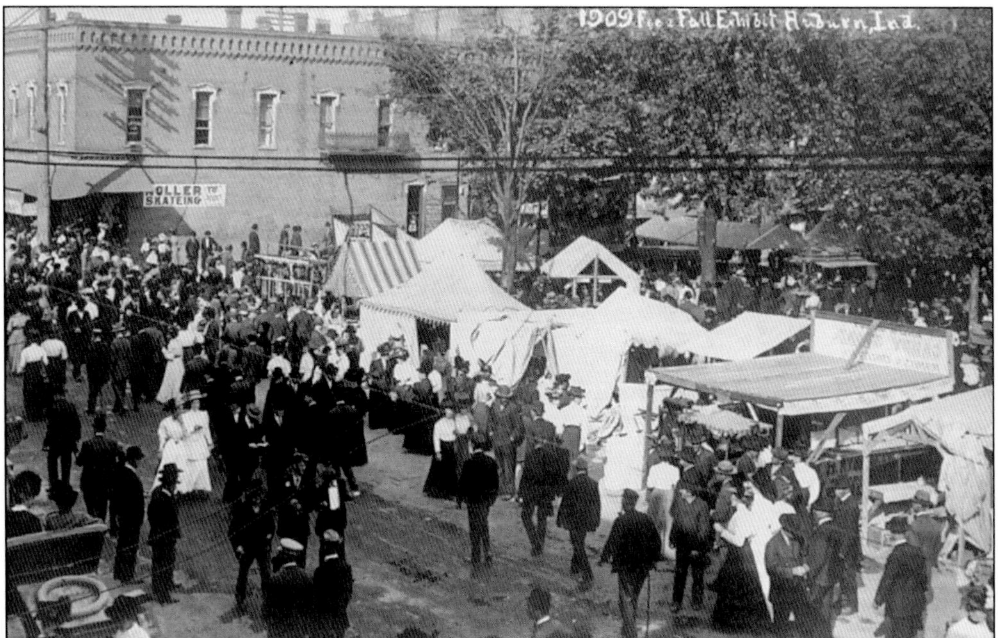

1909 Free Fall Exhibit, Auburn, Indiana. Tents and buildings lined the square. This view is at the intersection of Main and Seventh Streets. Note the "roller skating" sign.

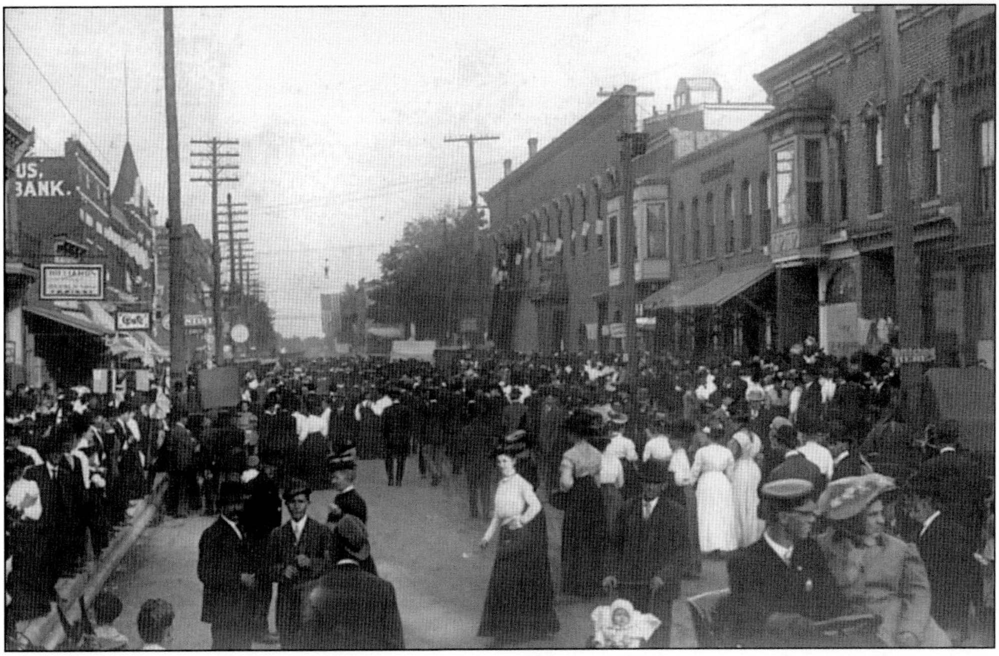

1909 FREE FALL EXHIBIT, AUBURN, INDIANA. This view looks east on Seventh Street from Jackson Street.

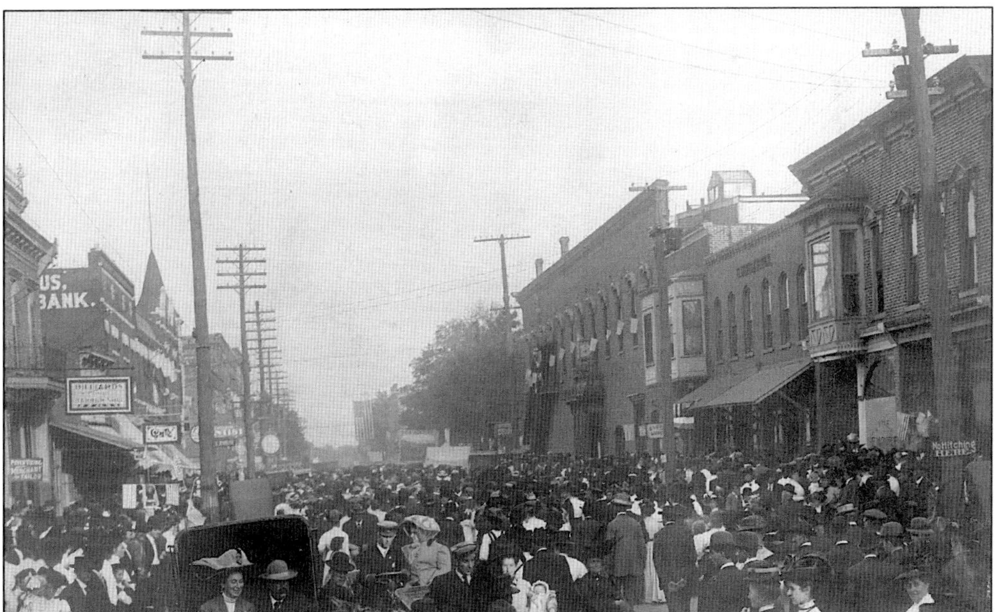

FREE FALL EXHIBIT, OCTOBER 6–8, 1909, AUBURN, INDIANA. The same view is shown with a different crowd. Note the monitor window on the top of the building on the right.

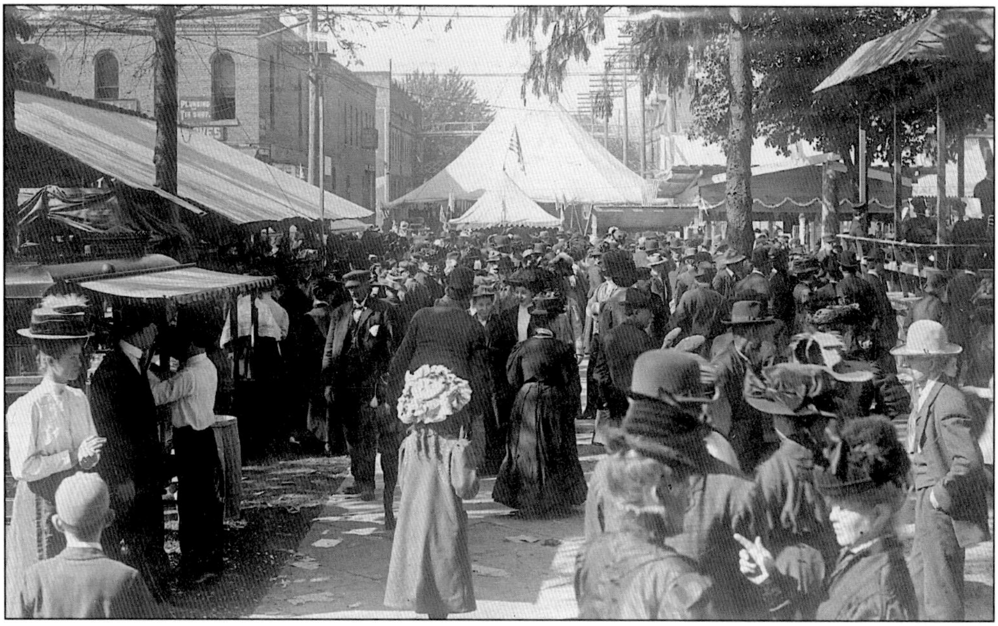

1909 Free Fall Exhibit, Auburn, Indiana. The crowd was dressed in their finest clothes complete with hats.

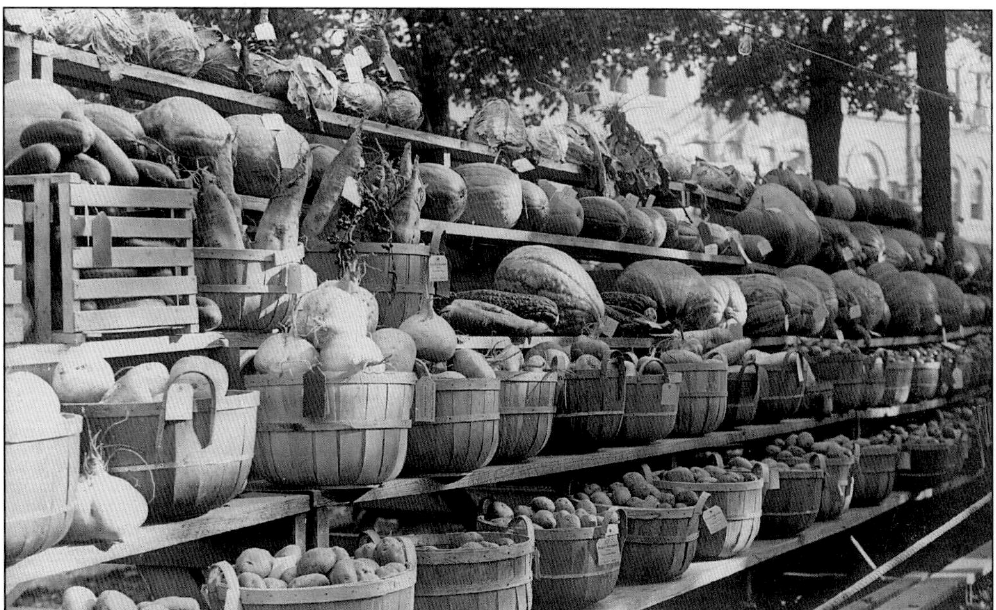

They "Are" the World at Free Fall Fair Exhibit, 1909, Auburn, Indiana. Cabbage, potatoes, onion, squash, and pumpkins are shown here.

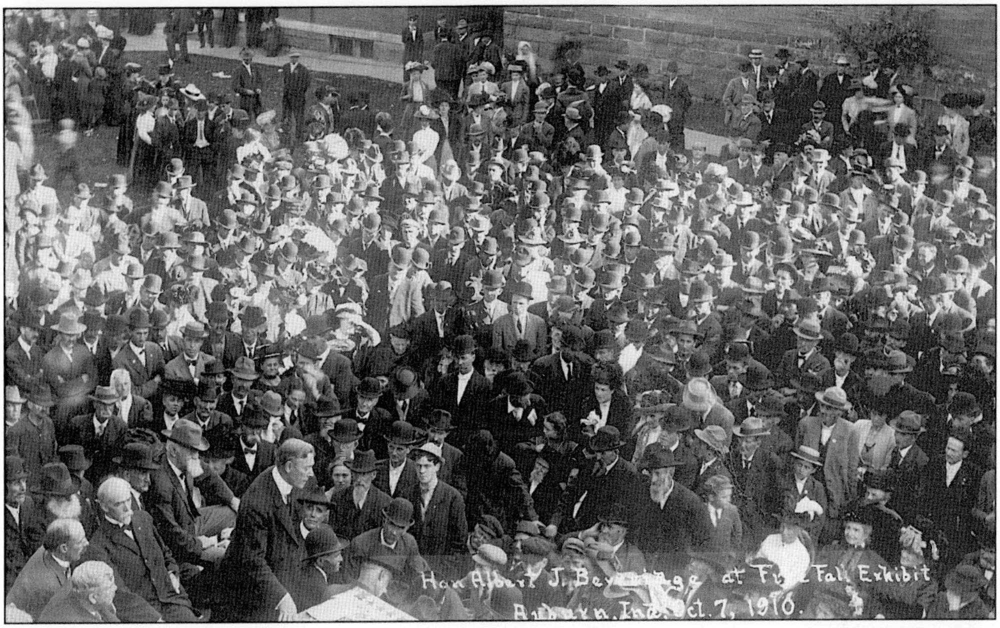

HON. ALBERT J. BEVERIDGE AT FREE FALL EXHIBIT, AUBURN, INDIANA, OCTOBER 7, 1910. Mr. Beveridge was a distinguished senator from Ohio, who later won a Pulitzer Prize for his biography of John Marshall.

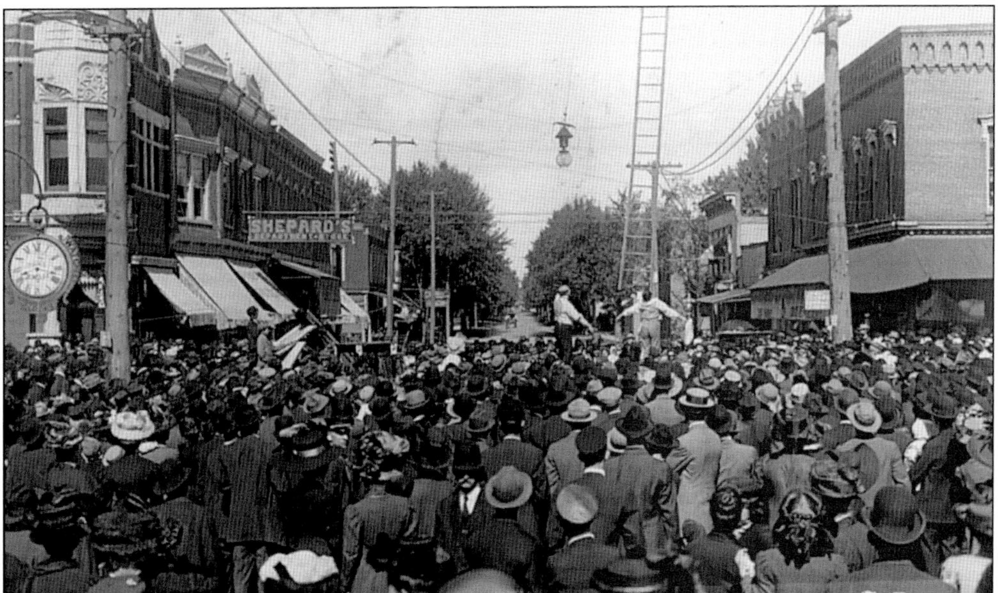

FREE FALL EXHIBIT 1910, AUBURN, INDIANA. "Free Acts" were a part of the DeKalb County Free Fall Fair. Trapeze artists were a common act. The view is north on Main Street from Seventh Street.

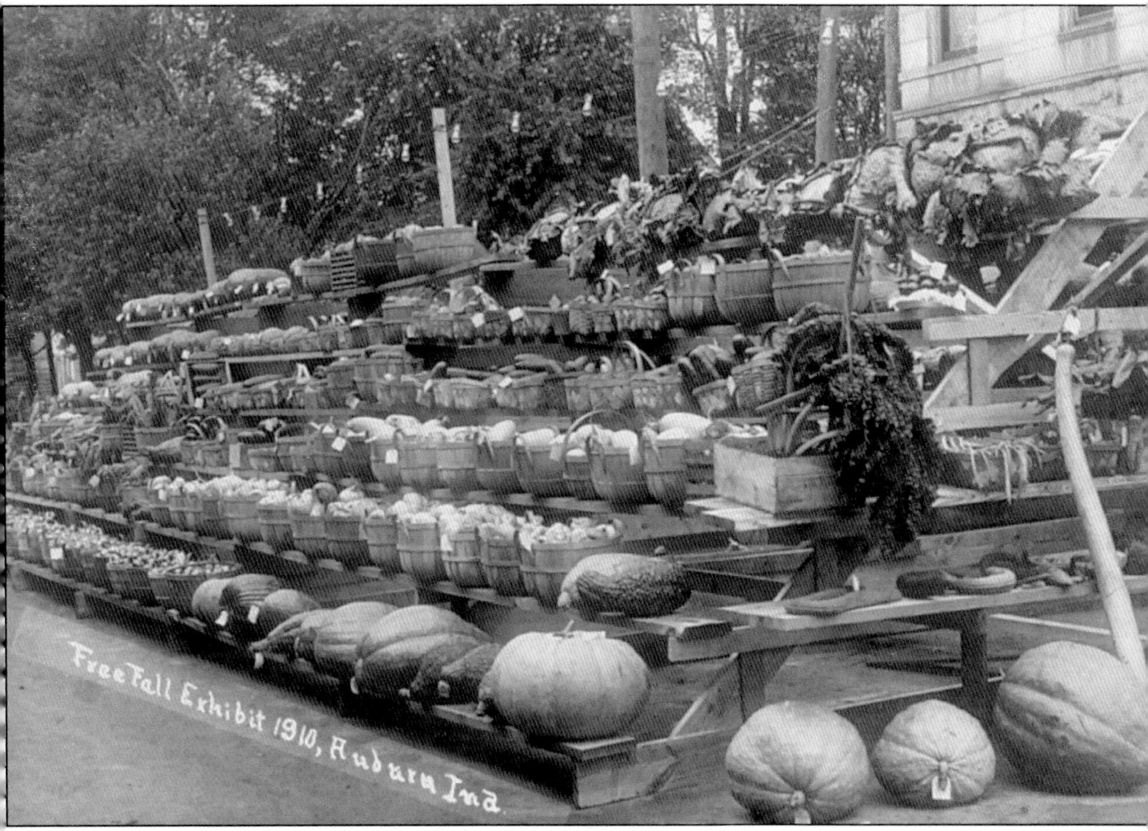

FREE FALL EXHIBIT, 1910, AUBURN, INDIANA. Huge exhibits of garden produce lined these racks. Note the string of light bulbs along the top.

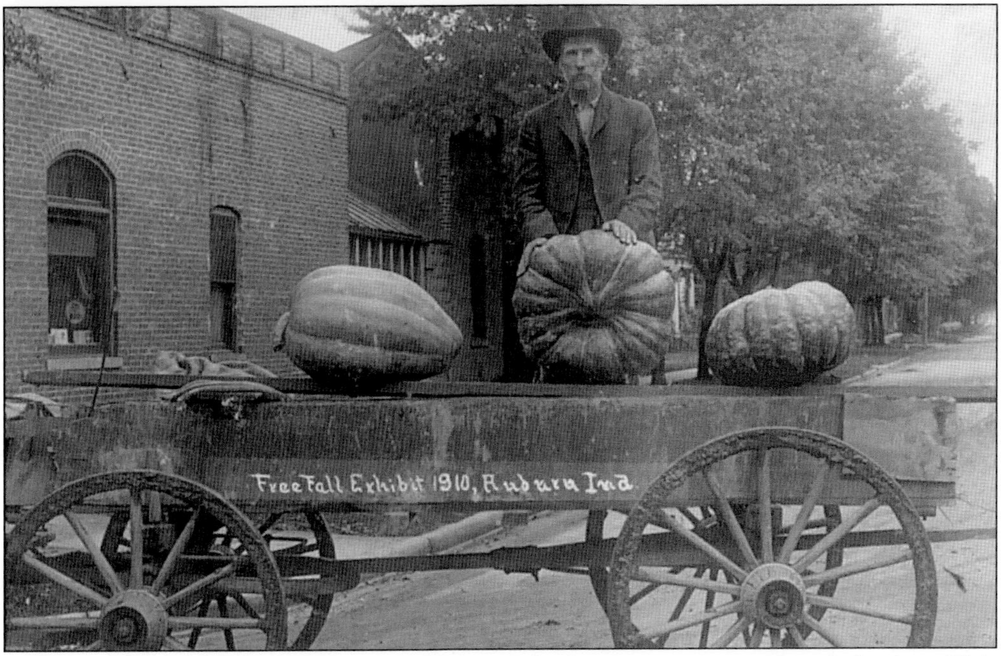

1909 FREE FALL, EXHIBIT, AUBURN, INDIANA. The largest items were awarded prizes. This gentleman proudly displays his pumpkins in front of the Schemmerhorn's Photo Studio, located at the southwest corner of South Jackson and West Seventh Streets. Note the glass area behind the left pumpkin. This was used by photographers to provide natural light for photographs.

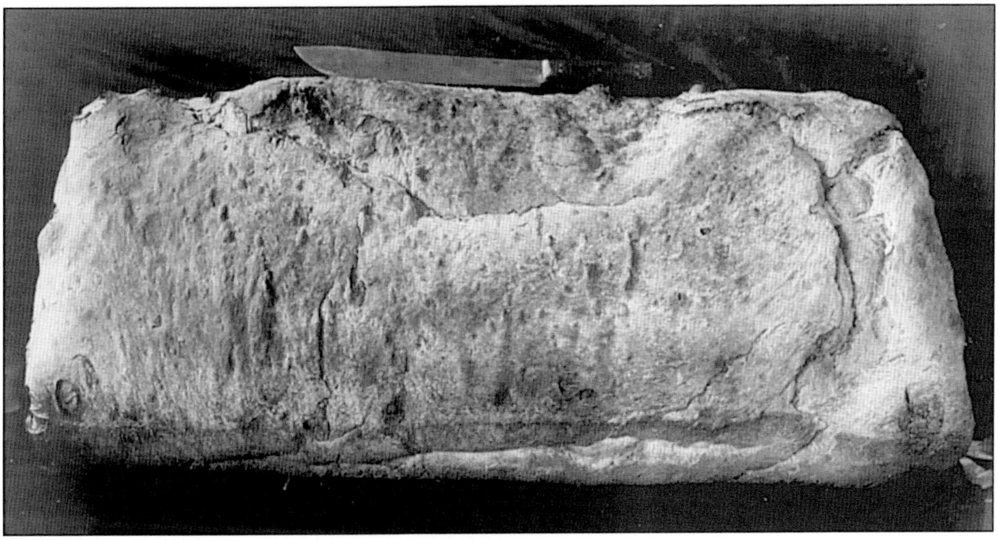

A DEKALB COUNTY FARM LOAF, 8 X 18 X 42 INCHES, 59 LBS. FREE FALL EXHIBIT OCTOBER 6–8, 1909, AUBURN, INDIANA. A 59-pound loaf of bread is pictured here.

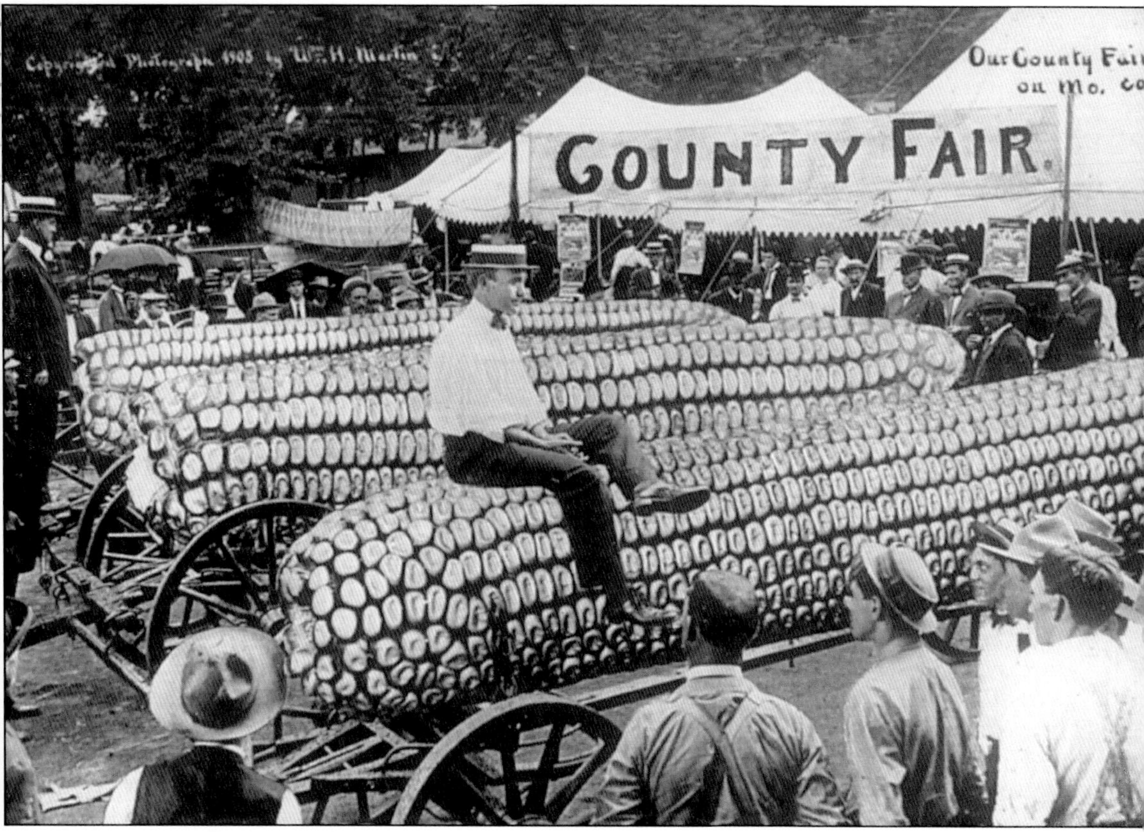

COUNTY FAIR LARGE CORN. Large crop postcards were made by "trick photography."

Six

GARRETT

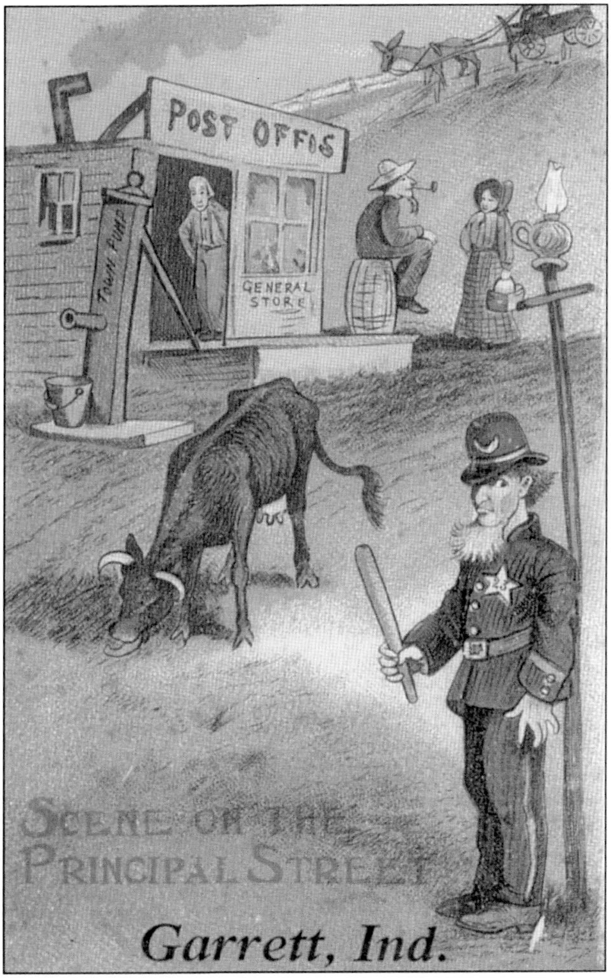

SCENE ON THE PRINCIPAL STREET, GARRETT, INDIANA. This comic card disparages the city of Garrett in a humorous way.

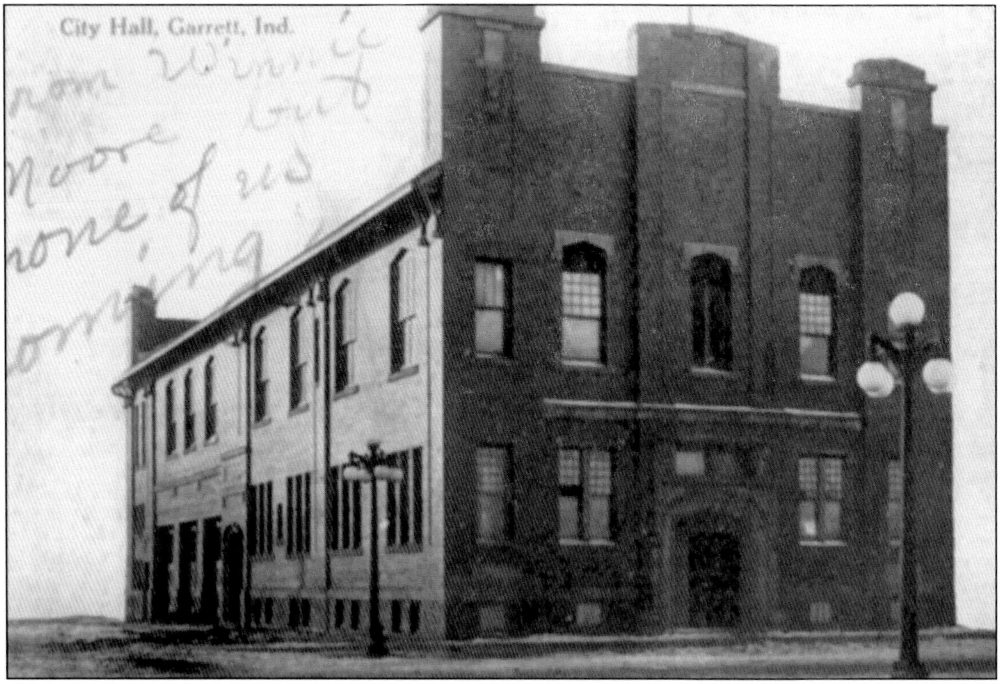

CITY HALL, GARRETT, INDIANA. The Garrett City Hall was an outstanding building in downtown Garrett.

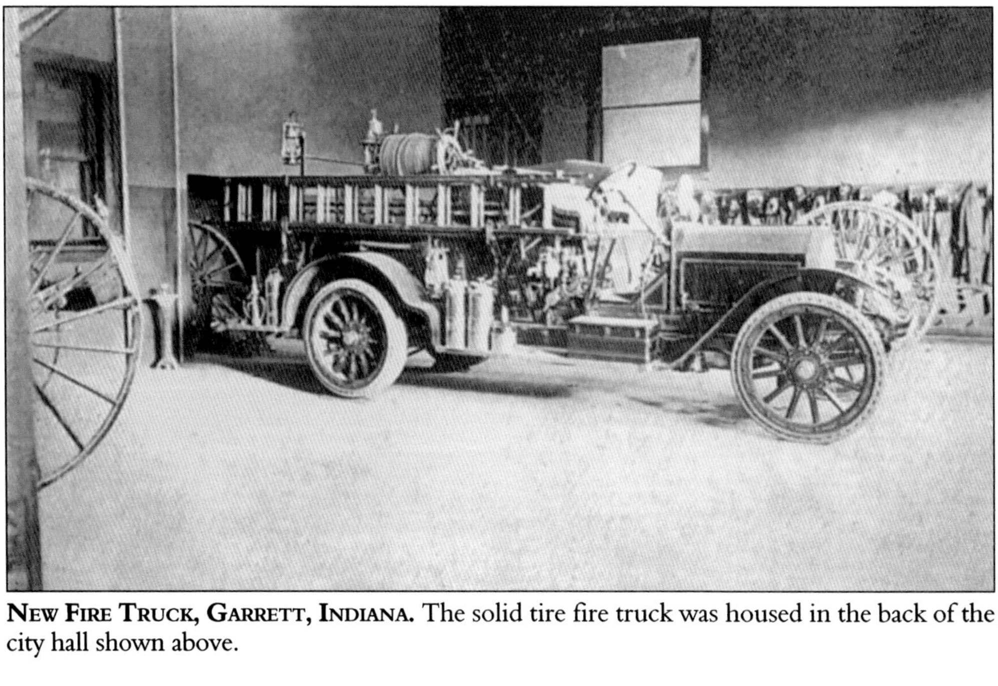

NEW FIRE TRUCK, GARRETT, INDIANA. The solid tire fire truck was housed in the back of the city hall shown above.

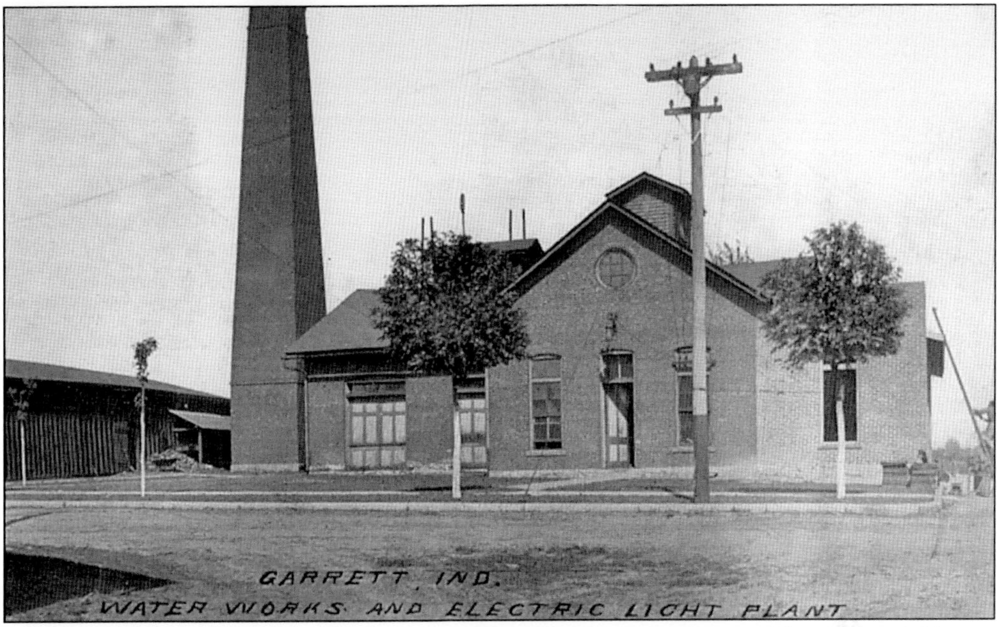

Garrett, Indiana, Water Works and Electric Light Plant. The City of Garrett generated its own power.

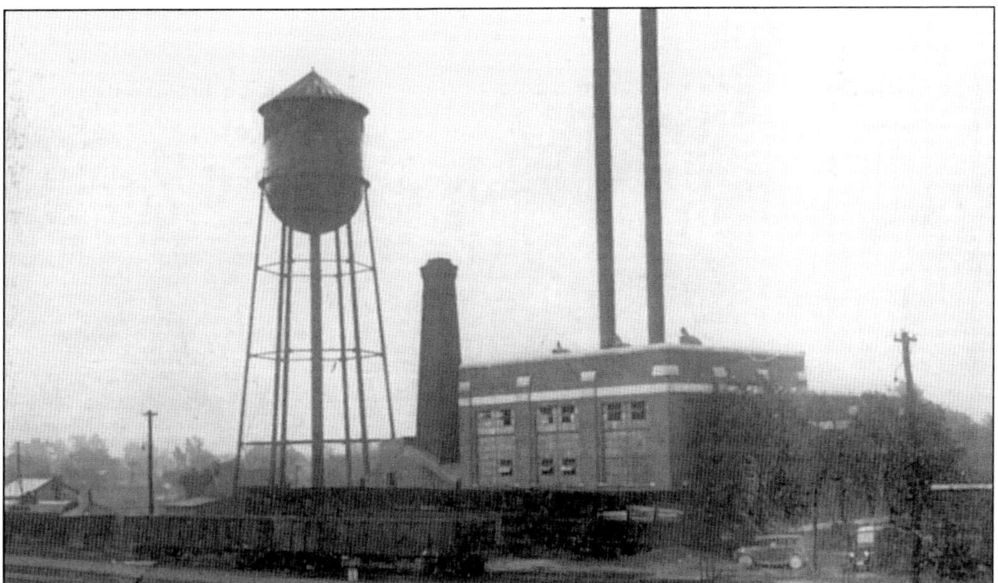

New Municipal Water and Light Plant, Garrett, Indiana. The "new" plant was state of the art at the time.

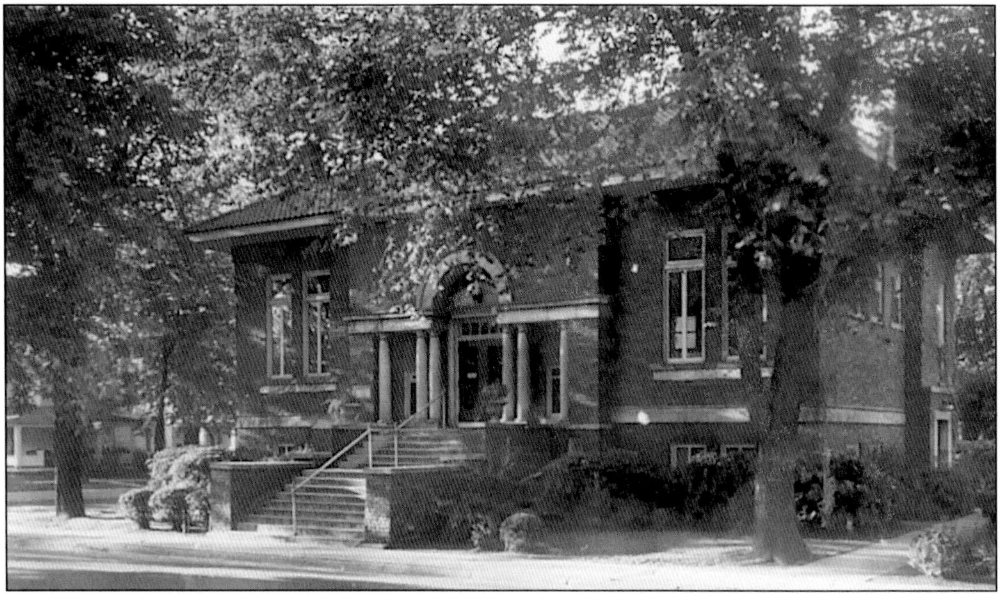

LIBRARY, GARRETT, INDIANA. The Garrett Library has served its citizens well.

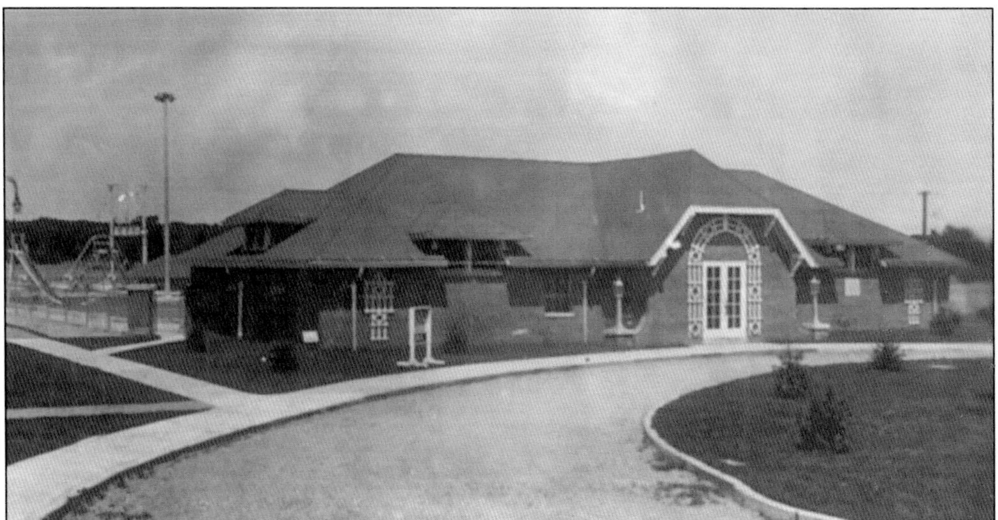

SWIMMING POOL, GARRETT, INDIANA. Garrett had a municipal pool long before most communities, thanks to prominent Democratic Mayor Fred Feick, who secured the structure through the Works Progress Administration during the Great Depression of the 1930s.

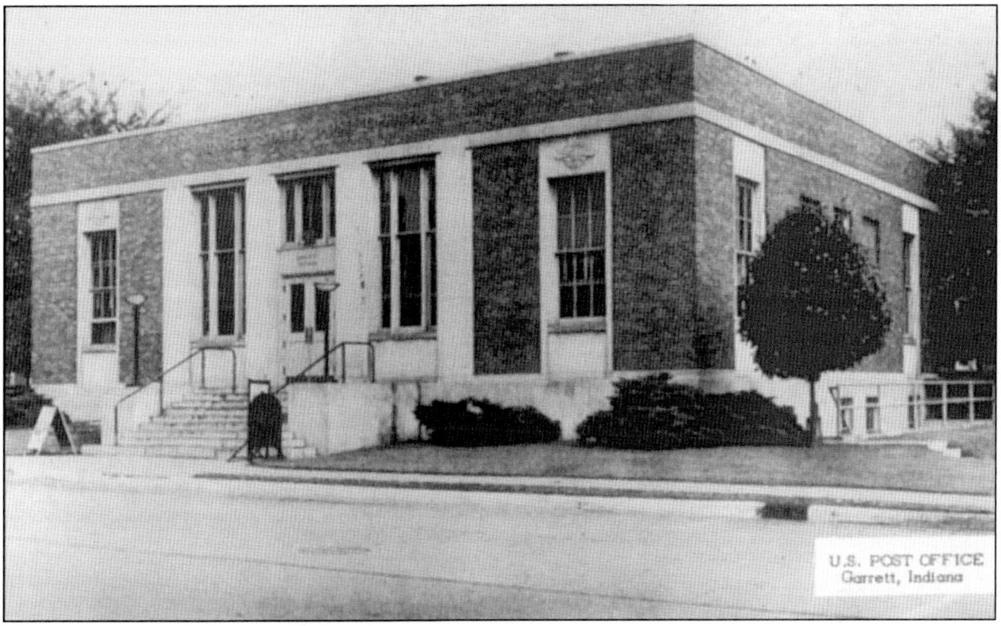

UNITED STATES POST OFFICE, GARRETT, INDIANA. The Garrett Post Office has several wonderful murals painted by WPA artists in its lobby.

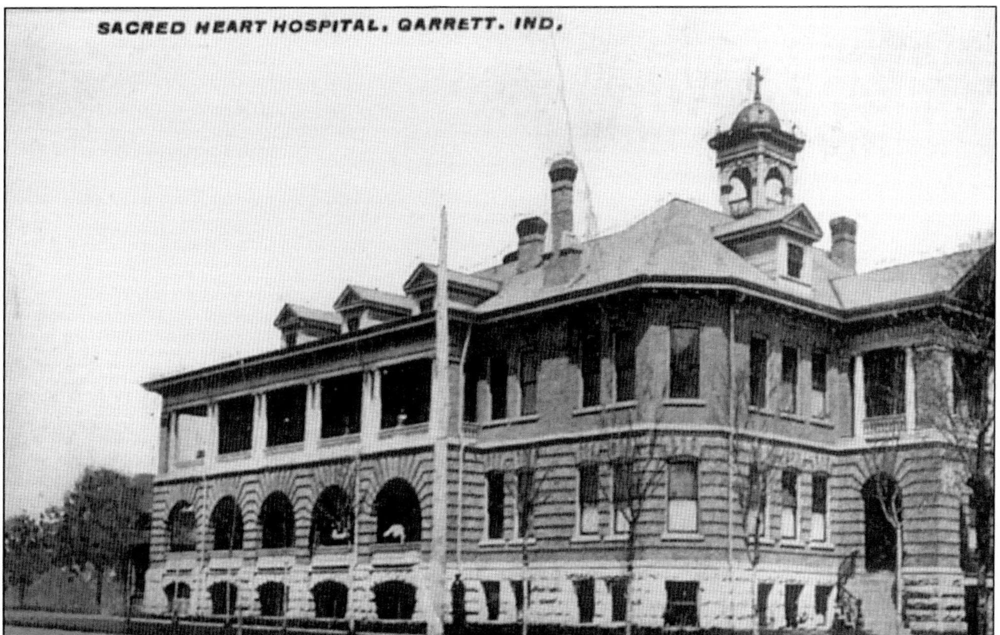

SACRED HEART HOSPITAL, GARRETT, INDIANA. The Sacred Heart Hospital was used by the doctors of the Garrett Clinic to provide excellent health care for DeKalb County citizens.

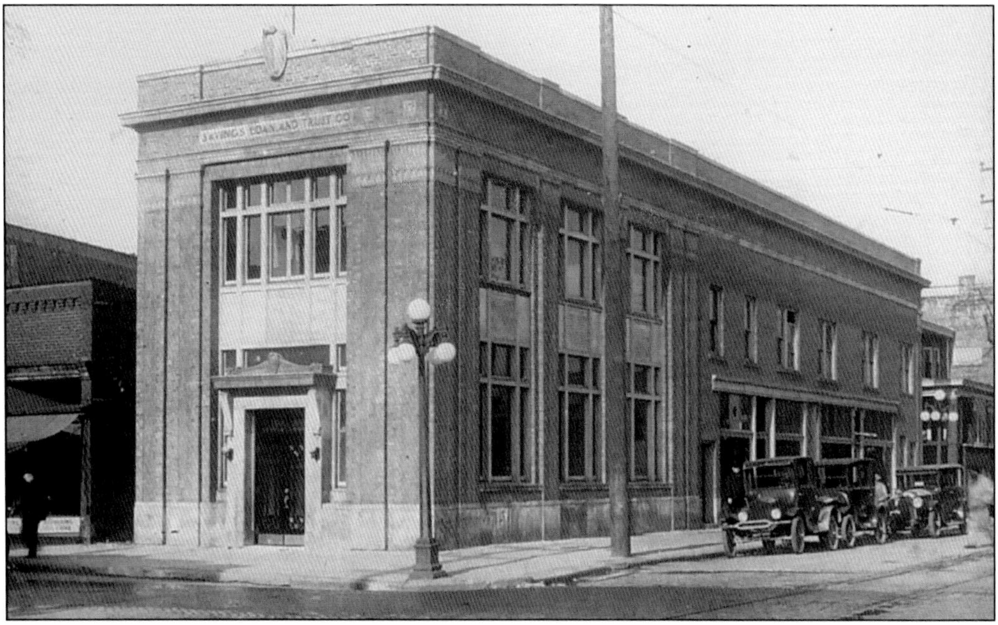

The Garrett State Bank. This stately building suggested safety and security for depositor's funds.

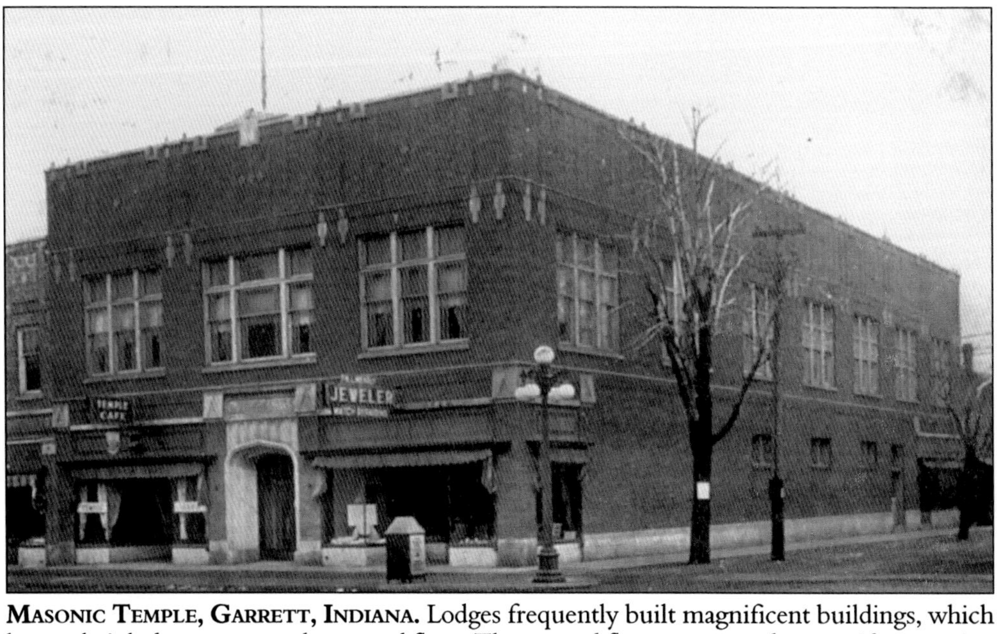

Masonic Temple, Garrett, Indiana. Lodges frequently built magnificent buildings, which house their lodge rooms on the second floor. The ground floor was rented to provide operating and maintenance funds. Ort Jewelers and the Temple Café were at street level.

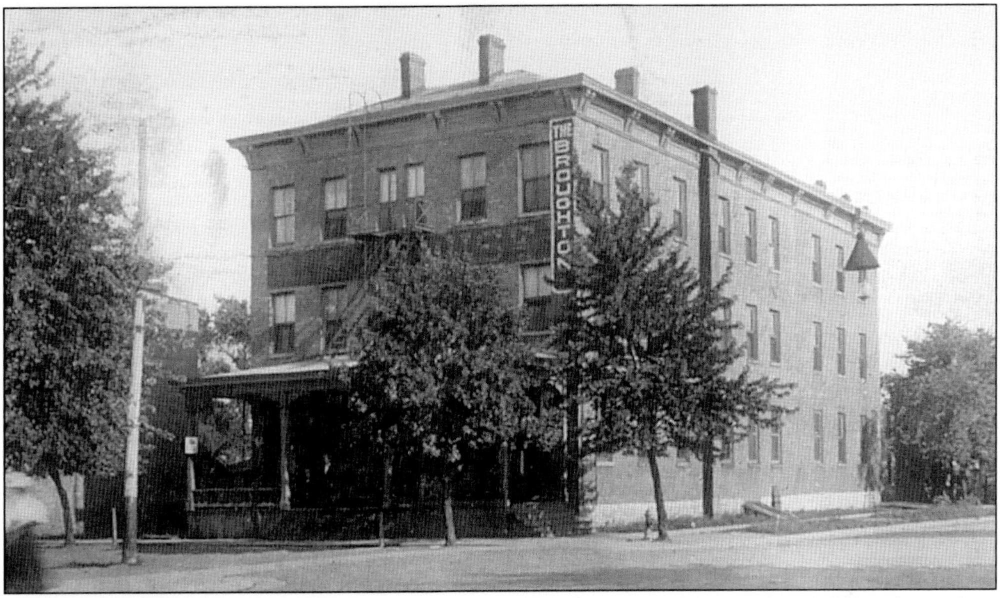

The Broughton Hotel, Garrett, Indiana. This large hotel housed and fed rail travelers who got off Baltimore and Ohio trains to spend the night.

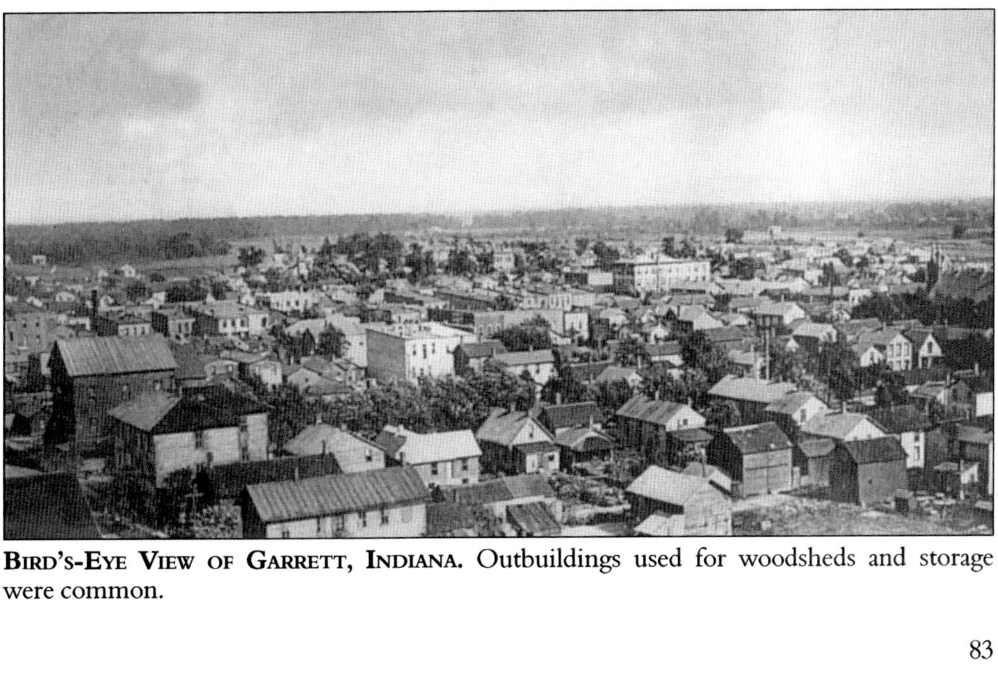

Bird's-Eye View of Garrett, Indiana. Outbuildings used for woodsheds and storage were common.

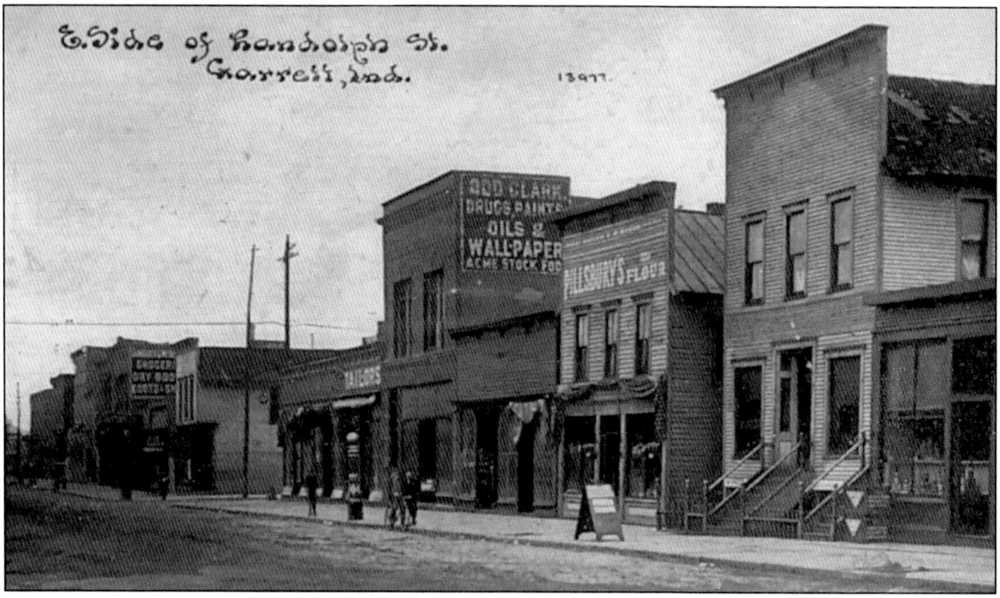

EAST SIDE OF RANDOLPH STREET GARRETT, INDIANA. Businesses include Pillsbury Flour; Add Clark, Drugs, Paints, Oils and Wallpaper, Acme Stock Food; Tailors and Groceries, and Dry Goods.

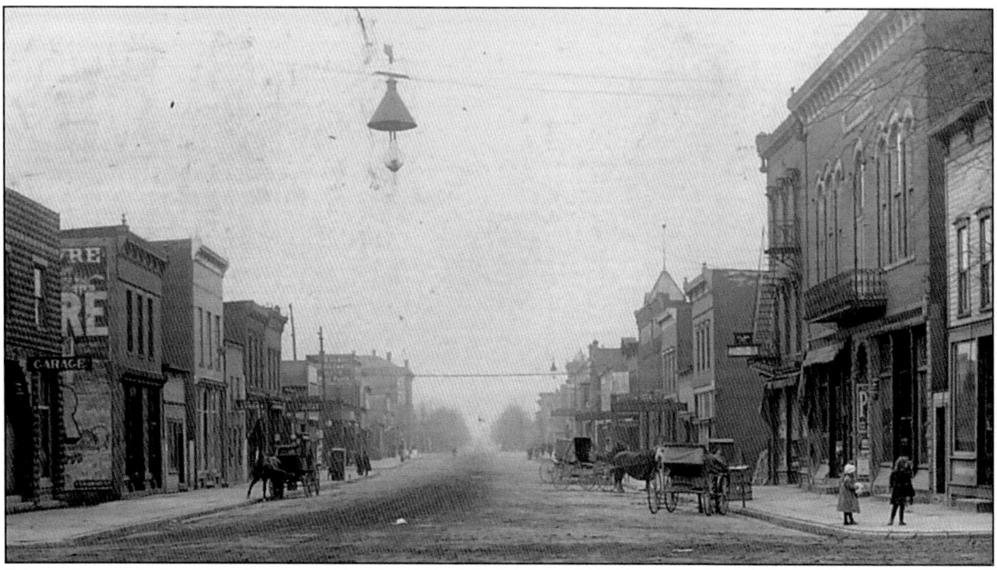

RANDOLPH STREET LOOKING SOUTH, GARRETT, INDIANA.

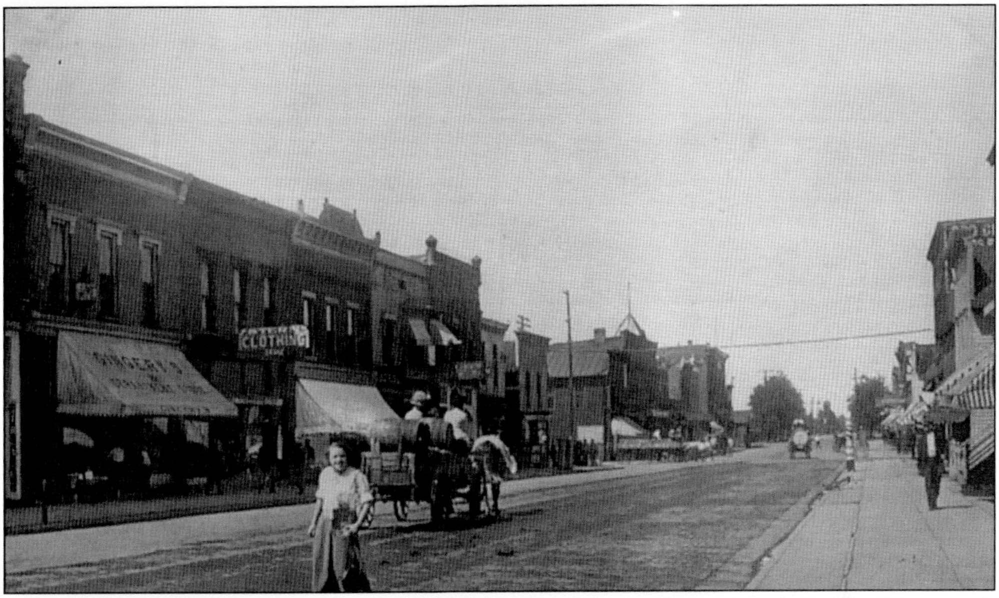

RANDOLPH STREET LOOKING NORTH, GARRETT, INDIANA. In this view, a lady is walking south in the street, and a team of horses is pulling a wagon loaded with two large wooden barrels. Gingery's Department Store and Stern Clothing Co. are on the west side of the street.

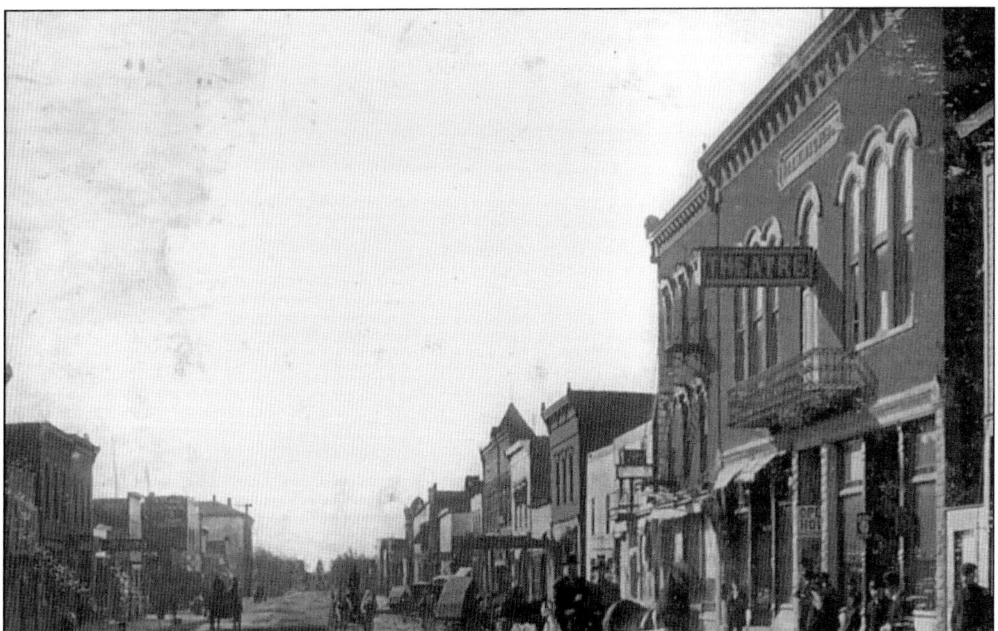

RANDOLPH STREET LOOKING SOUTH FROM QUINCY STREET, GARRETT, INDIANA. The theatre is on the right with an "Open House" sign in the window.

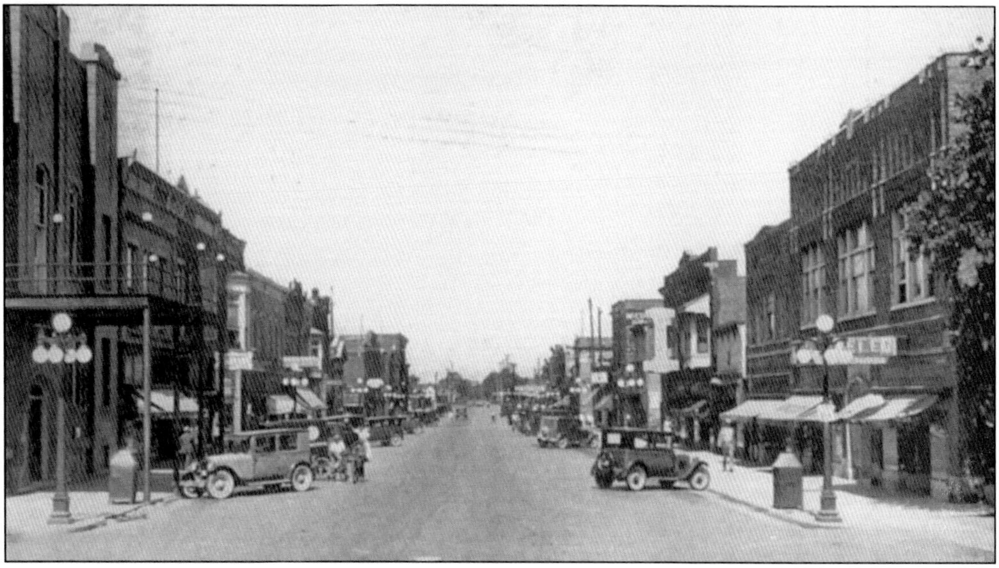

RANDOLPH STREET NORTH FROM KEYSER STREET, GARRETT, INDIANA. This is a later view, with *c.* 1920s cars. The Garret City Hall is on the left with a balcony. The Masonic Building is on the left.

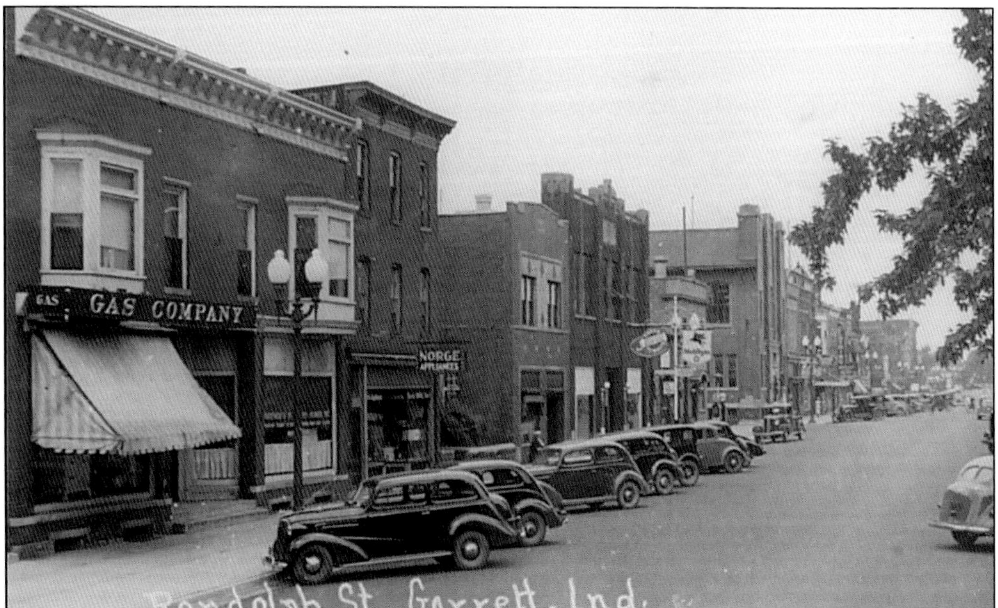

RANDOLPH STREET, GARRET, INDIANA. The gas company and Heinzerling Hardware are on the left with a Mobilgas "Flying Horse" sign.

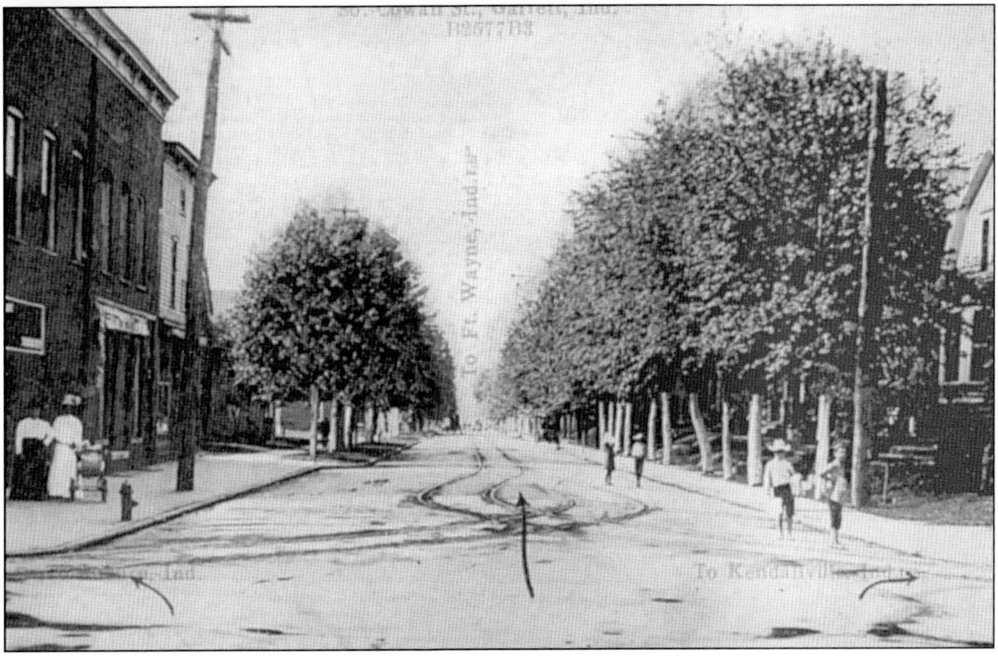

South Cowan Street, Garrett, Indiana. This view shows the convergence of the interurban tracks from Auburn and Kendallville, which then lead to Fort Wayne.

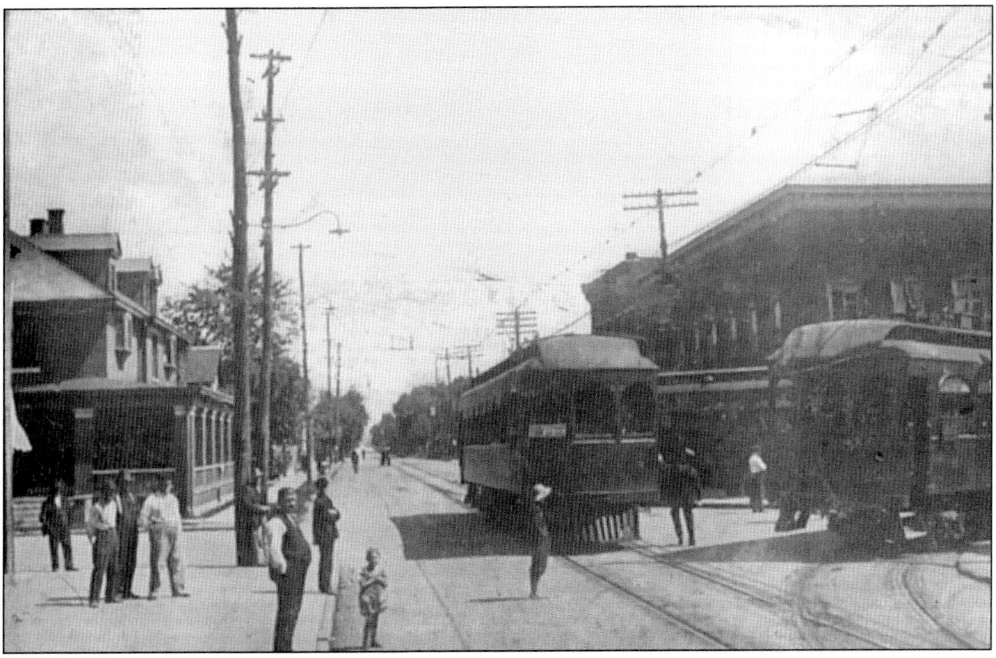

King Street at Interurban Station, Garrett, Indiana. Three interurban cars meet at the Interurban Station so that passengers can transfer to a different car to continue their journey. Note the overhead wires which supplied the cars with electricity.

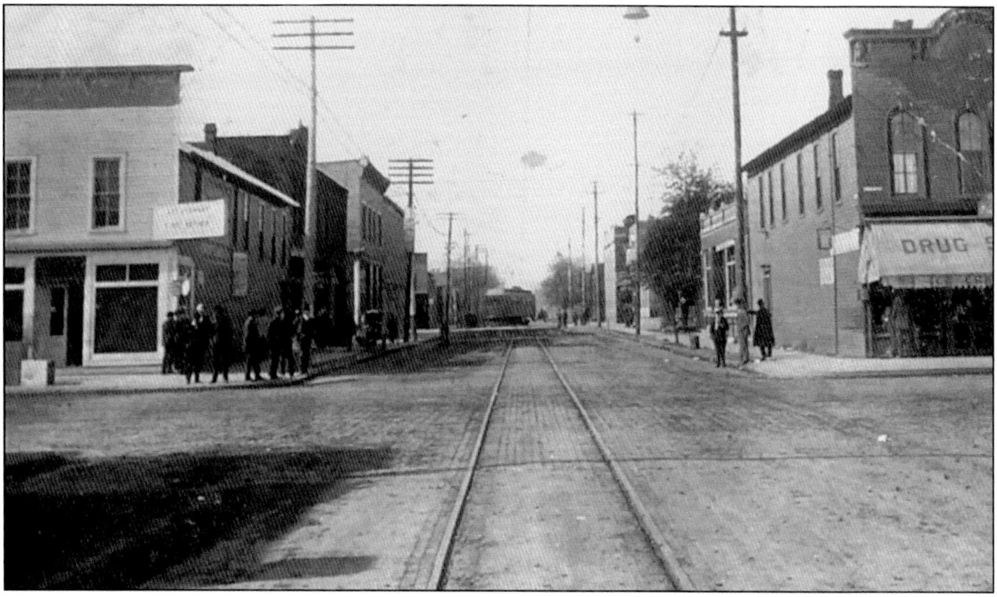

King Street, Garrett, Indiana. The interurban tracks are laid down the middle of the brick street. An interurban can be seen in the distance.

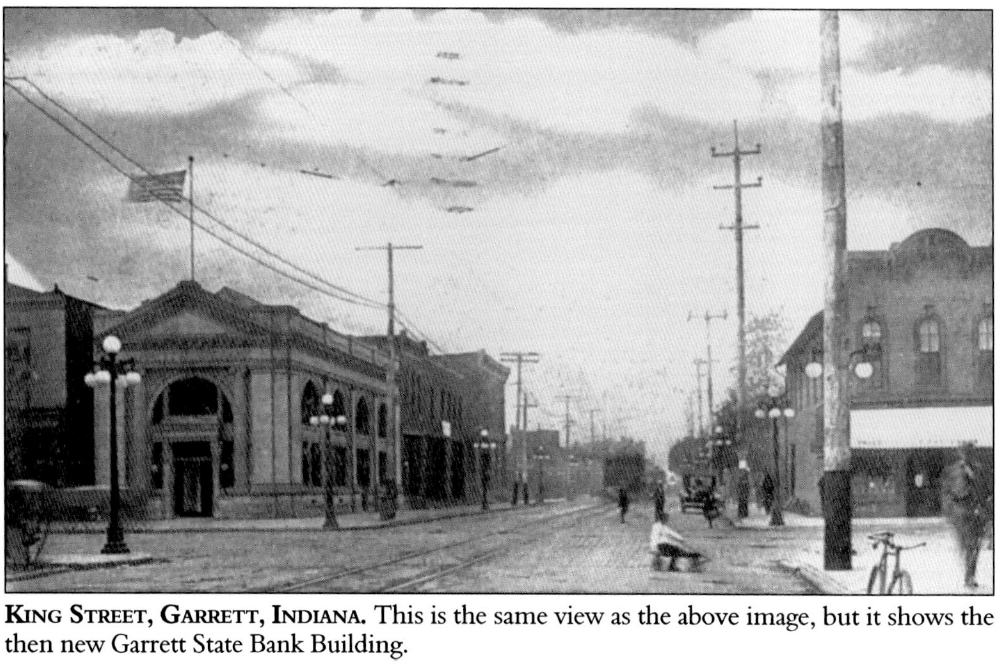

King Street, Garrett, Indiana. This is the same view as the above image, but it shows the then new Garrett State Bank Building.

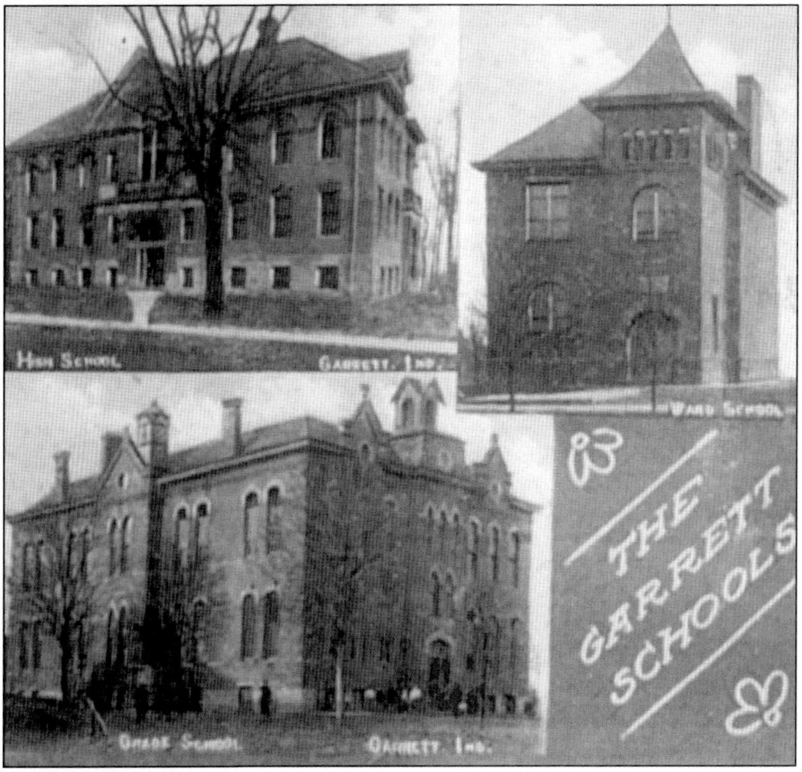

The Public Schools, Garrett, Indiana. The high school is in the upper left, the grade school is in the lower left, and the Ward School is in the upper right.

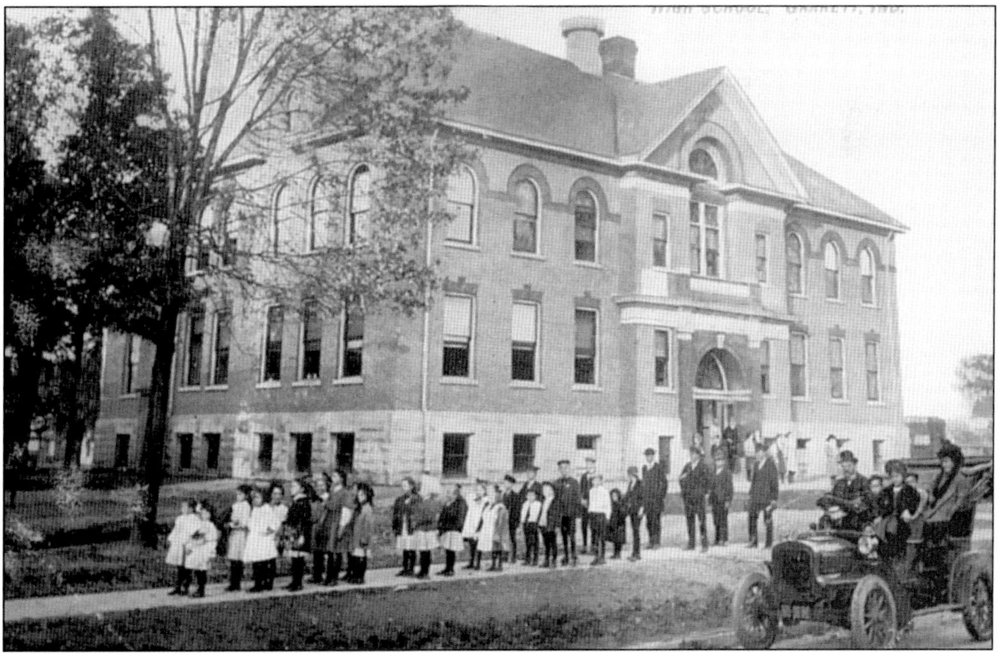

High School, Garrett, Indiana. School children and teachers watch a *c.* 1905 Auburn Automobile pass by the high school.

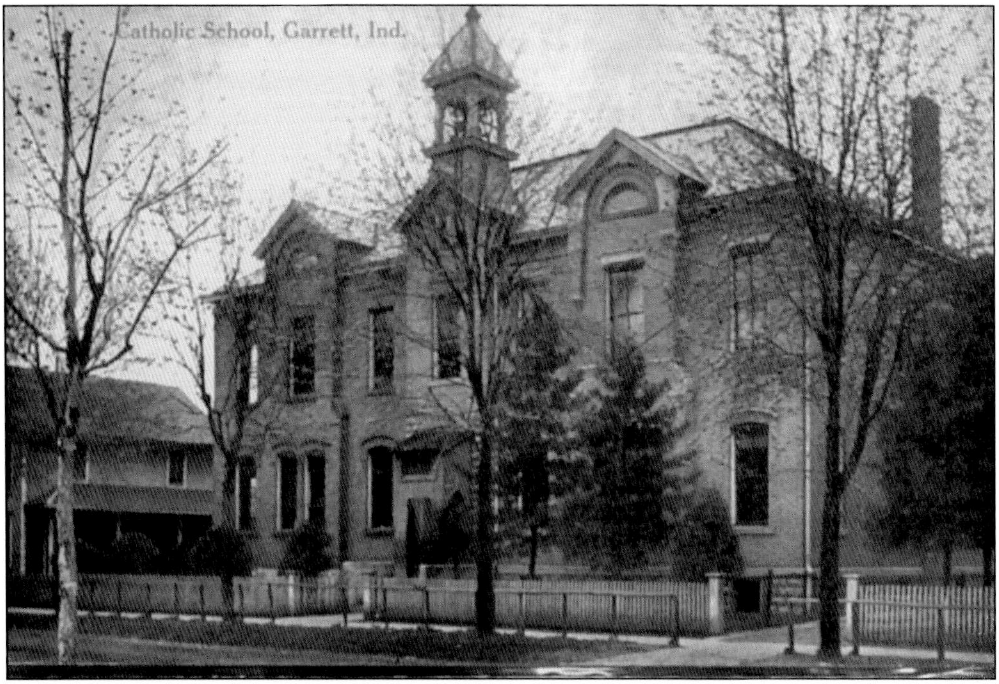

Catholic School, Garrett, Indiana. The Catholic school was surrounded by a fence. Hitching racks for horses were at curbside.

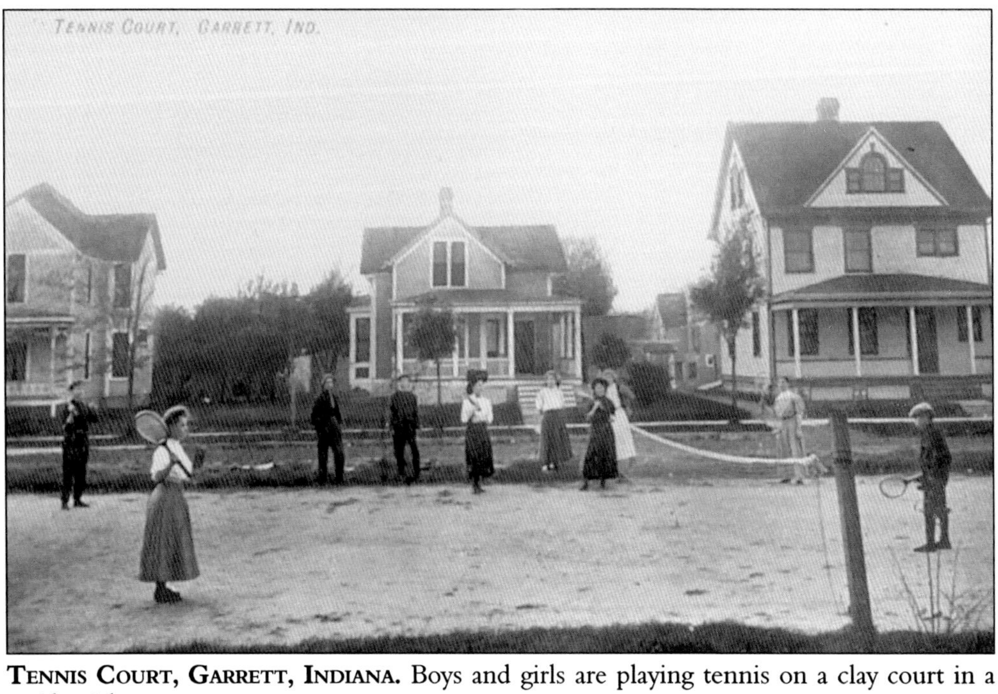

Tennis Court, Garrett, Indiana. Boys and girls are playing tennis on a clay court in a residential area.

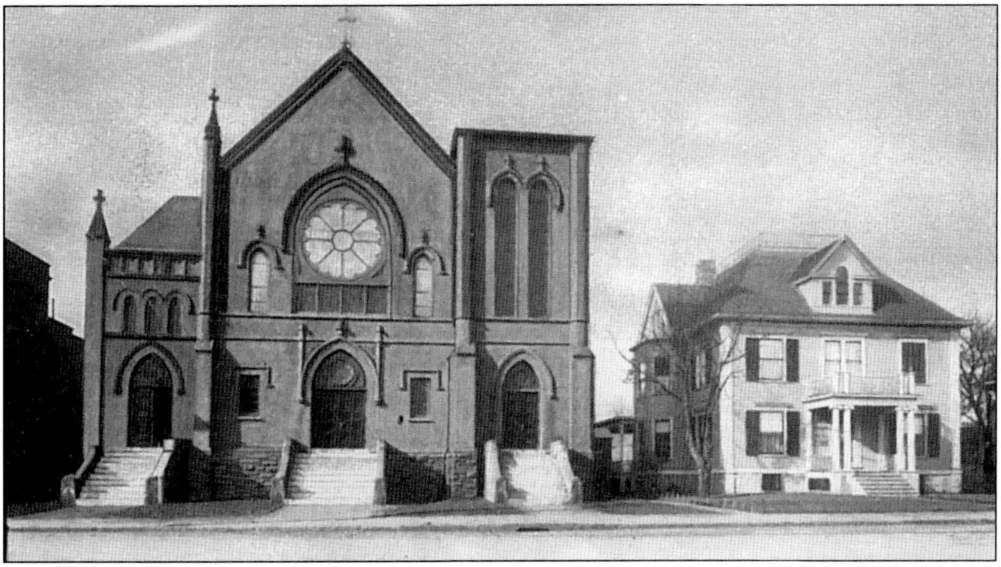

ST. JOSEPH'S CHURCH AND RECTORY. The large Catholic population of Garrett built a fine church and rectory.

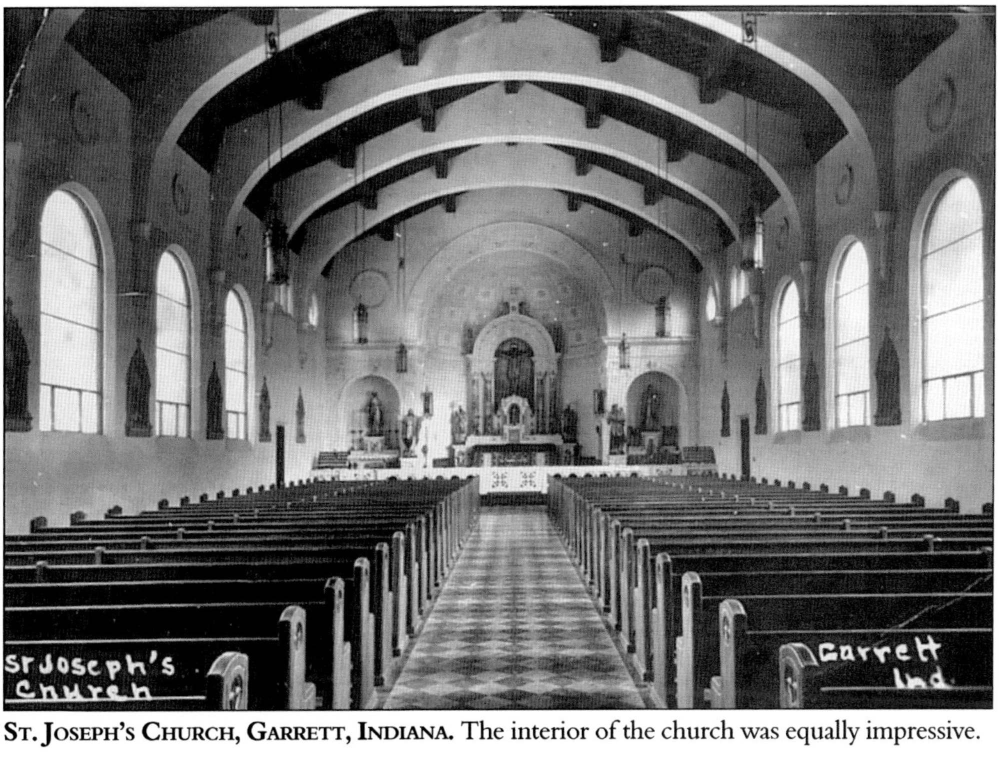

ST. JOSEPH'S CHURCH, GARRETT, INDIANA. The interior of the church was equally impressive.

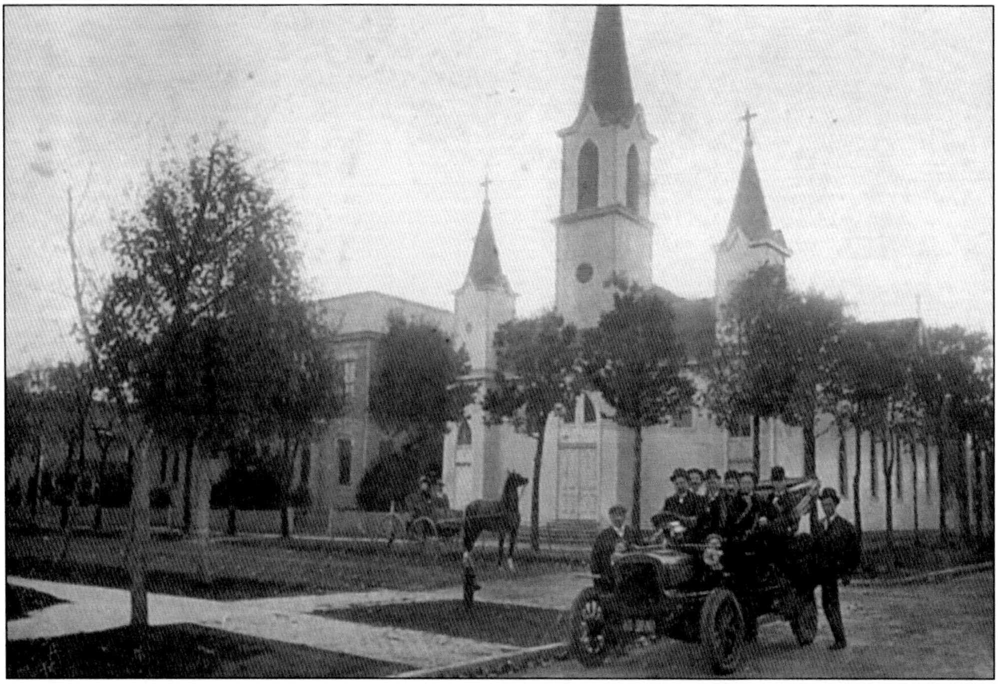

ST. PETER AND PAUL CHURCH, GARRETT, INDIANA. Five gentlemen are riding in the *c.* 1905 Auburn automobile.

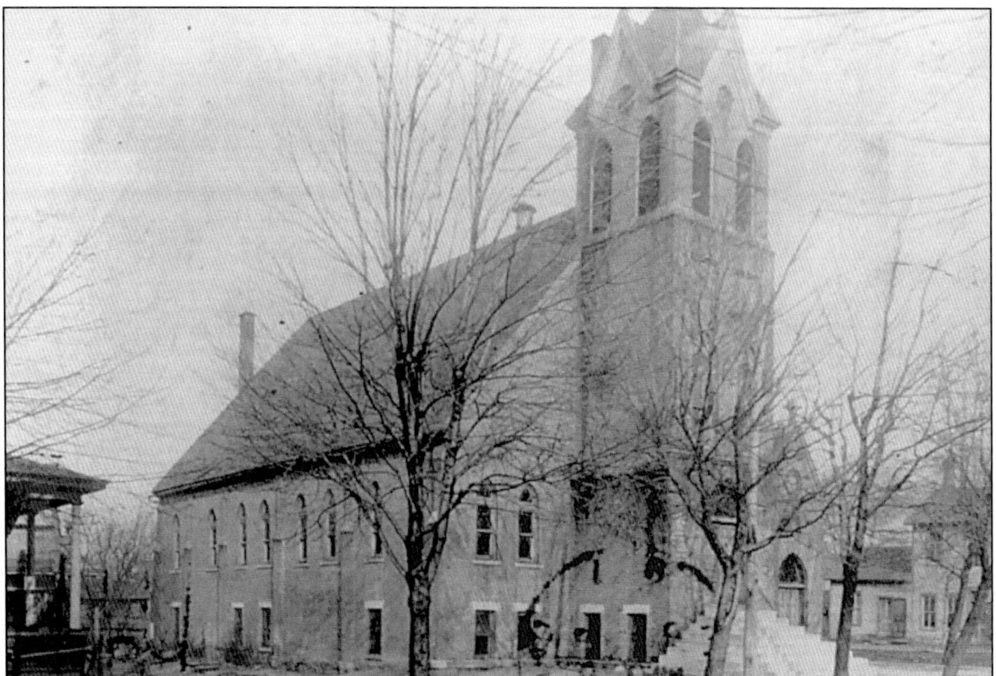

FIRST BAPTIST CHURCH, GARRETT, INDIANA. The First Baptist Church was one of the largest in Garrett.

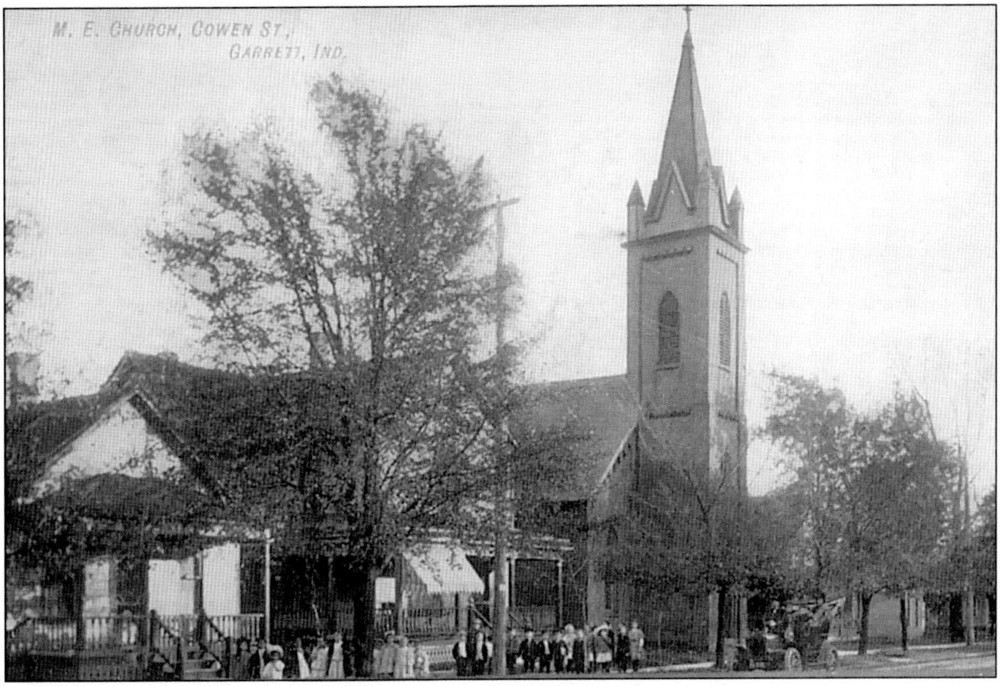

M.E. CHURCH, DOWEN STREET, GARRETT, INDIANA. The original Methodist Episcopal Church is shown with parishioners and a *c.* 1905 Auburn automobile.

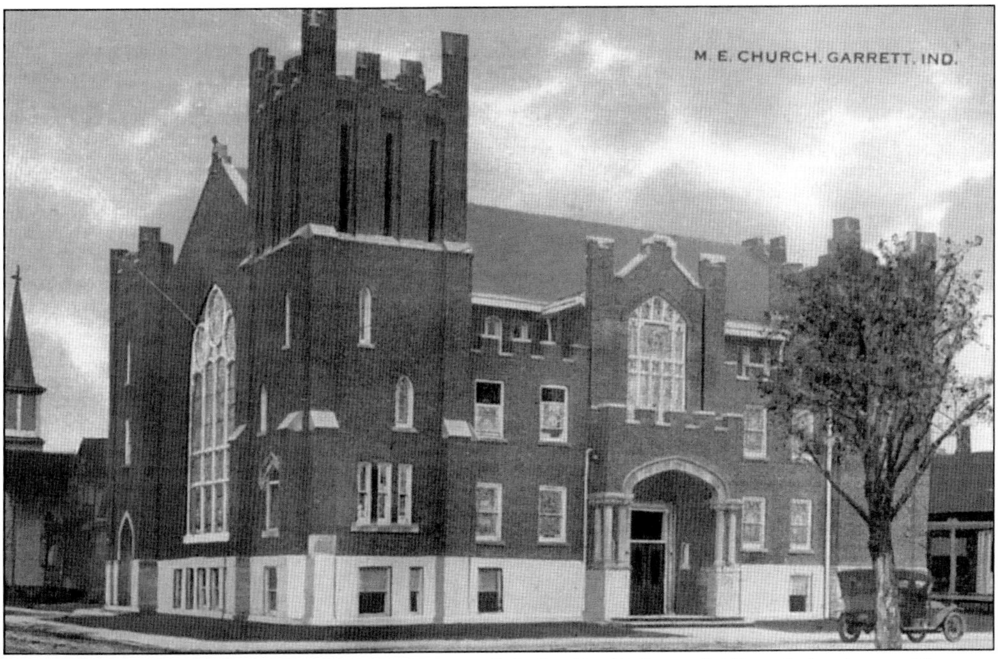

M.E. CHURCH, GARRETT, INDIANA. The new Methodist Episcopal Church is pictured here.

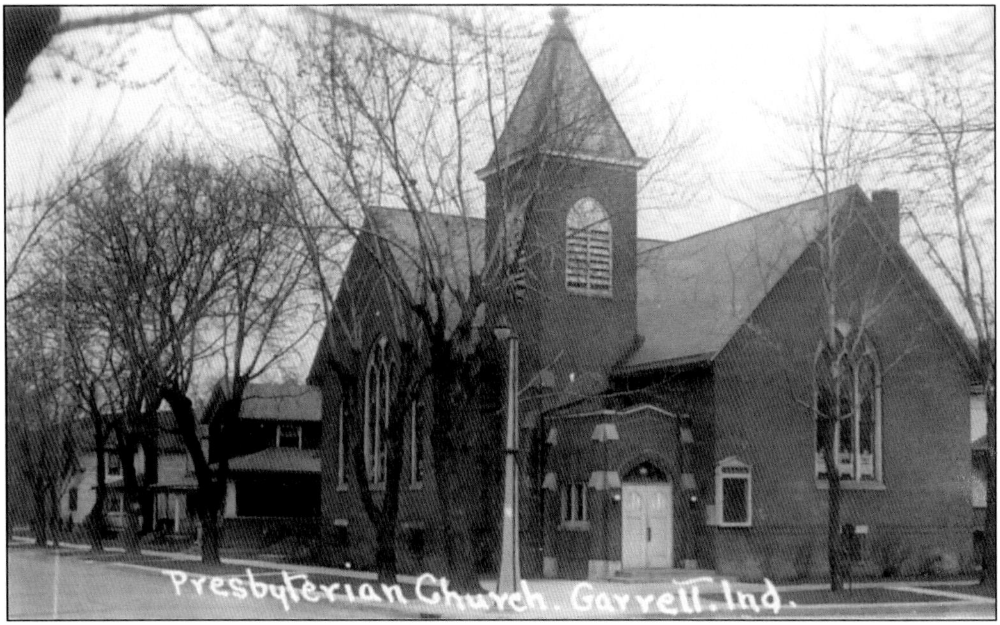

PRESBYTERIAN CHURCH, GARRETT, INDIANA.

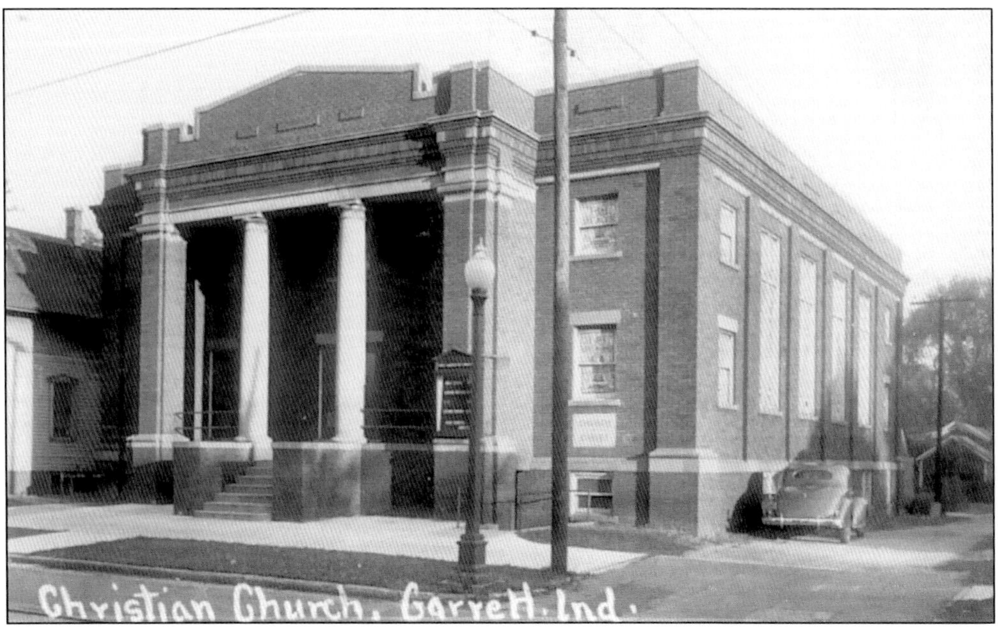

CHRISTIAN CHURCH, GARRETT, INDIANA.

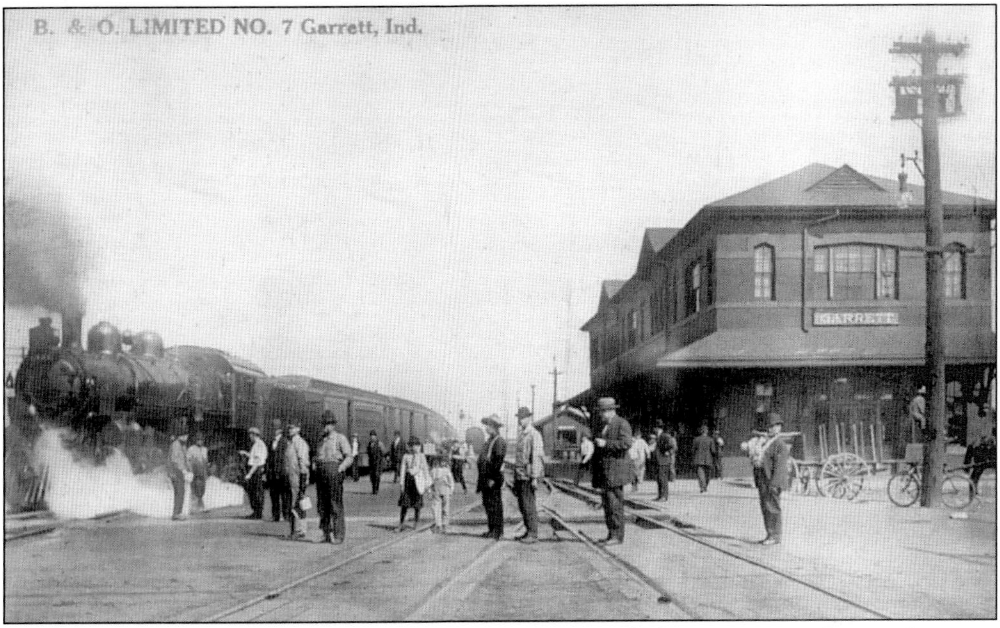

B&O Limited No. Seven, Garrett, Indiana. The arrival of a passenger train was always an exciting event.

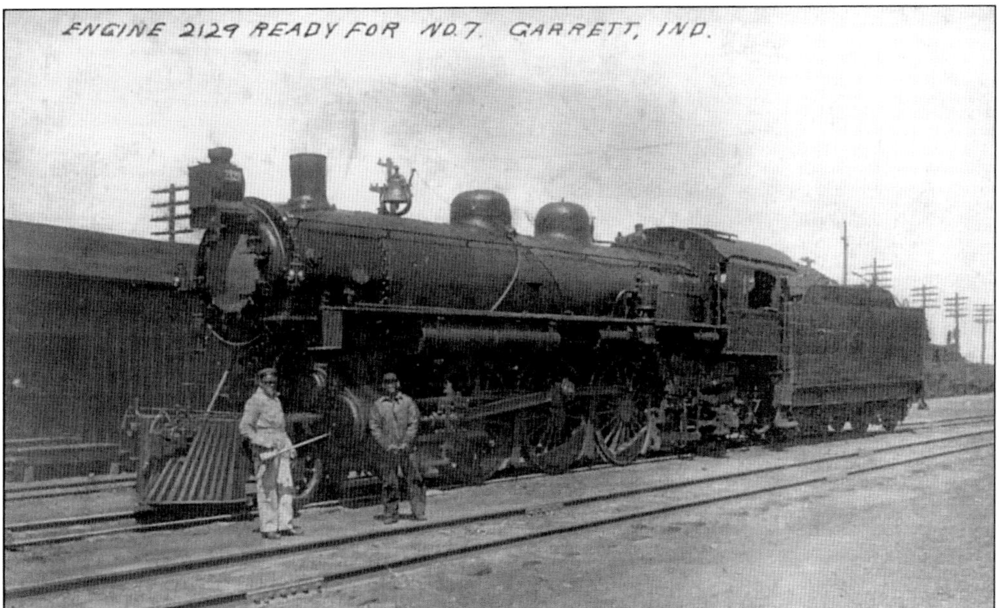

Engine 2129 Ready for No. Seven, Garrett, Indiana. A railroad worker with a huge oil can has prepared the engine for service.

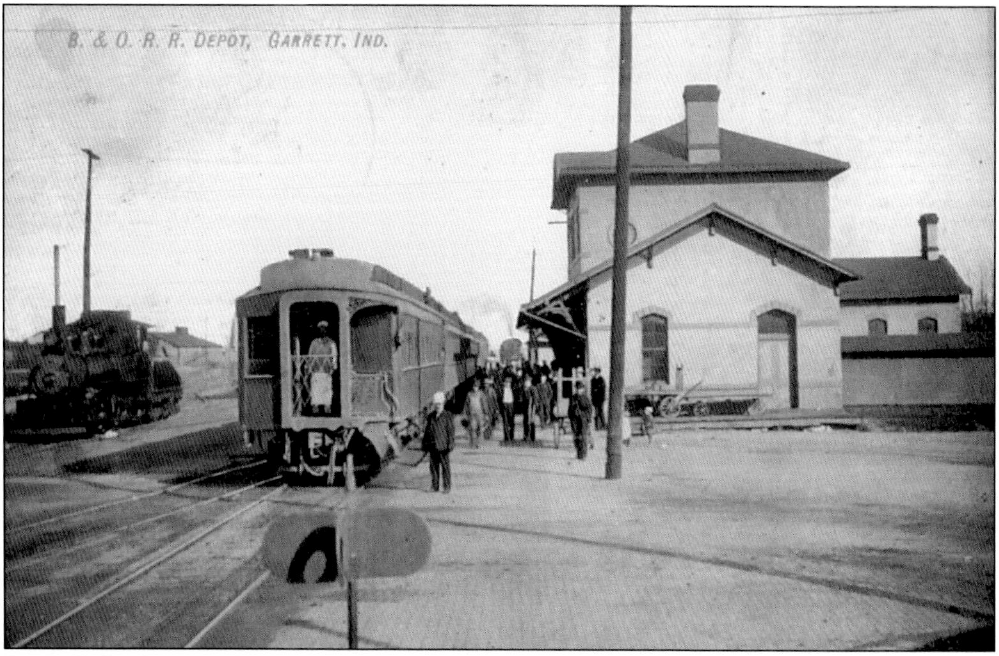

B&O R.R. DEPOT, GARRETT, INDIANA. An eastbound train is stopped at the depot. What appears to be a dining car employee is at the rear of the train.

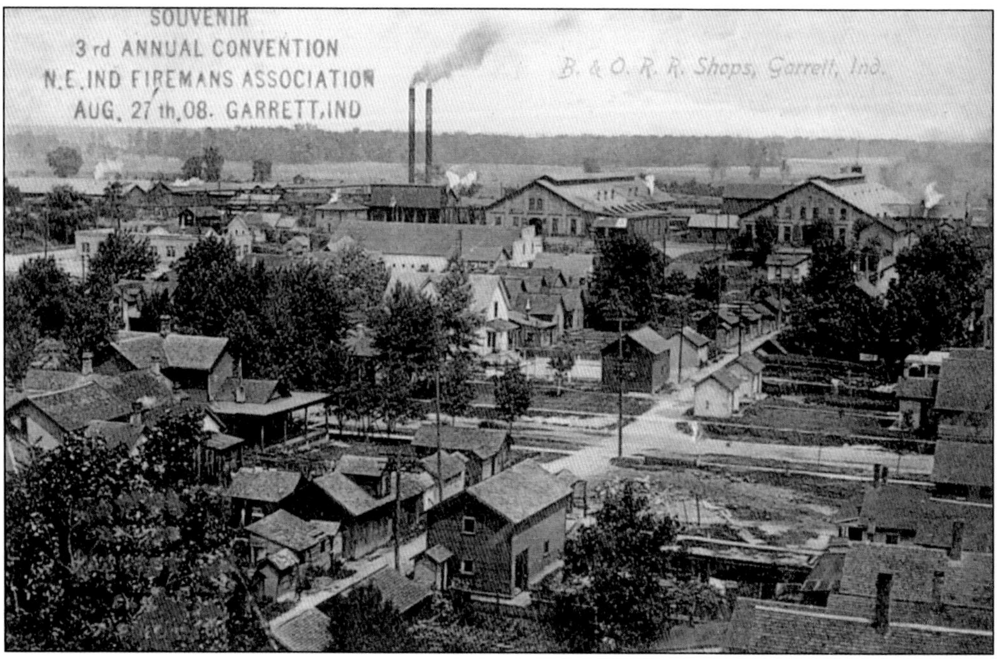

SOUVENIR, THIRD ANNUAL CONVENTION NORTHEAST INDIANA FIREMAN ASSOCIATION, AUGUST 27, 1908, GARRETT, INDIANA. Many railroad trade and fraternal associations were located at Garrett. The shops are in the background.

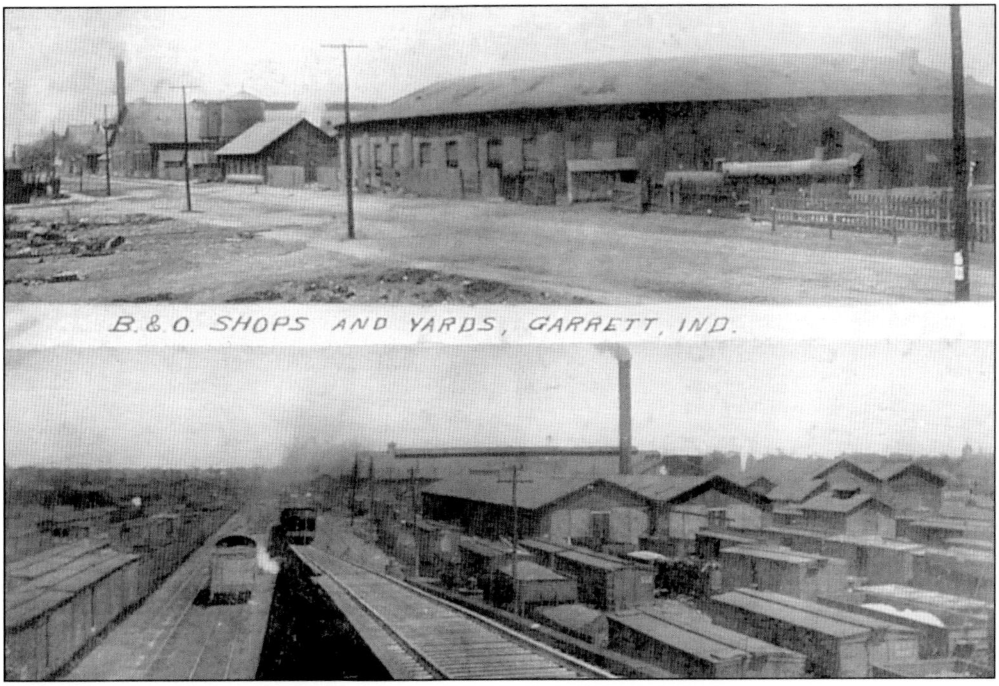

B&O Shops and Yards, Garrett, Indiana. Garrett was a division point for the Baltimore and Ohio Railroad. The roundhouse is in the upper left. The message states: "Am in Garrett now, Come with C.W. posting bills like you seen at Auburn last Sat are a peach of a day raining here all the time, hope we make home all right for the roads are slippery." "Bill posters" went from town to town posting "handbills" on poles and trees. These handbills advertised events and products.

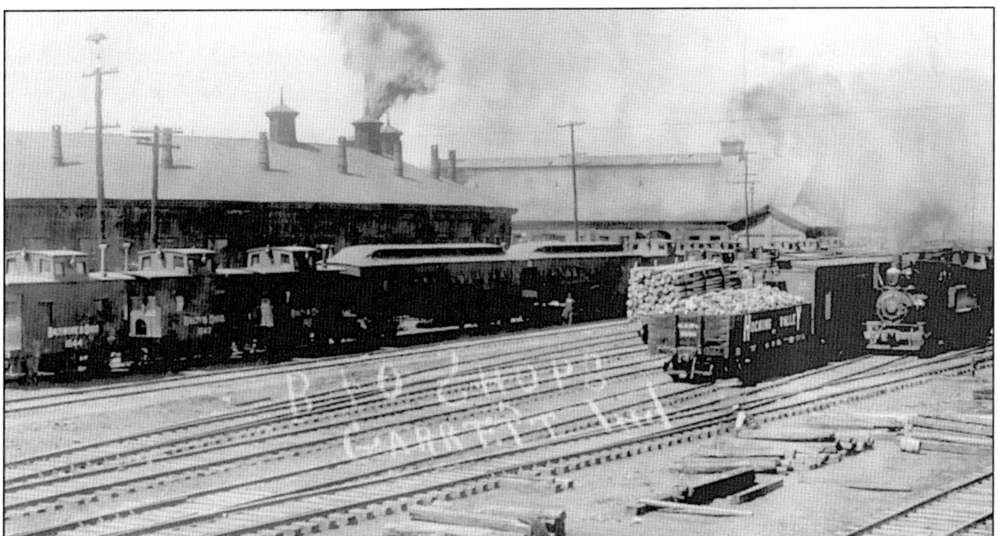

B&O Shops, Garrett, Indiana. Coal smoke was prevalent in the era of steam locomotives. The roundhouse is on the left. Each "stall" had a chimney so that smoke from the locomotive could escape.

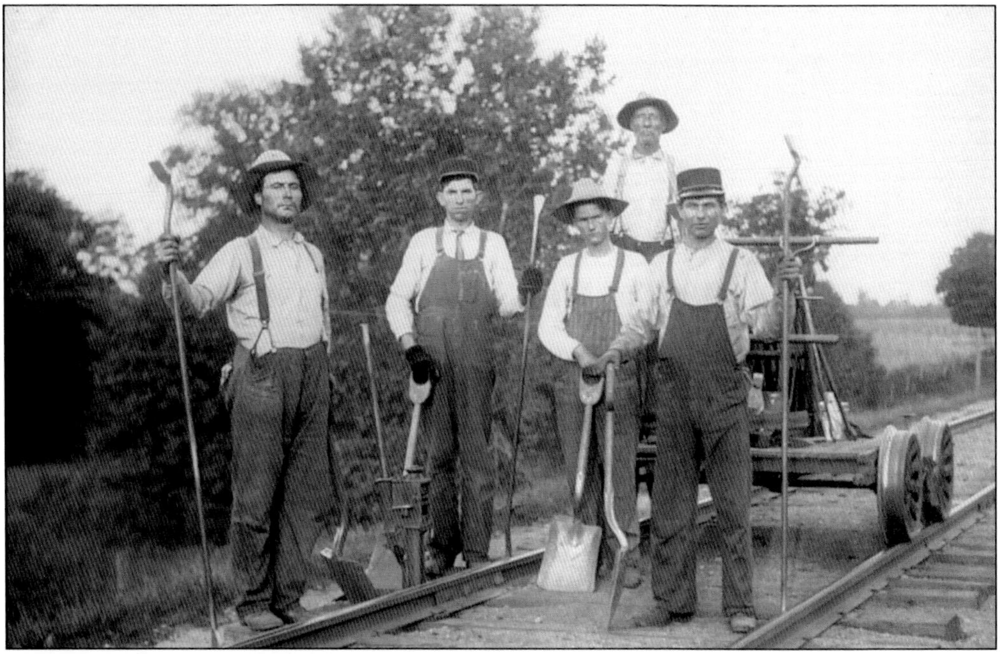

SECTION CREW ON B&O RAILROAD NEAR GARRETT. The foreman is on the right. Such a crew was responsible for the maintenance of a section of tracks.

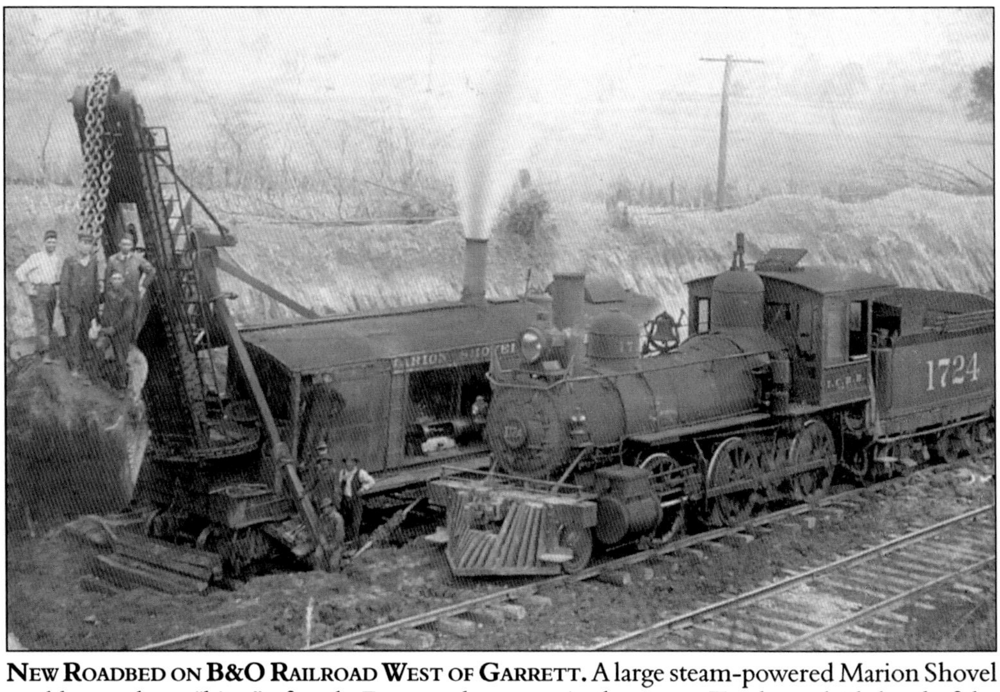

NEW ROADBED ON B&O RAILROAD WEST OF GARRETT. A large steam-powered Marion Shovel could move large "bites" of earth. Four workers pose in the scoop. Track was laid ahead of the unit as it dug out a hill for right of way.

Seven

SPENCERVILLE

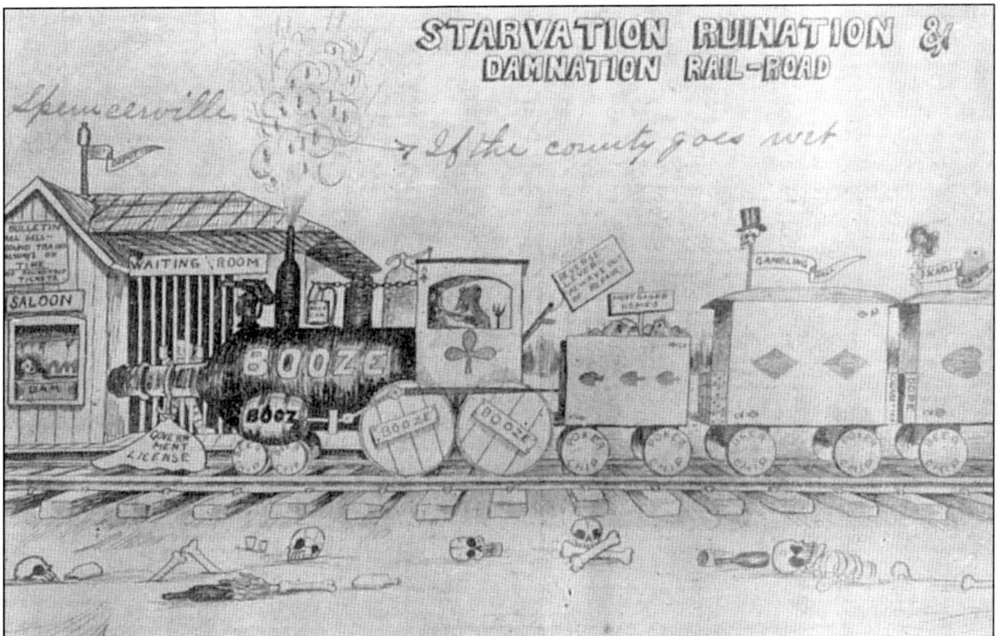

STARVATION, RUINATION, AND DAMNATION RAILROAD. Postcards were used to make social and political statements. The handwritten comment states "Spencerville—if the county goes wet," an apparent reference to a referendum on alcoholic beverages in an era of local option. The bulletin board above the window of the saloon states: "All hell bound trains always on time, no round-trip tickets." A prisoner is looking between the bars of a jail/waiting room. The banners on the train state "Reverse lever always out of repair—mortgage homes—gambling halls—scarlet women."

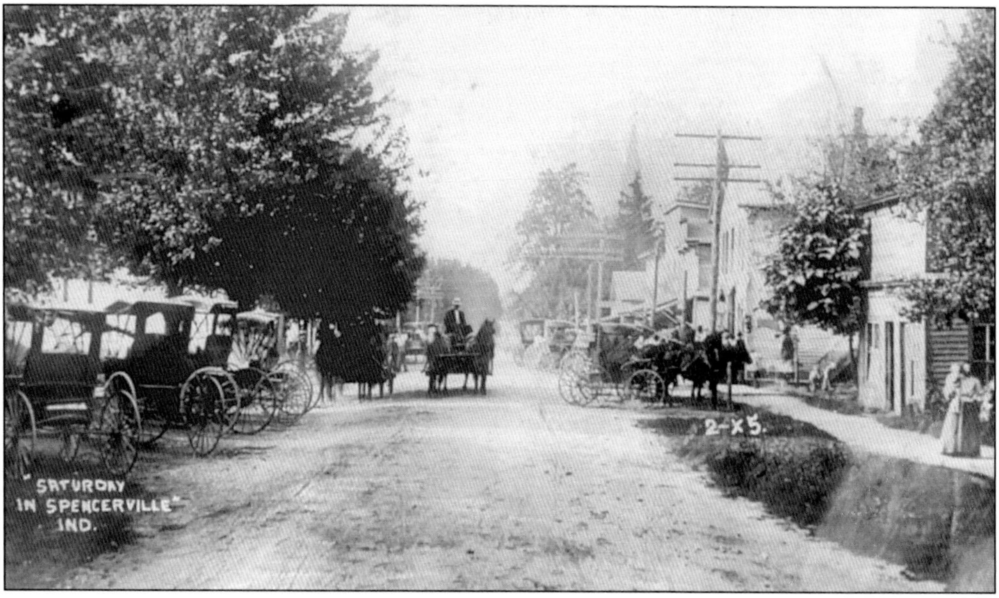

SATURDAY IN SPENCERVILLE, INDIANA. Most rural people went to the nearest town on Saturday to shop for the week.

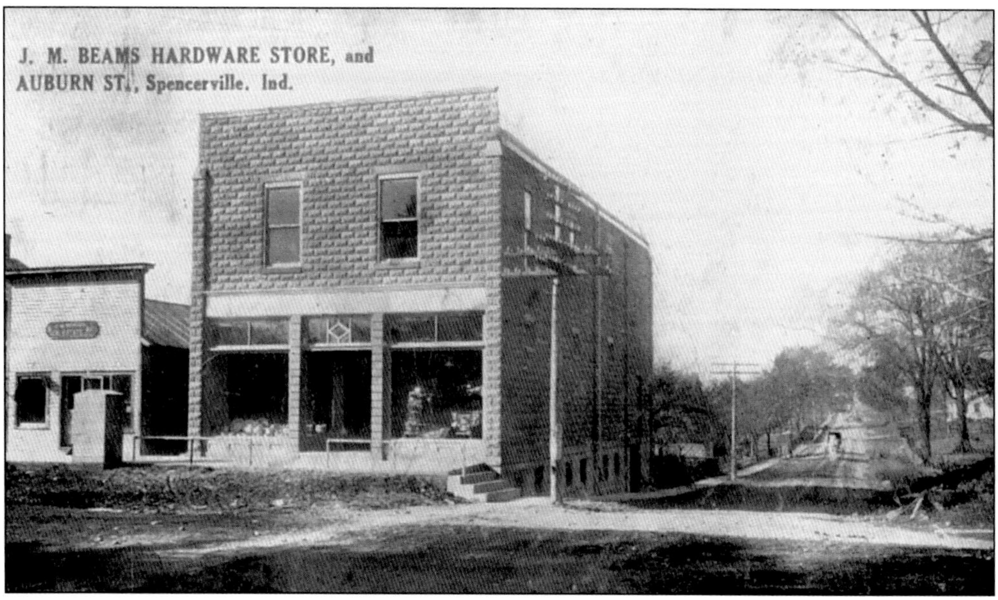

J.M. BEAM'S HARDWARE STORE AND AUBURN STREET, SPENCERVILLE, INDIANA. The hardware was an essential source of tools and supplies for farmers of the area.

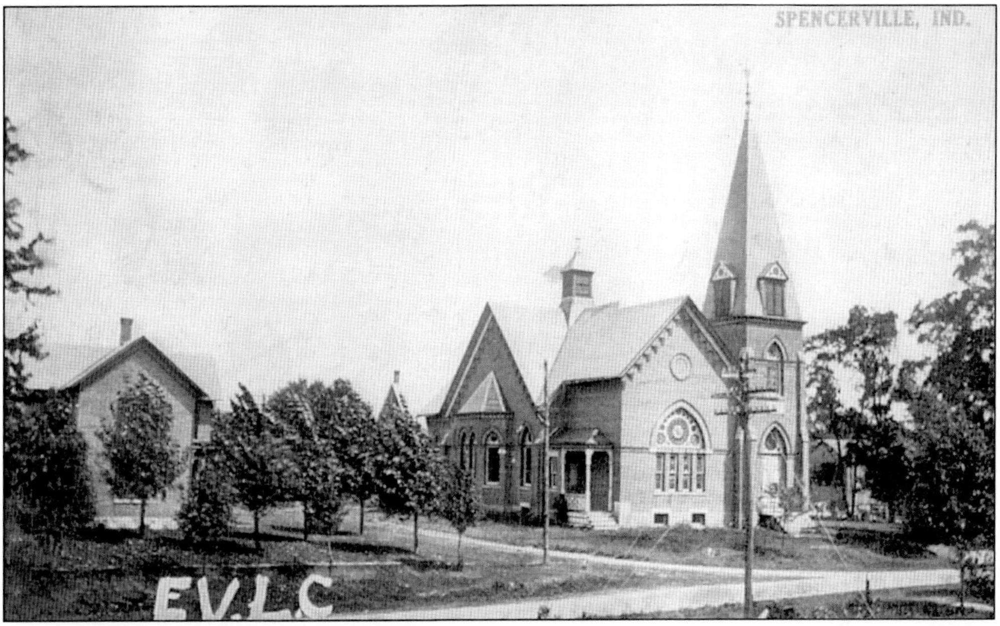

Evangelical Lutheran Church, Spencerville, Indiana.

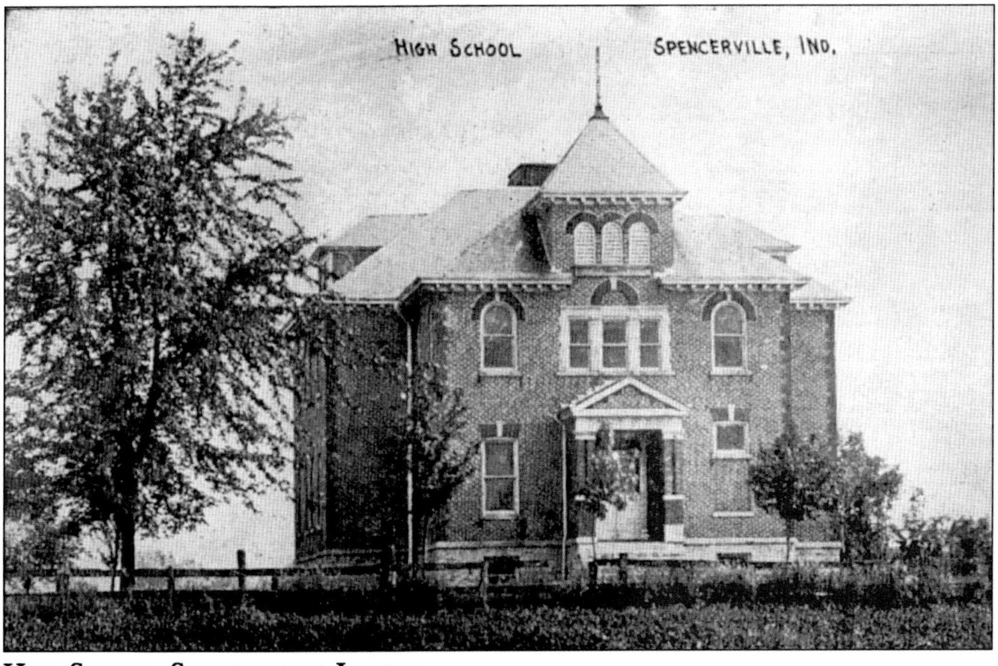

High School, Spencerville, Indiana.

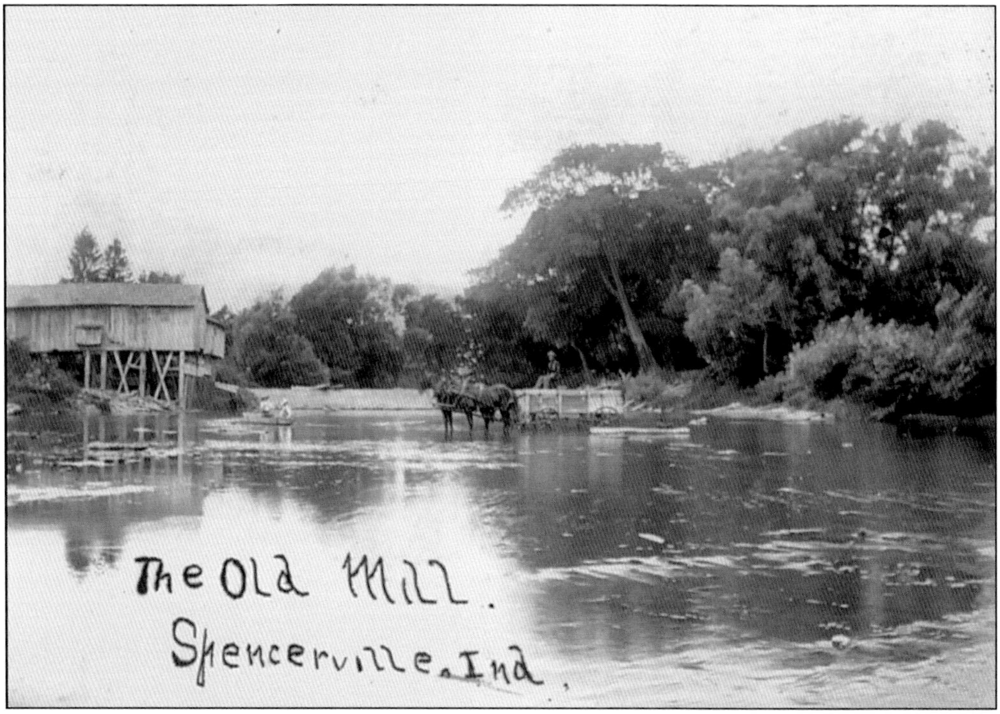

THE OLD MILL, SPENCERVILLE, INDIANA. A team of horses fords the St. Joseph River in low water. The dam is in the background.

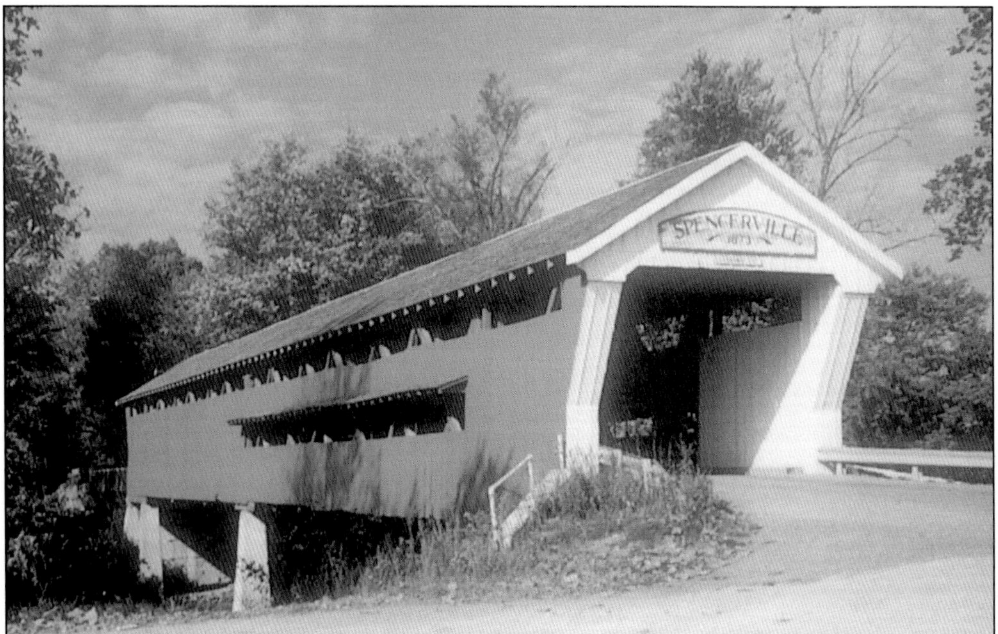

"THE ONLY COVERED BRIDGE IN DEKALB COUNTY." The Spencerville Covered Bridge is the northernmost covered bridge in Indiana. It has been restored and maintained by the DeKalb County Commissioners.

Eight

ST. JOE

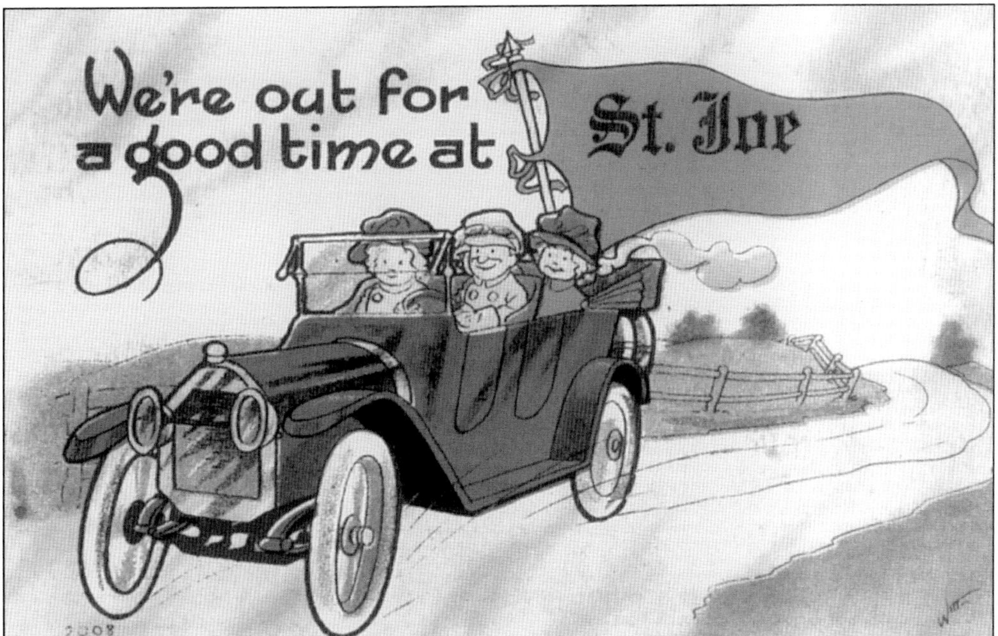

WE'RE OUT FOR A GOOD TIME AT ST. JOE.

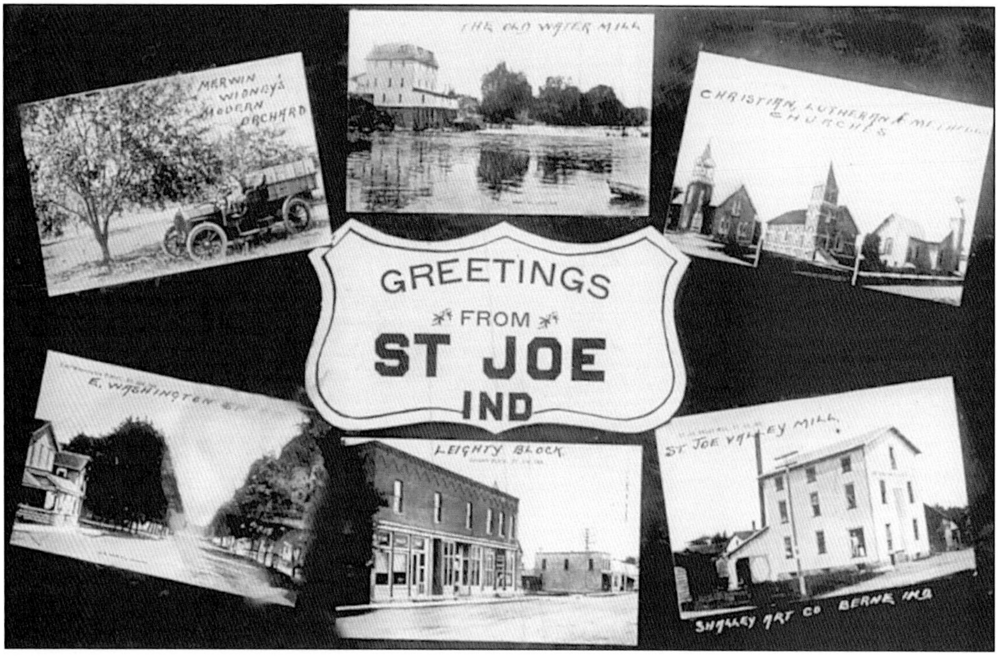

Greetings from St. Joe, Indiana. Clockwise from upper left are: "Merwin Widney's Modern Orchard; The Old Water Mill; Christian, Lutheran, and Methodist Churches; East Washington Street; Leighty Block; and St. Joe Valley Mill.

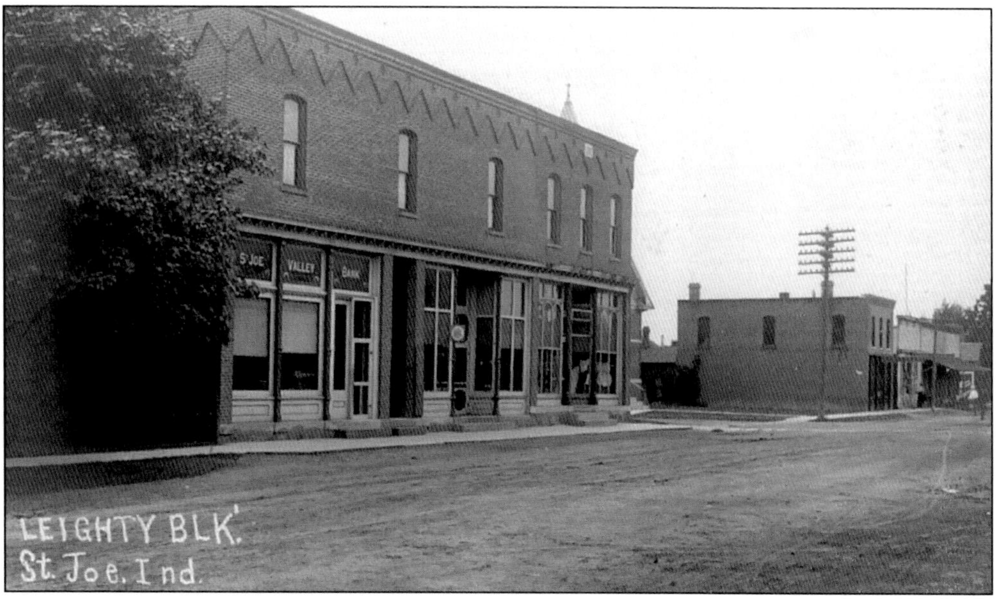

Leighty Block, St. Joe, Indiana. The Leighty Block housed the St. Joe Valley Bank, the Milliman Drug Store, and the Johnston Store.

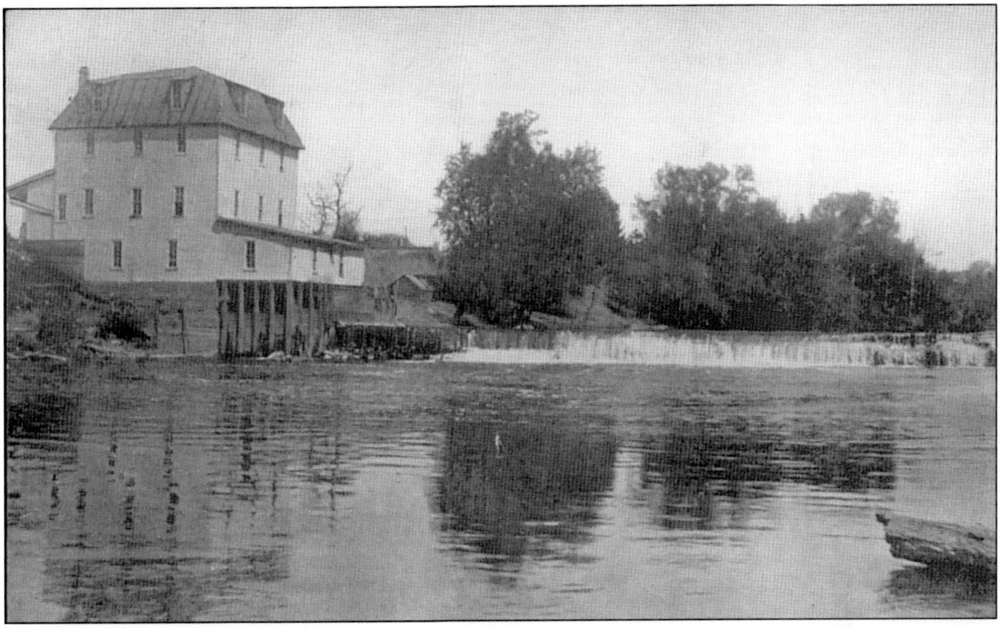

The Old Water Mill, St. Joe, Indiana. The mill was powered by water impounded by the dam on the St. Joseph River. It was inoperable in periods of low water.

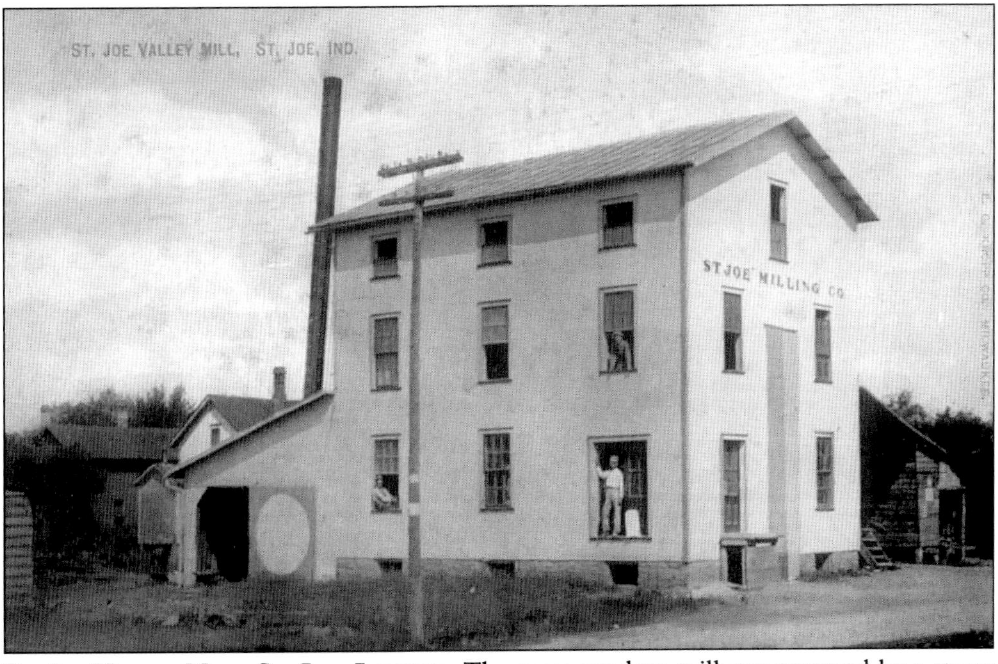

St. Joe Valley Mill, St. Joe, Indiana. The more modern mill was powered by a steam engine, located in the building at the rear. Note the large smokestack.

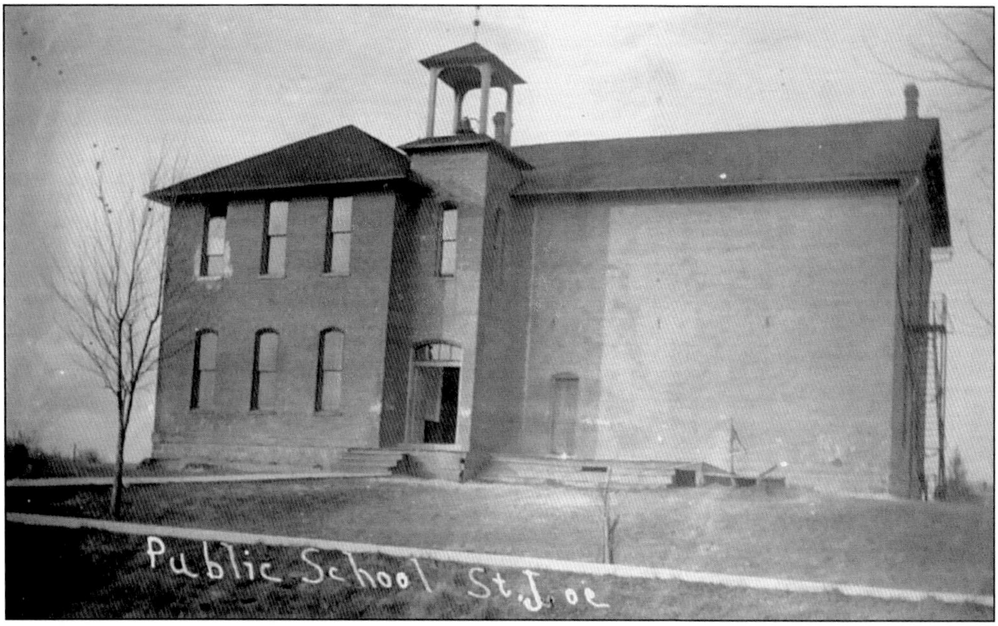

PUBLIC SCHOOL, ST. JOE, INDIANA. The school design was unusual with its large windowless wall. Note the bell in the tower capped with a lightning rod and the iron fire escape on the right.

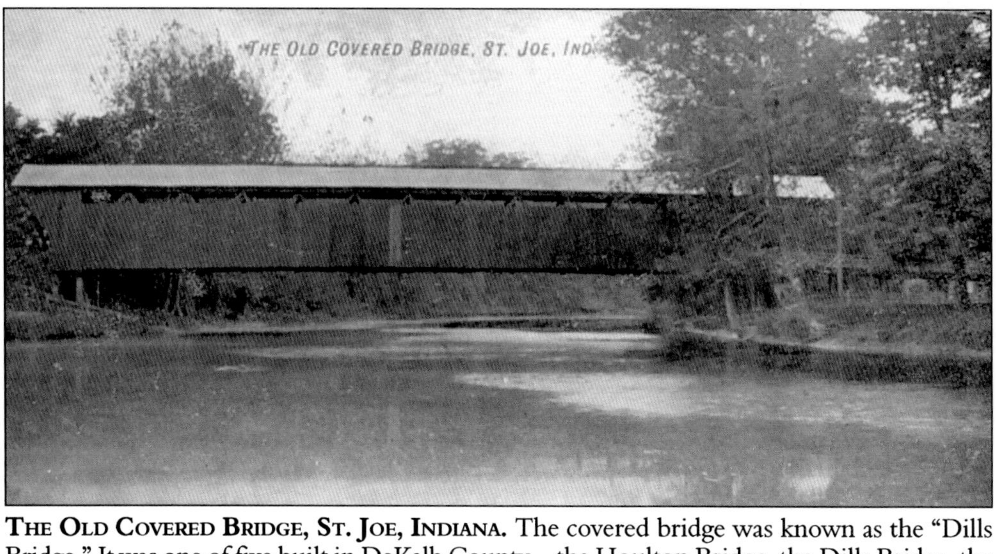

THE OLD COVERED BRIDGE, ST. JOE, INDIANA. The covered bridge was known as the "Dills Bridge." It was one of five built in DeKalb County—the Houlton Bridge, the Dills Bridge, the Newville Bridge, the Spencerville Bridge, and the Cedar Chapel Bridge.

Nine

WATERLOO

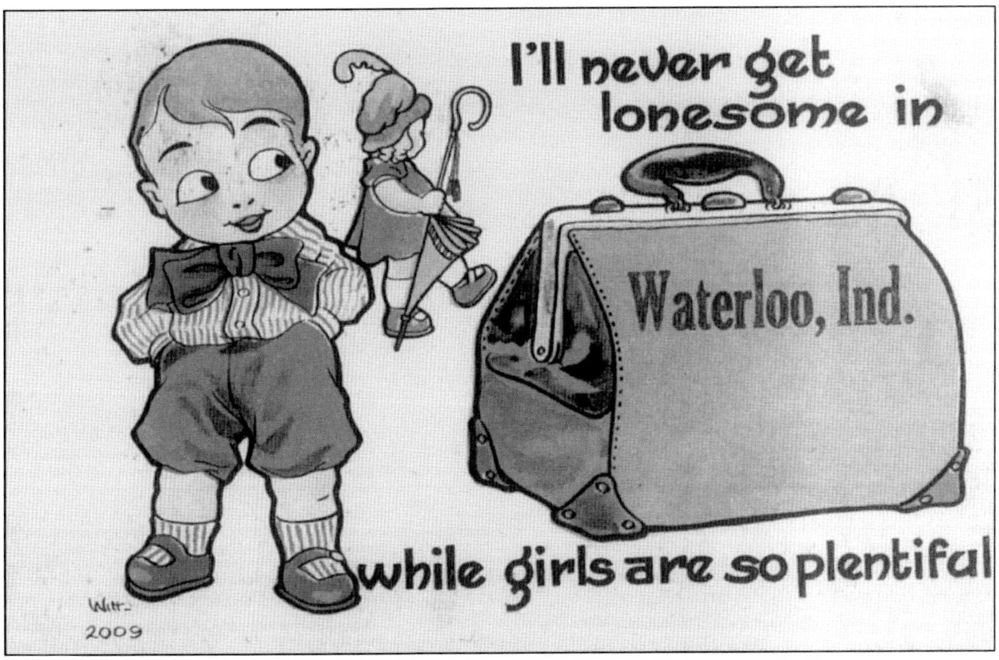

I'LL NEVER GET LONESOME IN WATERLOO, INDIANA, WHILE GIRLS ARE SO PLENTIFUL.

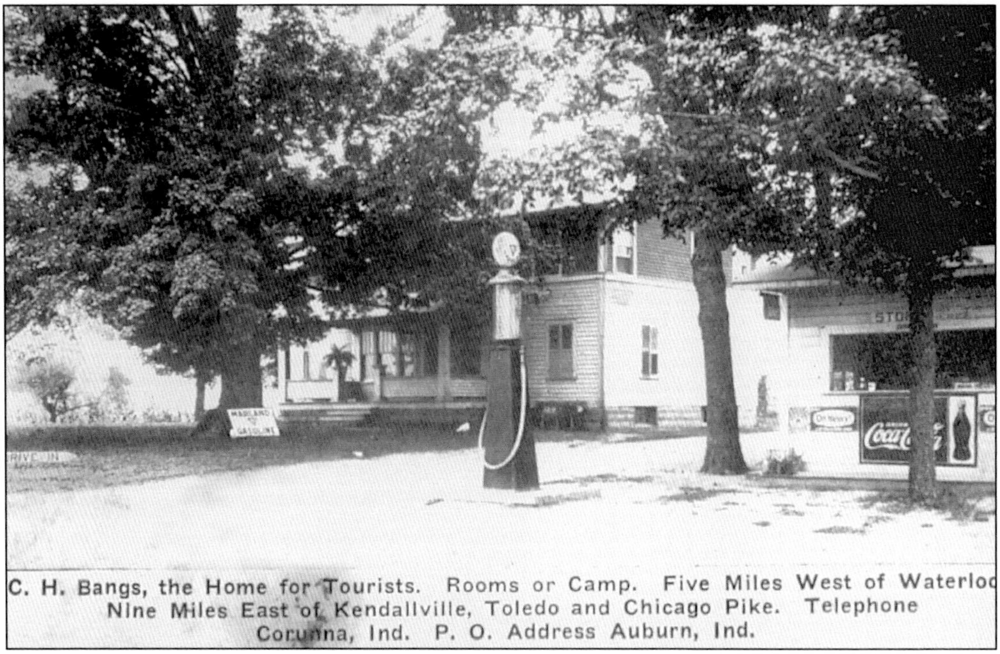

C.H. BANGS, THE HOME OF TOURISTS; ROOMS OR CAMP, FIVE MILES WEST OF WATERLOO, NINE MILES EAST OF KENDALLVILLE; TOLEDO, AND CHICAGO PIKE. The Toledo and Chicago Pike was a major route for travelers. It later became U.S. Six.

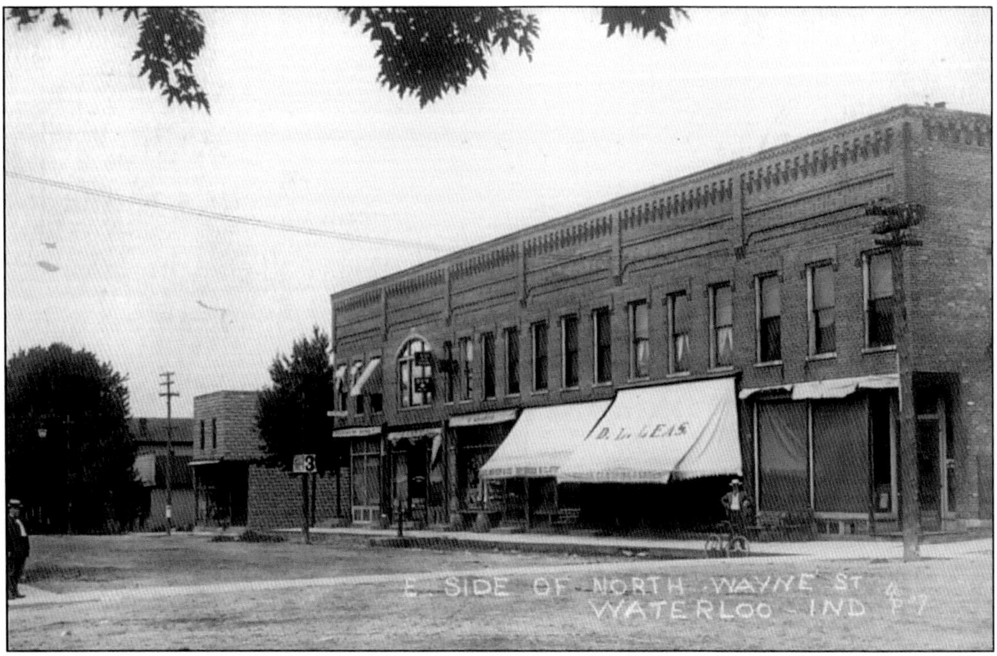

EAST SIDE OF NORTH WAYNE STREET, WATERLOO, INDIANA. This block housed the D.L. Leas Clothing Store, Dry Goods Store, and the Waterloo State Bank.

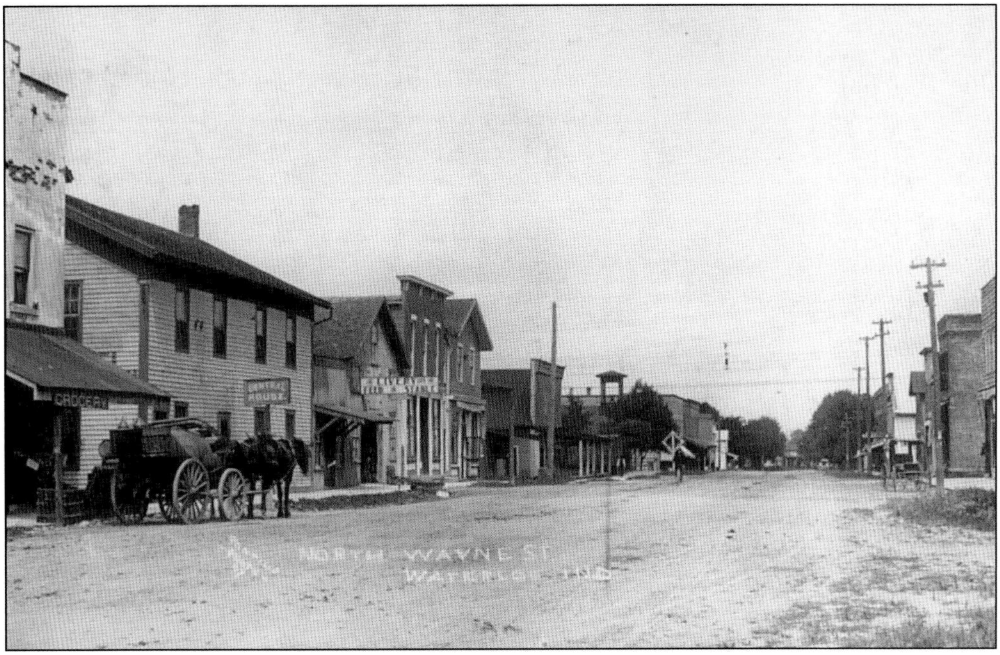

NORTH WAYNE STREET, WATERLOO, INDIANA. A horse-drawn wagon is in front of the grocery. The Central House and "Livery—Feed—Stable" are on the left.

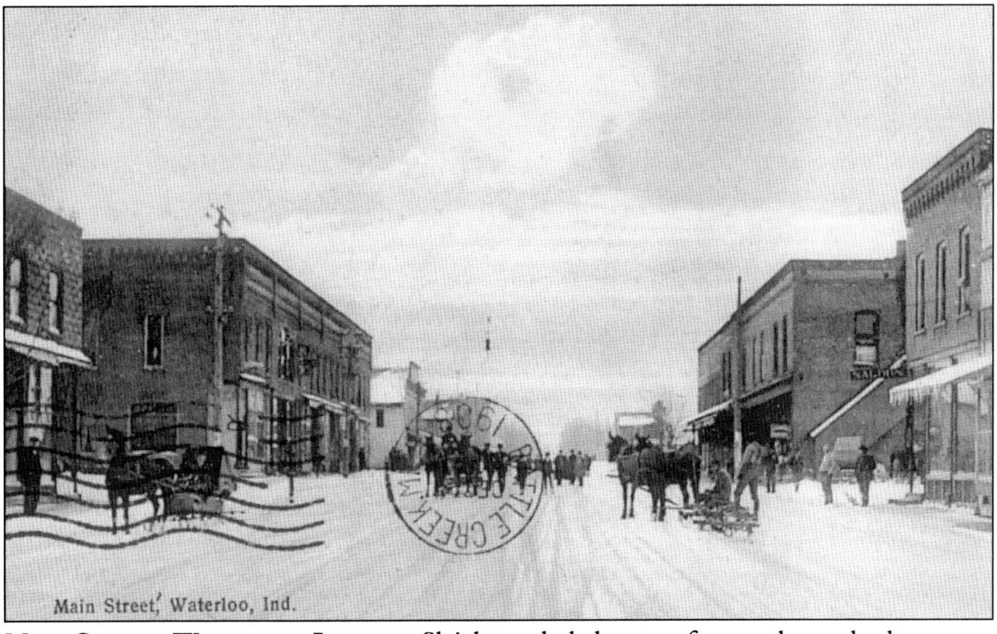

MAIN STREET, WATERLOO, INDIANA. Sleighs and sleds were frequently used when snow covered the roads and streets.

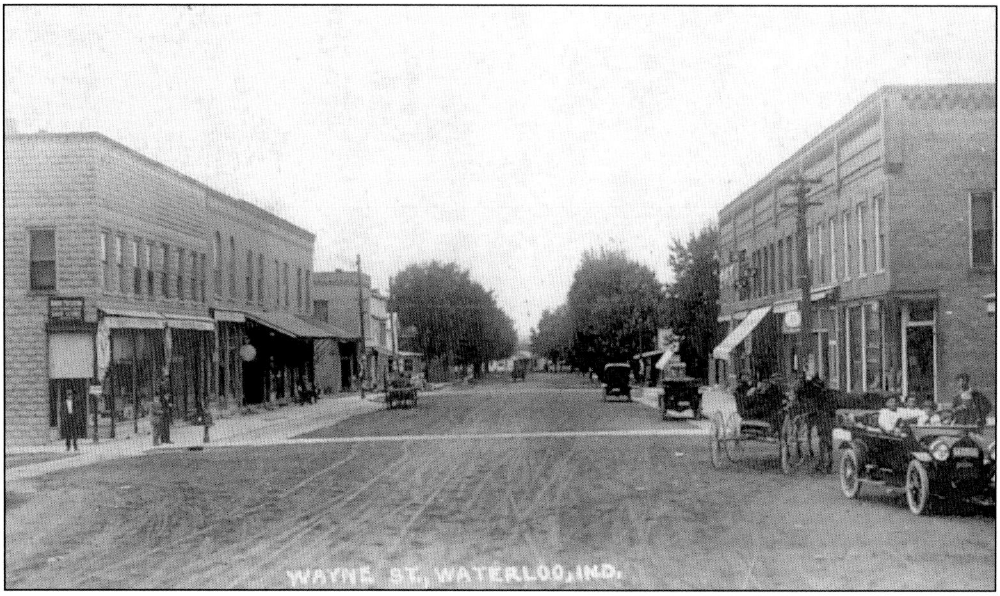

WAYNE STREET, WATERLOO, INDIANA. Buggies, wagons, and cars are shown on the dirt street.

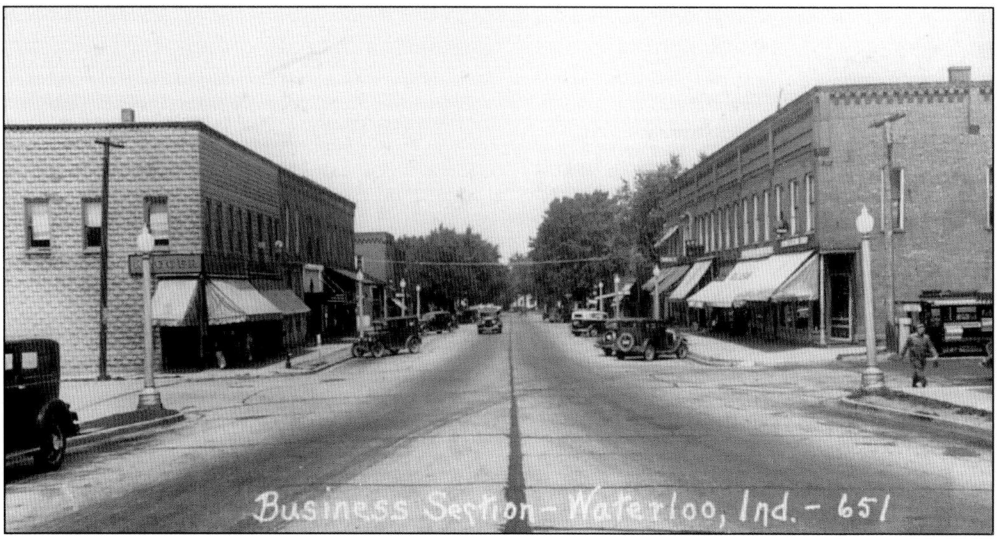

BUSINESS SECTION, WATERLOO, INDIANA. This is the same scene as above after the streets were paved. The Kroger Store is on the left. There is a popcorn wagon on the right.

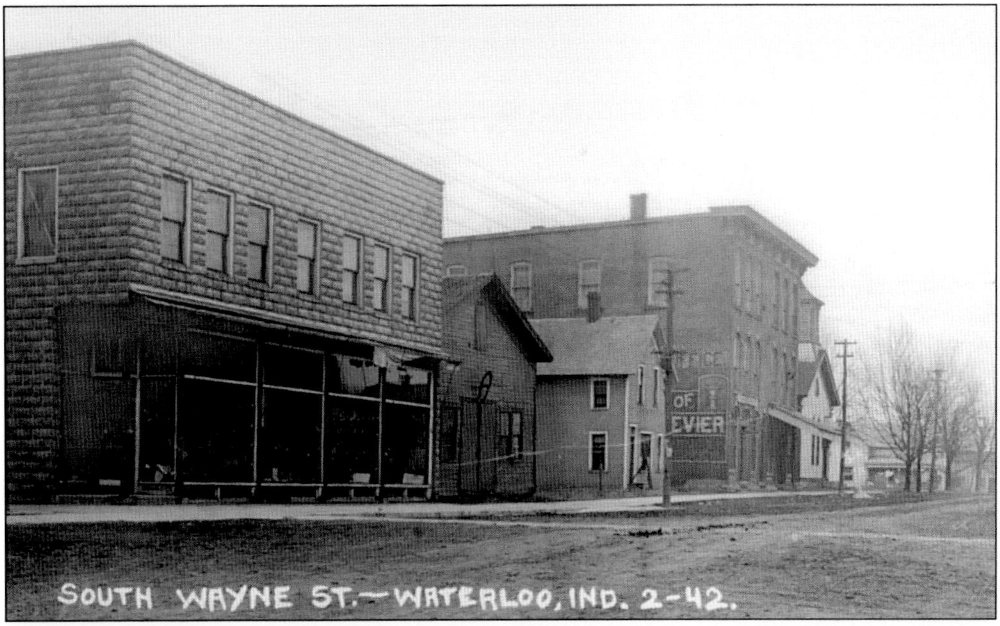

SOUTH WAYNE STREET, WATERLOO, INDIANA. This view is the east side of the street looking south from the railroad. The three-story building was the home of the homeopathic medical practice of Frank Bevier. He purchased various herbs from local residents, processed and packaged them, and then sold them to druggists and doctors. He carried on a large mail order medical practice.

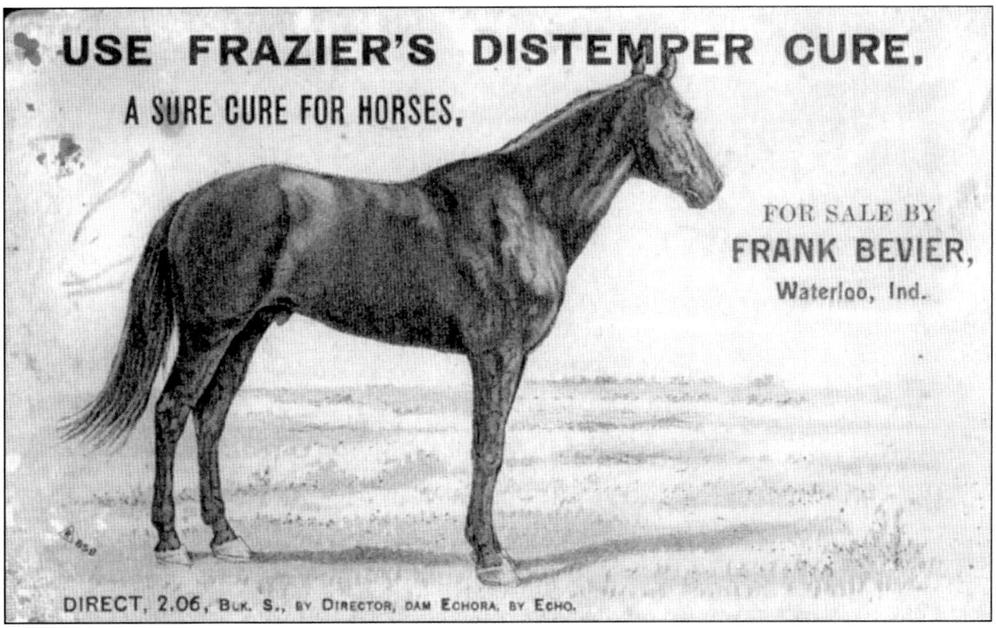

USE FRAZIER'S DISTEMPER CURE. A SURE CURE FOR HORSES. FOR SALE BY FRANK BEVIER, WATERLOO, INDIANA. Dr. Bevier also treated farm animals.

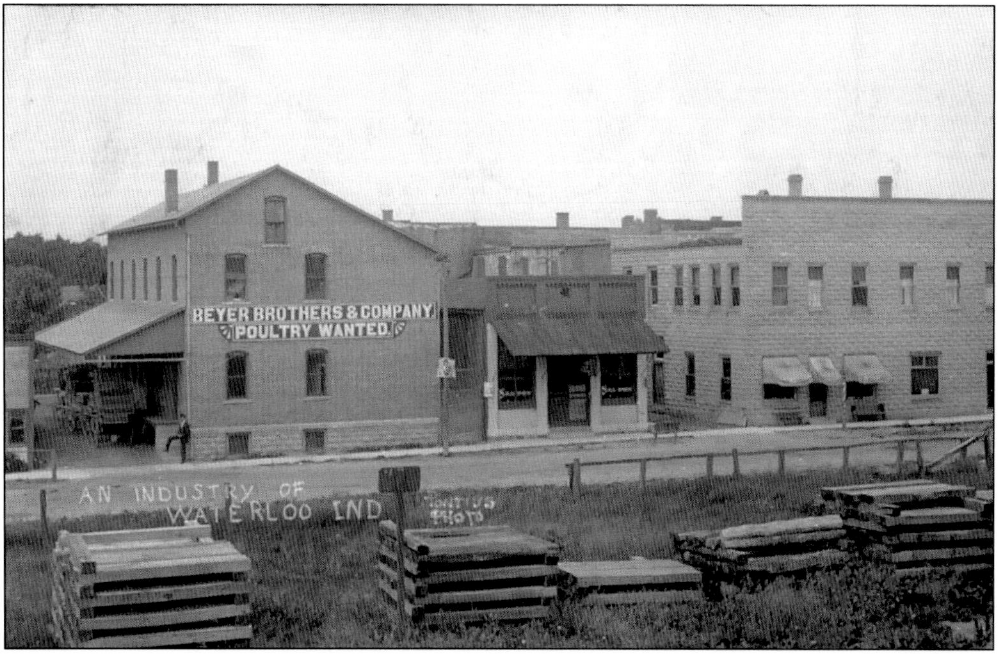

An Industry of Waterloo, Indiana. Beyer Brothers purchased chickens from local farmers and then brokered and shipped them to wholesalers and retailers by rail on the New York Central Railroad. The wagon at this loading dock on the left is stacked with wooden chicken crates. The middle building was a saloon.

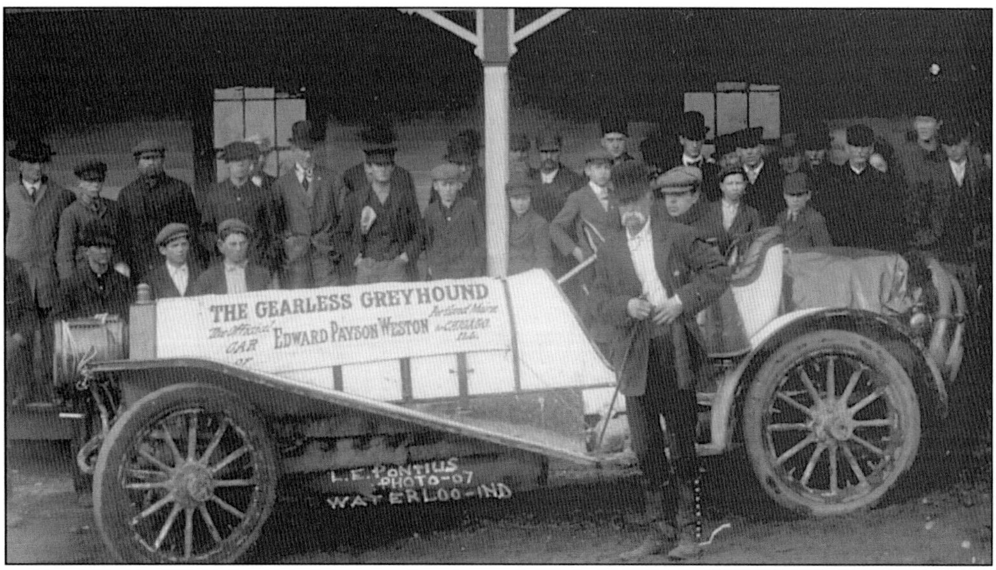

The Gearless Greyhound—The Official Car of Edward Payson Weston—Portland, Maine, to Chicago, Illinois. Many car companies sponsored major trips to demonstrate the reliability and economy of their cars for interstate travel.

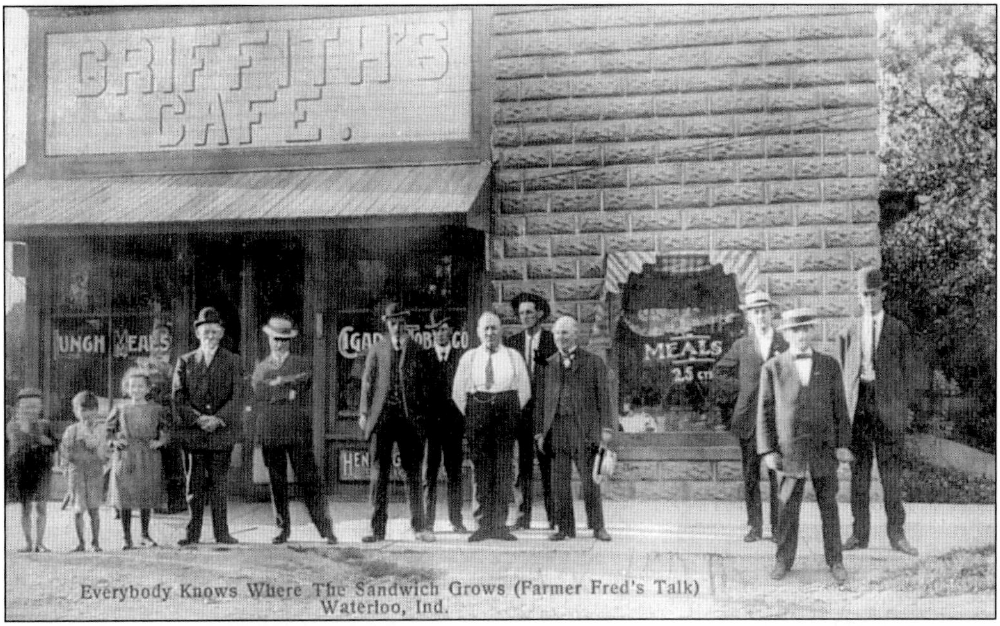

EVERYBODY KNOWS WHERE THE SANDWICH GROWS (FARMER FRED'S TALK). Griffith's Café was a popular restaurant at Waterloo. The signs in the window state: "Lunch—Meals—Cigars—Tobacco—Meals 25¢." "Farmer Fred" was a publisher of postcards located at Battle Creek, Michigan.

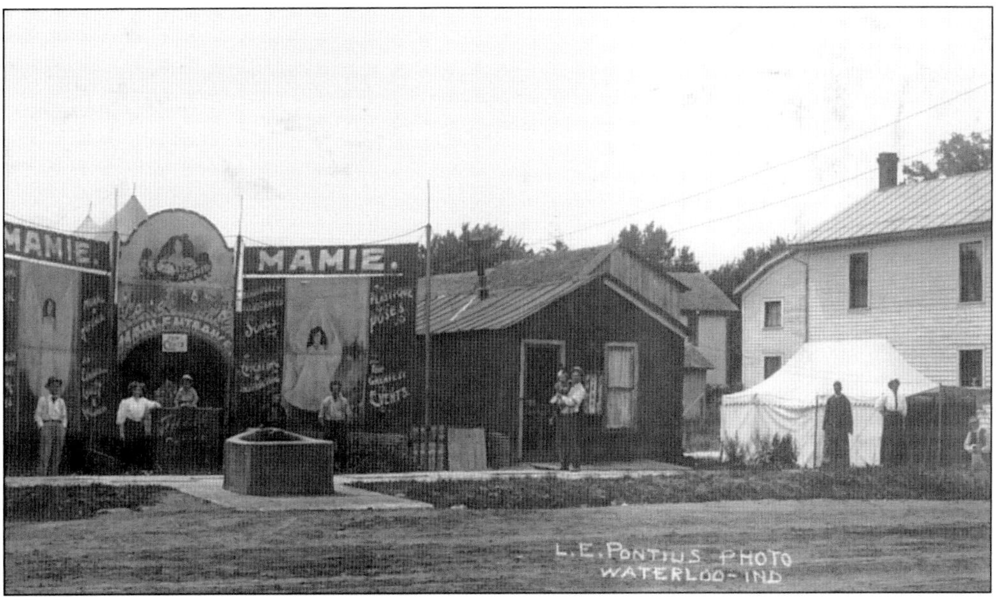

MAMIE. A tent show was set up in Waterloo. The signs state: "Beautifully Illustrated Songs—Plastique Poses—The Greatest Events."

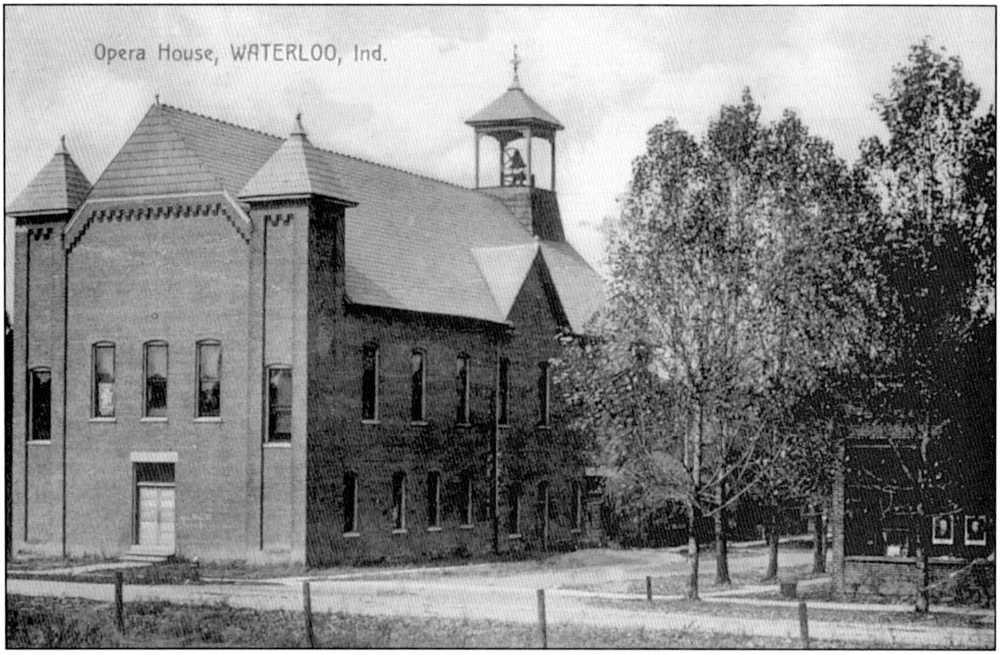

OPERA HOUSE, WATERLOO, INDIANA. The message states: "The picture on the other side was the Opera House before it was destroyed by the storm. . . ."

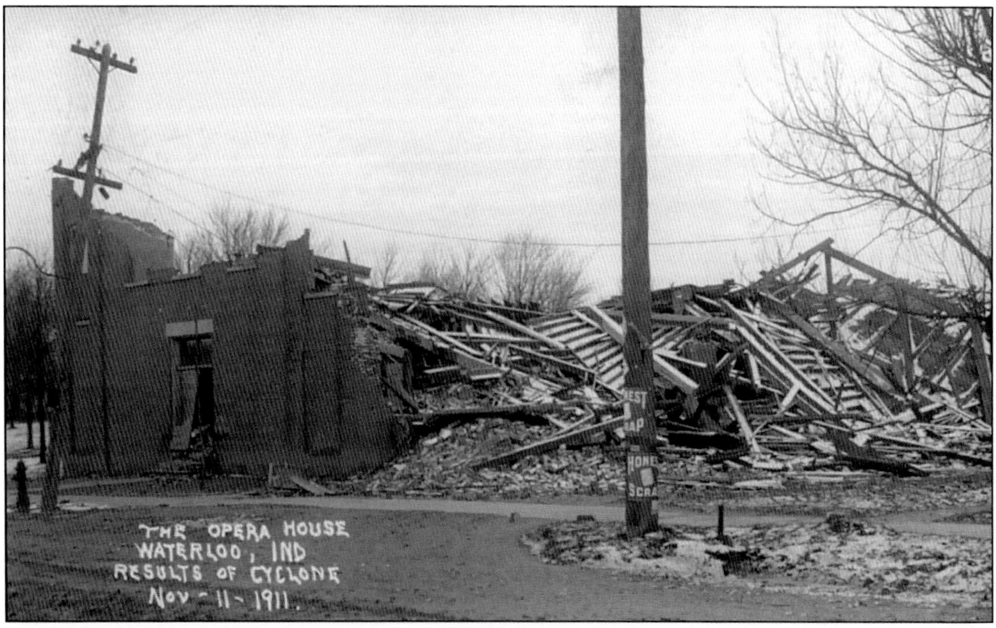

THE OPERA HOUSE, WATERLOO, INDIANA, RESULTS OF CYCLONE, NOVEMBER 11, 1911. A cyclone (tornado) destroyed the Waterloo Opera House at 11:00 a.m. November 11, 1911. The message states: "Dear Cousin: Children just recovering from mumps. Mother Mom died and now buried the 7th. We were not hurt by storm not much damage south of R.R. $50,000 North of R.R. Yours truly J.E.S."

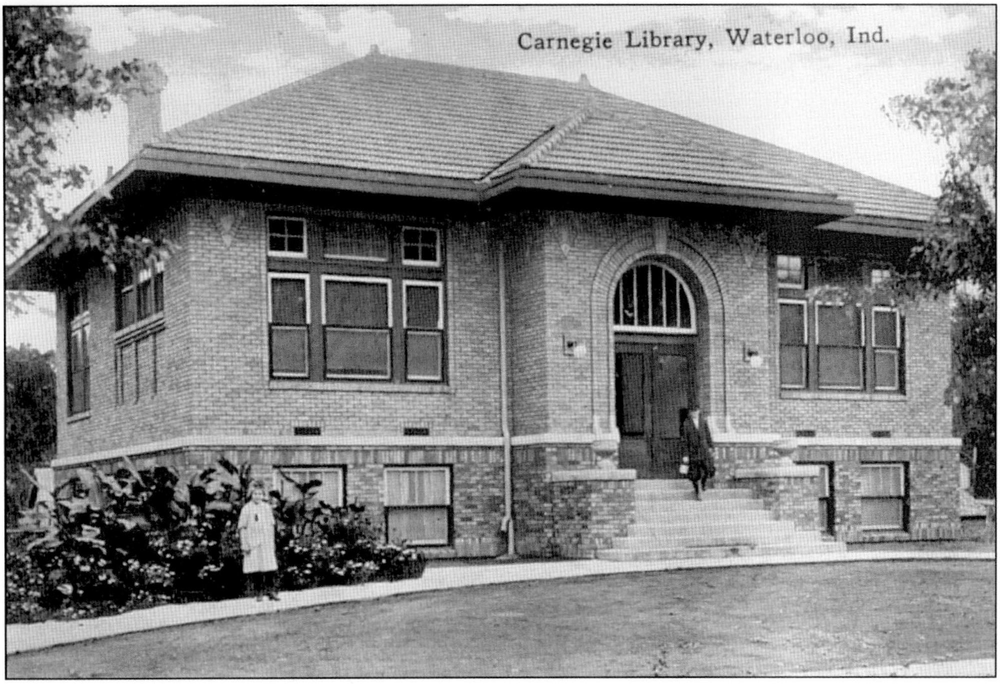

Carnegie Library, Waterloo, Indiana. Philanthropist Andrew Carnegie provided funds for Carnegie Libraries at Butler, Garrett, and Waterloo.

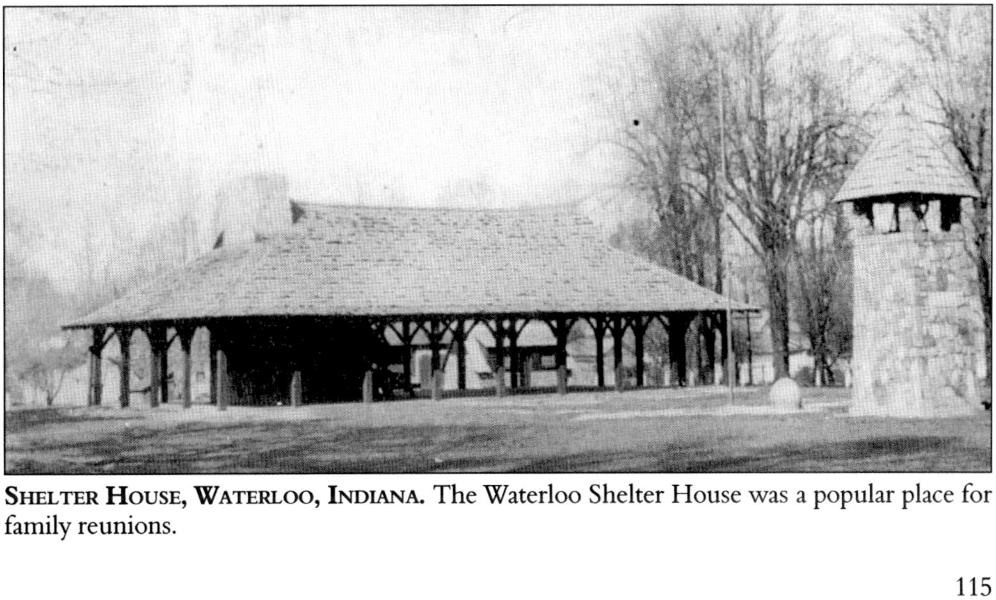

Shelter House, Waterloo, Indiana. The Waterloo Shelter House was a popular place for family reunions.

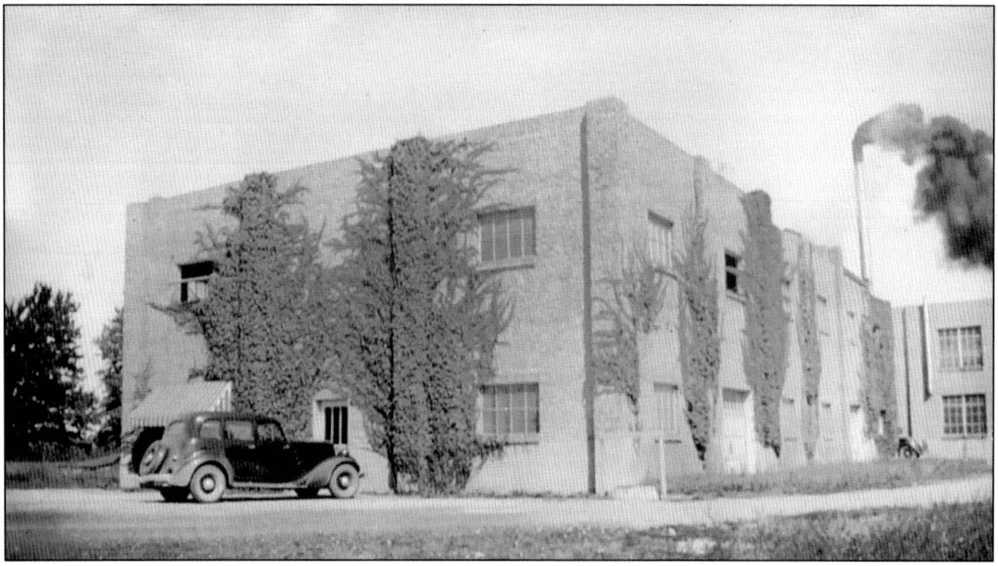

HALL-STINGLE CANNING FACTORY, WATERLOO, INDIANA. This company canned various vegetables in season. The automobile is a 1934 Auburn four-door sedan.

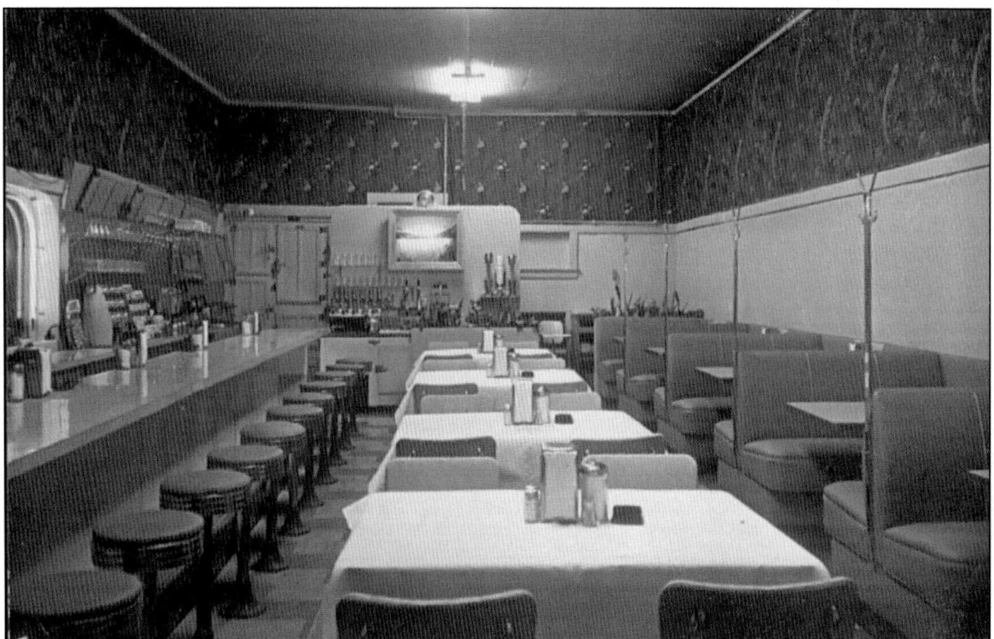

THE GREEN PARROT. "On U.S. 27 and U.S. 427—4 Blocks So. of U.S. 6, Waterloo, Ind.—Phone 8211. Open 7 Days a Week. Steaks—Chicken Dinners—Short Orders—Sandwiches. Mr. and Mrs. Austin Feller (A.B. and Ann)."

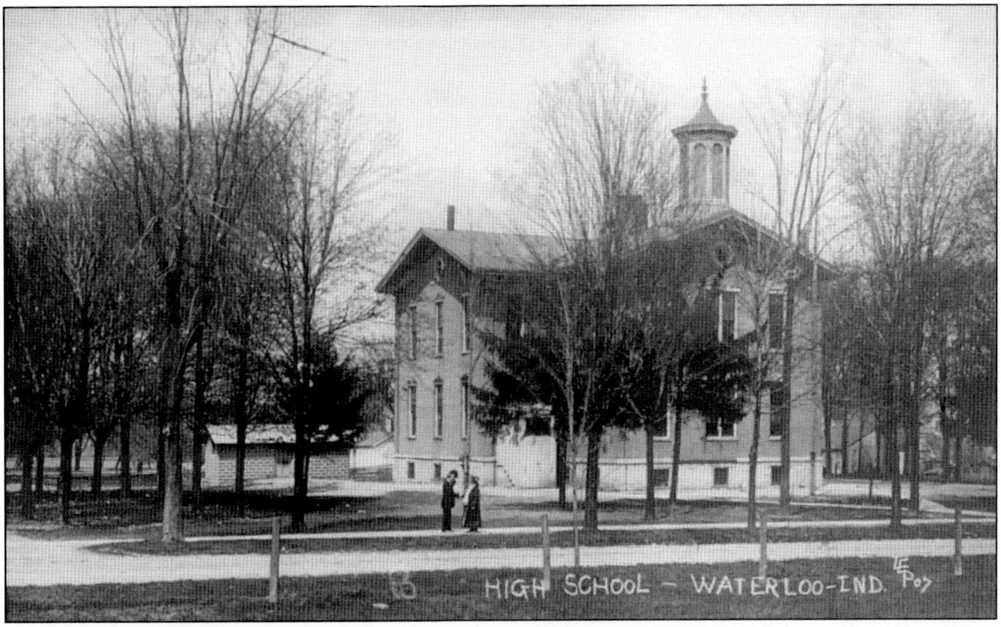

High School, Waterloo, Indiana. The original Waterloo High School was capped with an octagonal bell tower. A large bell, which could be heard throughout the town, was rung to call children to school.

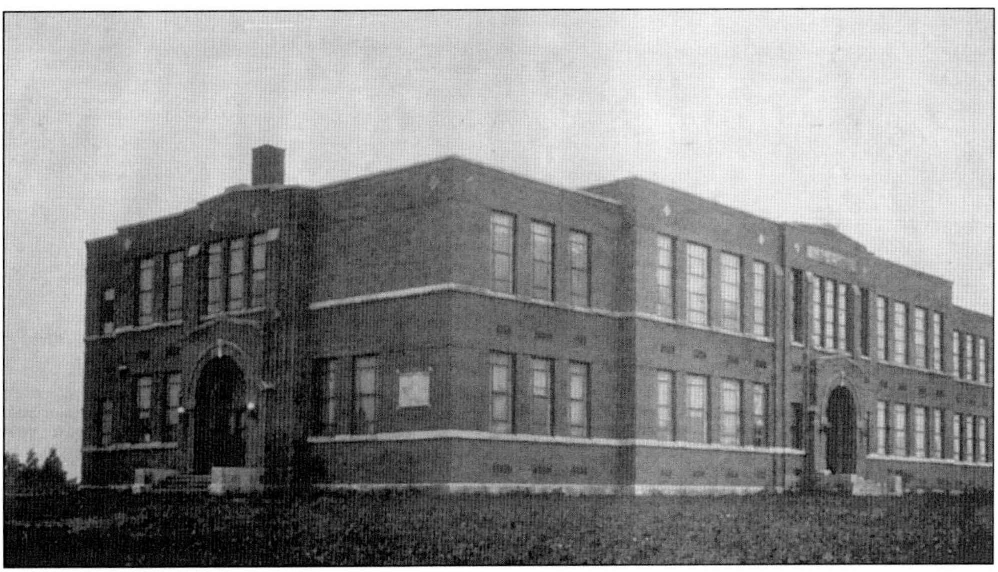

Waterloo High School, Waterloo, Indiana. The "new" school building was a state of the art educational facility when it was built.

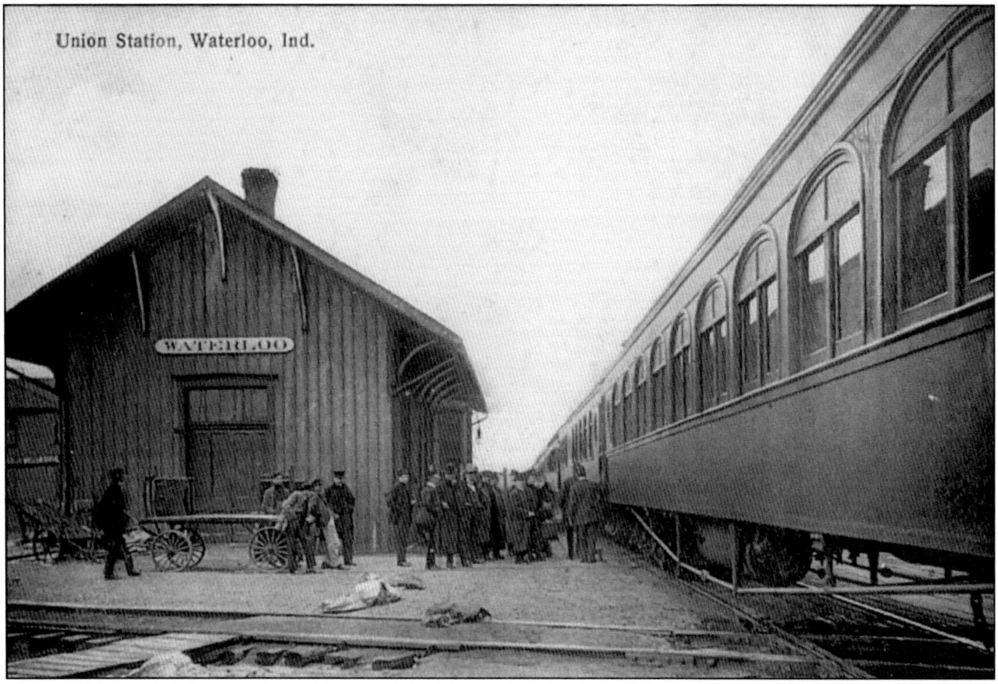

UNION STATION, WATERLOO, INDIANA. Waterloo's Union Station served the New York Central, Fort Wayne and Jackson, and Interurban Railroads. The track in the foreground is the Fort Wayne and Jackson Railroad.

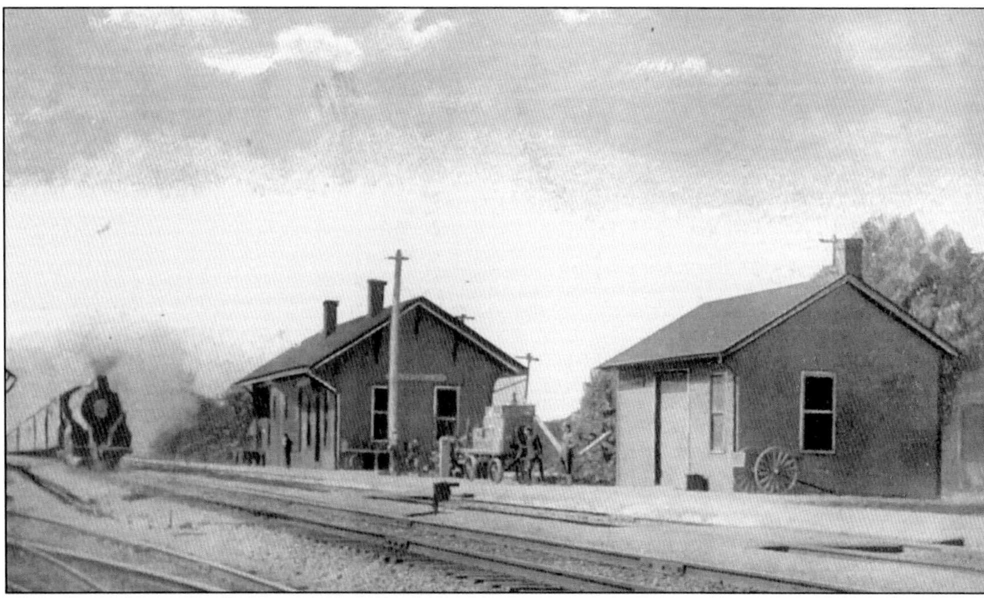

ARRIVING AT WATERLOO, INDIANA. The double-track mainline of the New York Central connected New York and Chicago. The tower on the left was manned by an employee who was responsible for the signals and the switches. The middle building is the passenger depot, and the building on the right is the freight house.

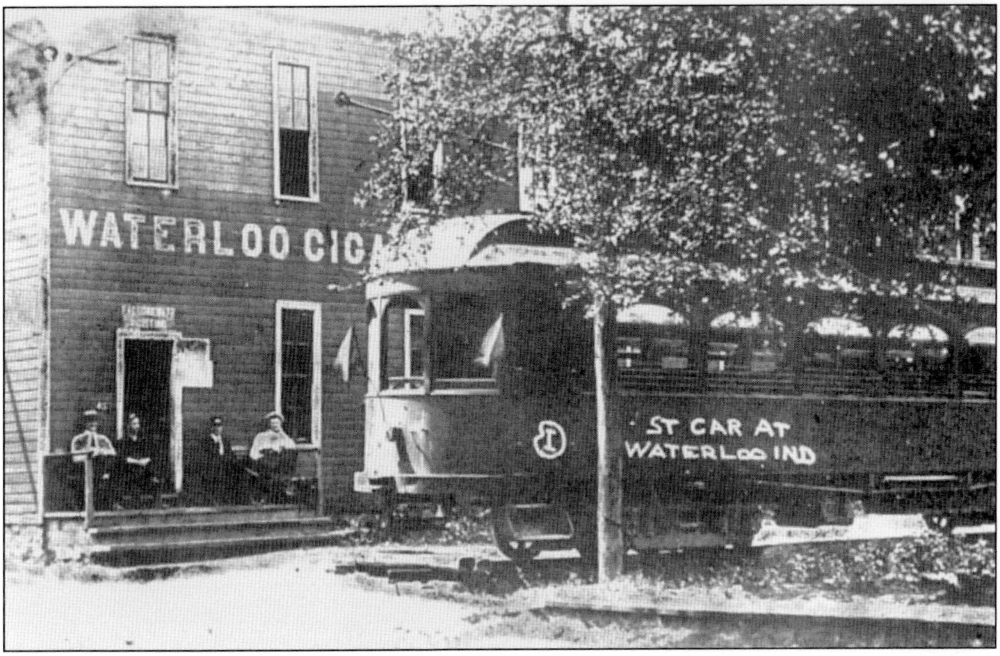

Street Car at Waterloo, Indiana. The interurban provided connections to Auburn, Garrett, and Fort Wayne. The northeastern terminus was south of the Waterloo Union Depot. The Waterloo Cigar Company was a local manufacturer of cigars. The sign above the door indicates that the factory was "Factory No. 77—N. Dist. Ind.," a reference to its federal license to manufacture cigars.

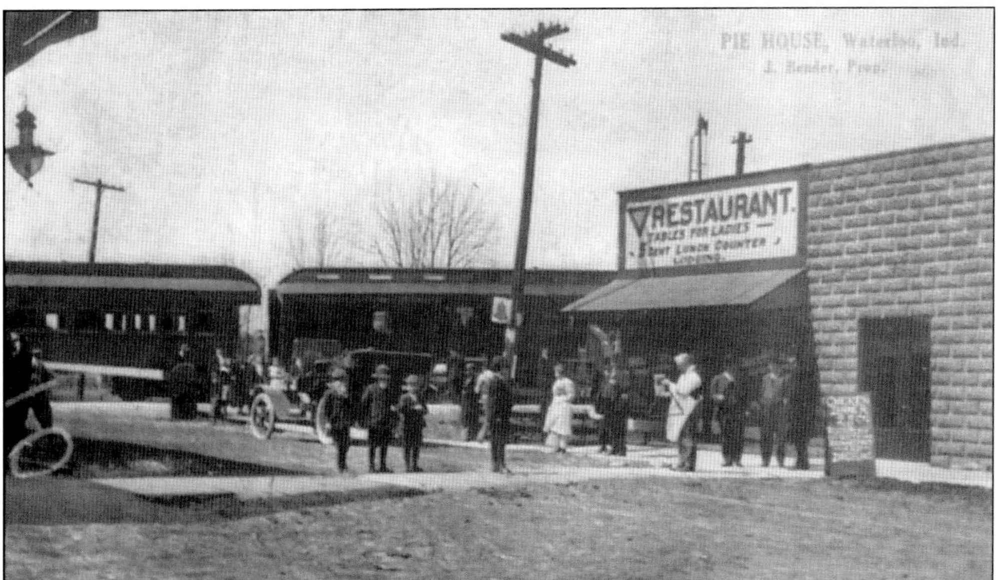

Pie House, Waterloo, Indiana. Some passenger trains stopped adjacent to restaurants for passengers to have meals. The sign states: "Restaurant—Tables for Ladies—5 cent Lunch Counter—Lodging."

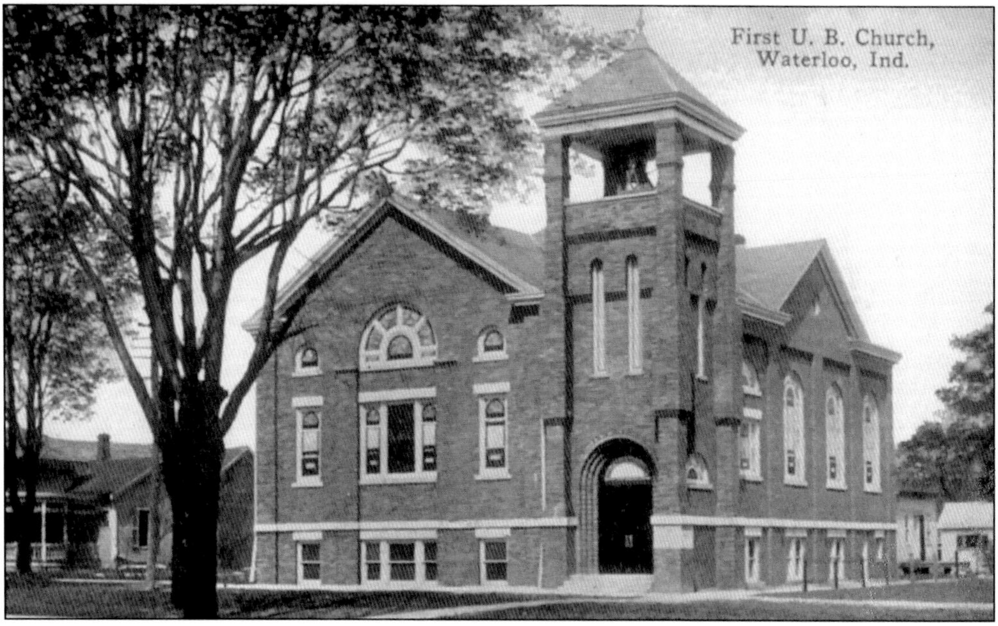

First U.B. Church, Waterloo, Indiana. The First United Brethren Church was graced by many stained glass windows.

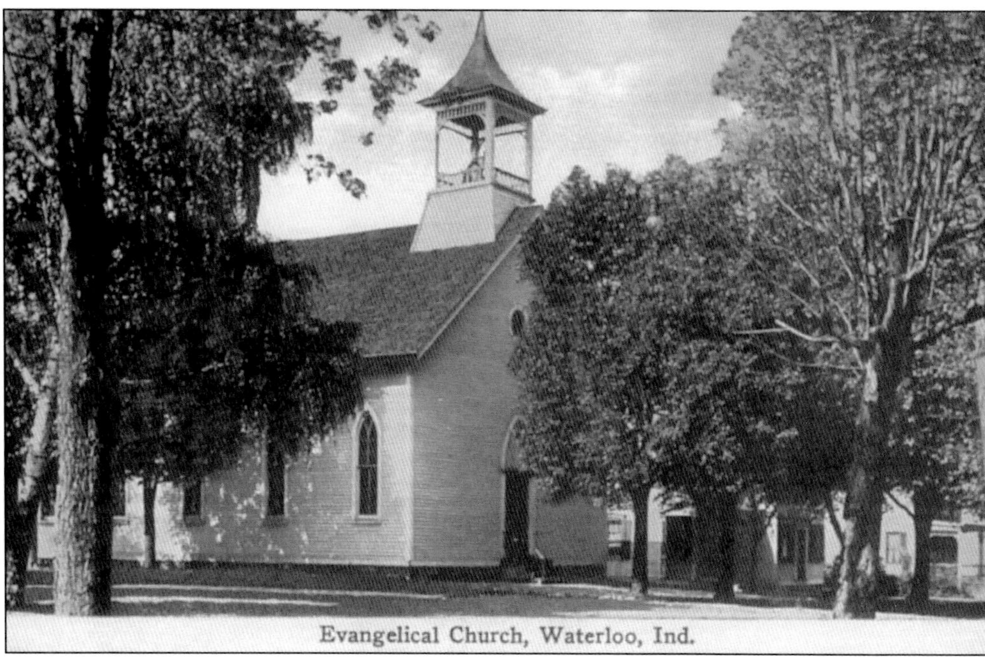

Evangelical Church, Waterloo, Indiana. The Evangelical Church was later merged with the United Brethren Church to create the Evangelical United Brethren Church.

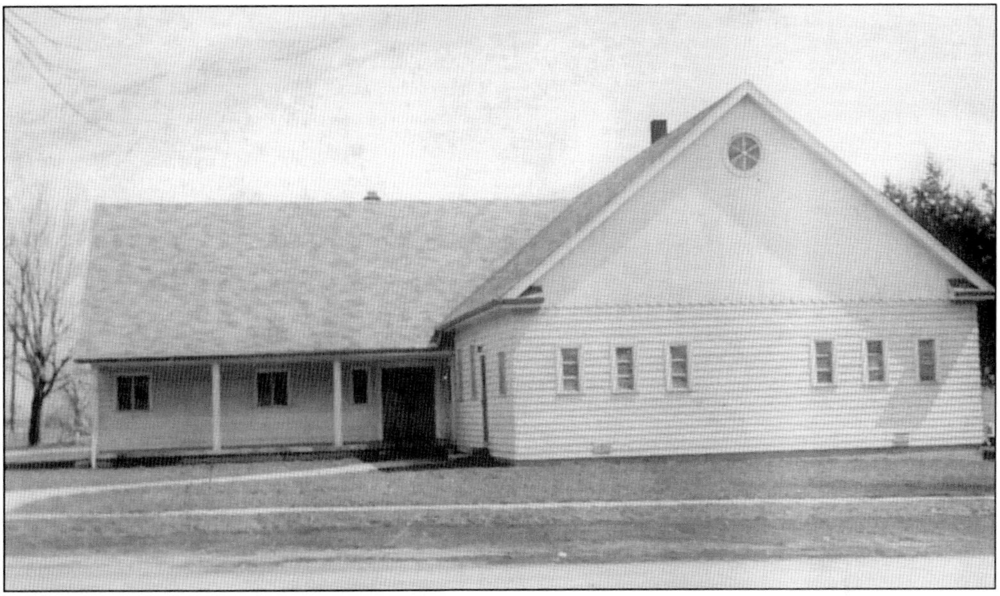

Church Of Christ, Waterloo, Indiana.

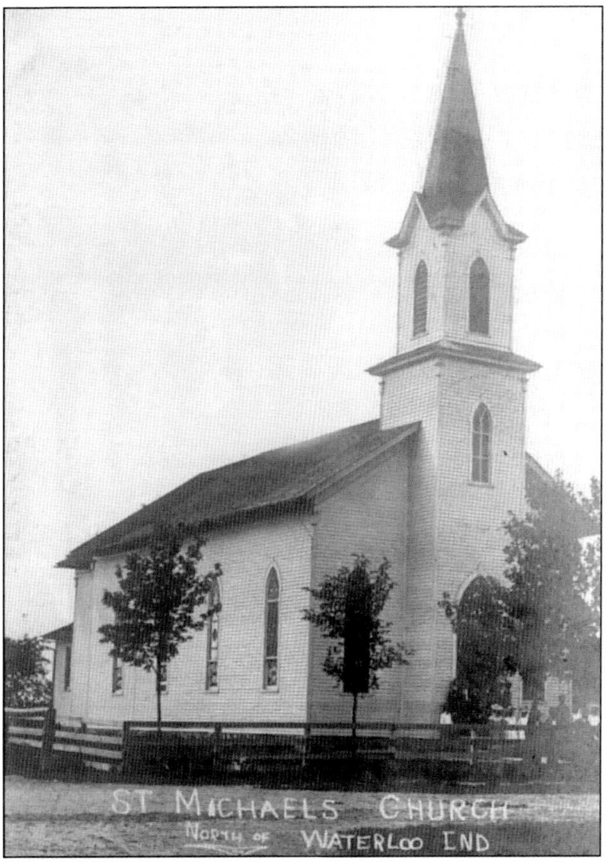

St. Michaels Church, Waterloo, Indiana. This is a view of the original frame building of the St. Michaels Church located north of Waterloo.

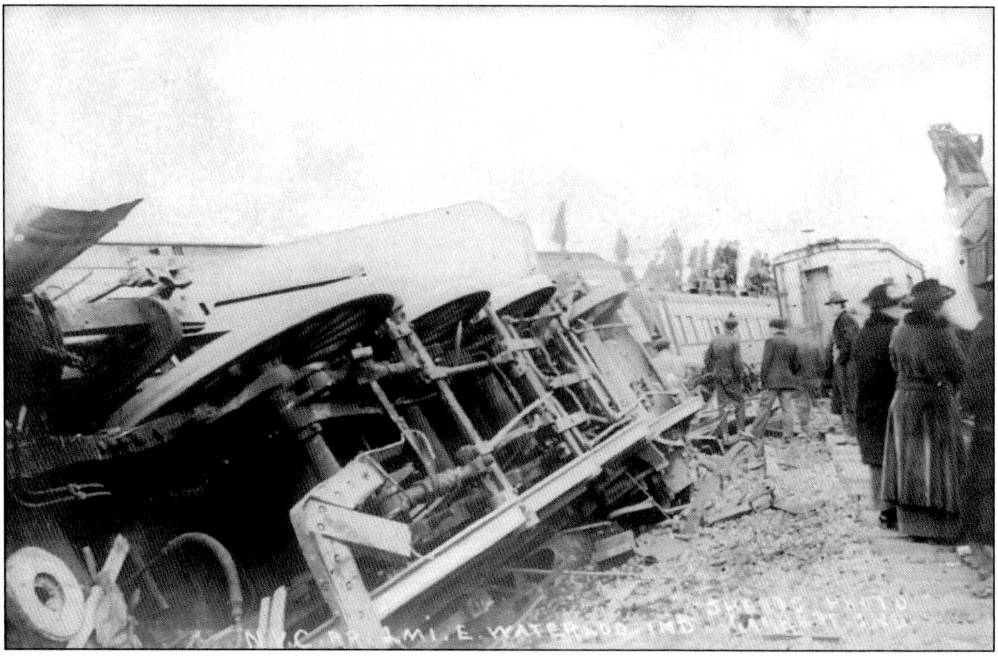

NYC R.R. 2 MILES EAST OF WATERLOO, INDIANA. Train wrecks were relatively common in the Waterloo area. Local photographers rushed to the scene and then created "real photo" postcards for residents to send to friends.

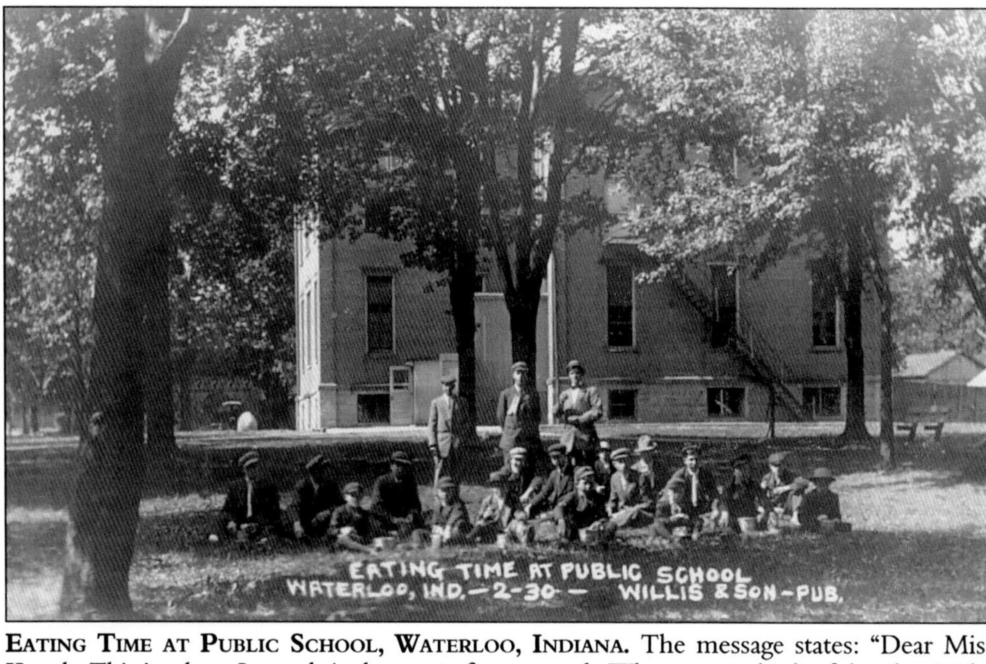

EATING TIME AT PUBLIC SCHOOL, WATERLOO, INDIANA. The message states: "Dear Miss Kouch: This is where I spend six days out of every week. What to you think of the place? The place I have marked (x) is the High School assembly room. And the place I have marked (v) is the Laboratory. Hope to hear from you soon."

Ten

Villages and Rural Areas

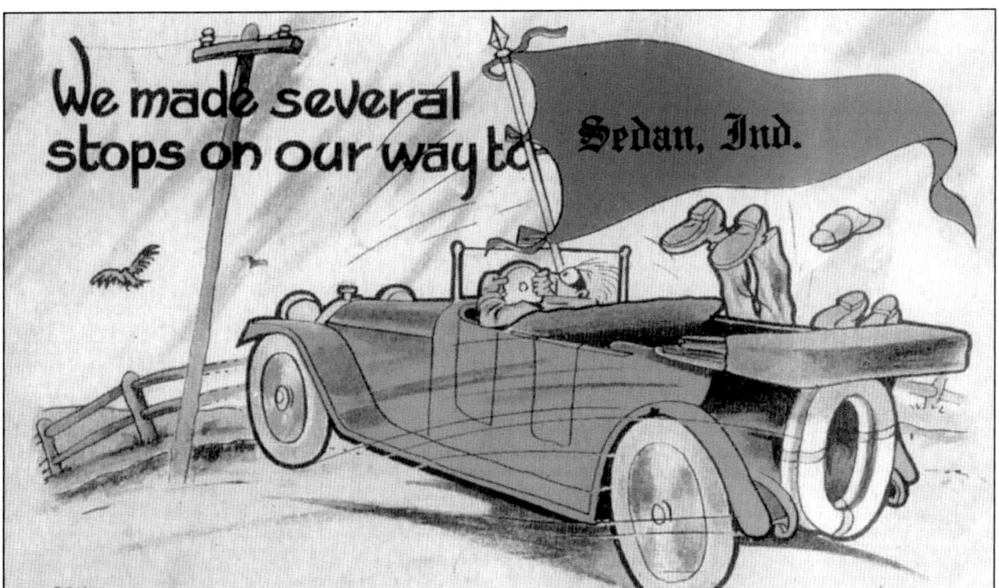

We Made Several Stops on Our Way to Sedan, Indiana. Sedan was a small village located on the New York Central Railroad between Waterloo and Corunna.

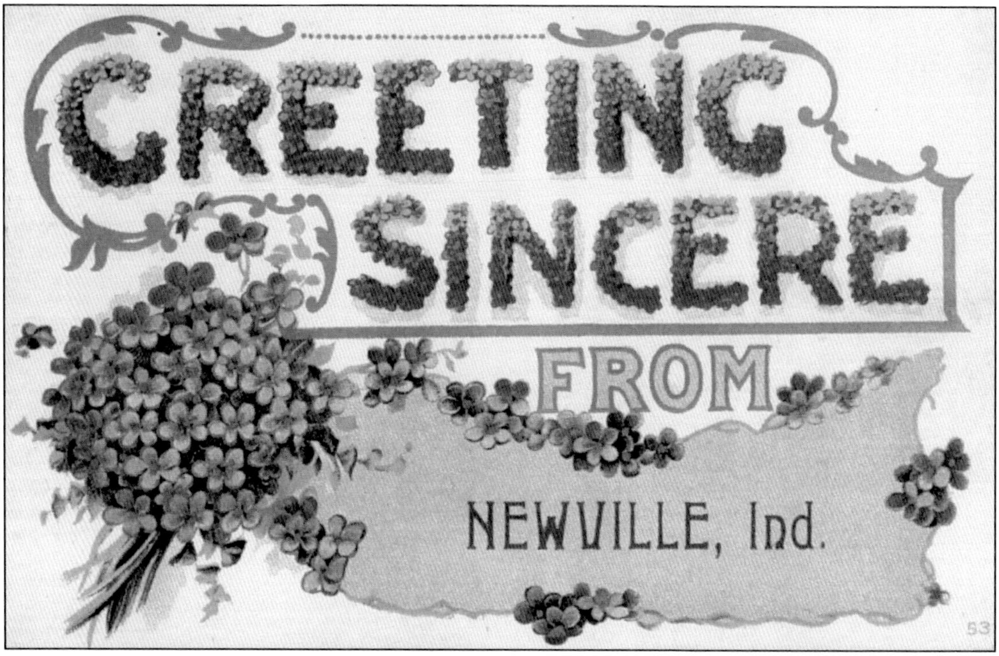

Greeting Sincere From Newville, Indiana. A stock card overprinted for Newville.

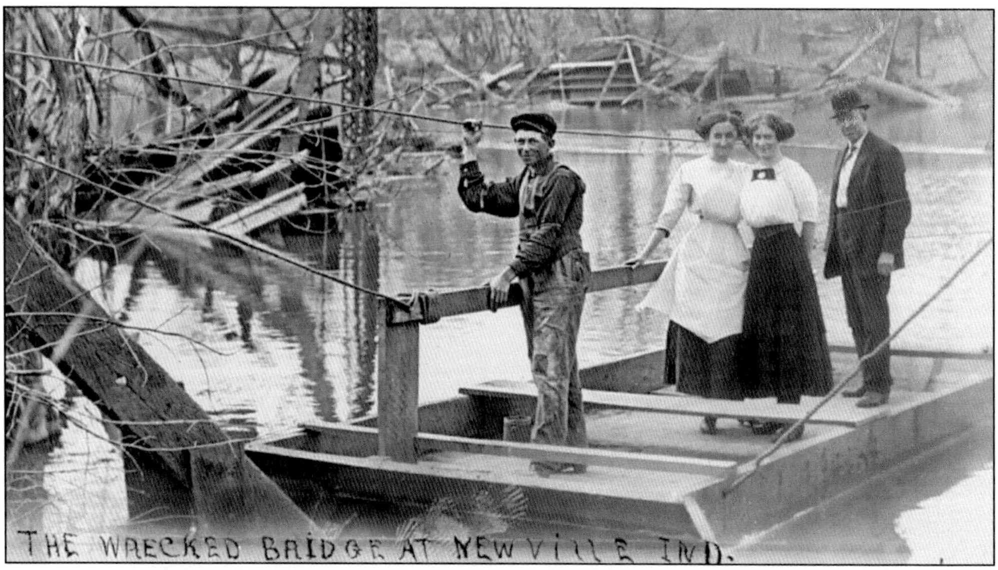

The Wrecked Bridge at Newville, Indiana. The bridge over the St. Joseph River is shown here. The small boat is rigged to a cable in such a way that the passengers could pull the boat across the river. The message states: "Hello received your car yesterday. I am fine and dandy. Was up to the church last eve to practicing for Children's day. I expect this picture looks natural does it? Forest and I was across it last night. The Reds are doing fine but I don't know who is ahead. Next Sun is the Sunday School convention at Ashley, Ind. Forest, Grace, Neva an I are to go as Delegates but I don't know whether I can go or not. I will have to quit or write on the table our commencement is the 11th June 'Harry Friend.'"

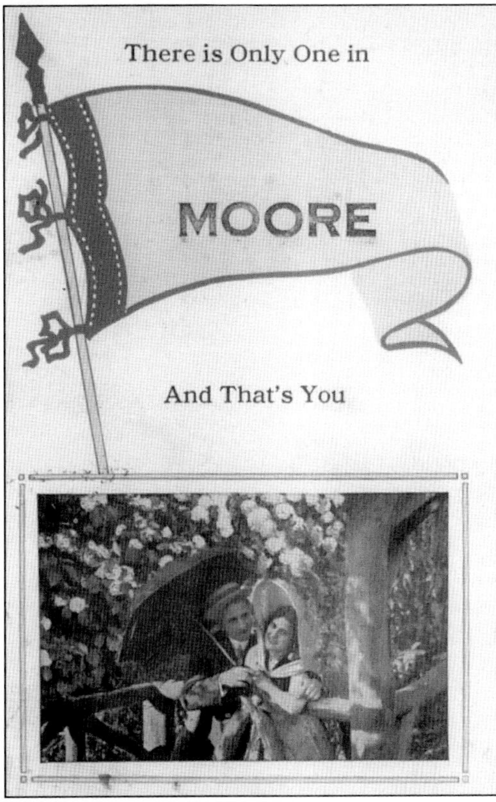

There is Only One in Moore and That's You. This is a sentimental card from Moore, Indiana.

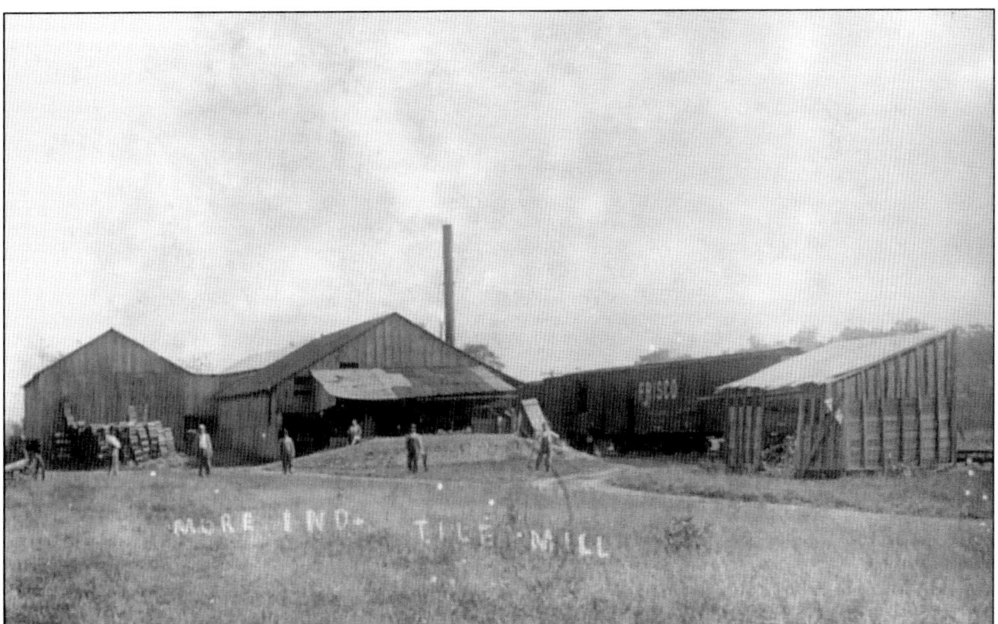

Moore, Indiana, Tile Mill. This mill was located on the Vandalia Railroad and manufactured clay field tile.

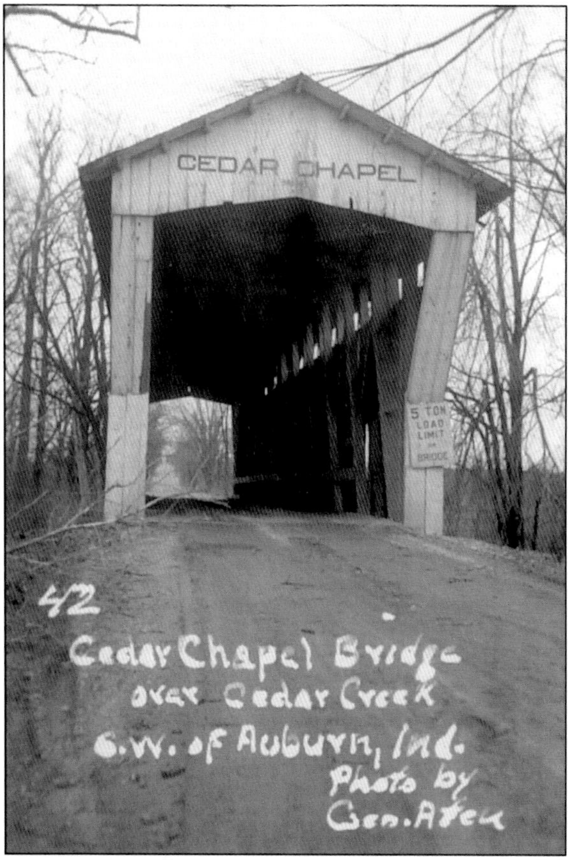

Cedar Chapel Bridge over Cedar Creek, Southwest of Auburn, Indiana. The bridge was located over Cedar Creek on what is now DeKalb County Road 68. The bridge has been moved to Conner Prairie near Noblesville, Indiana.

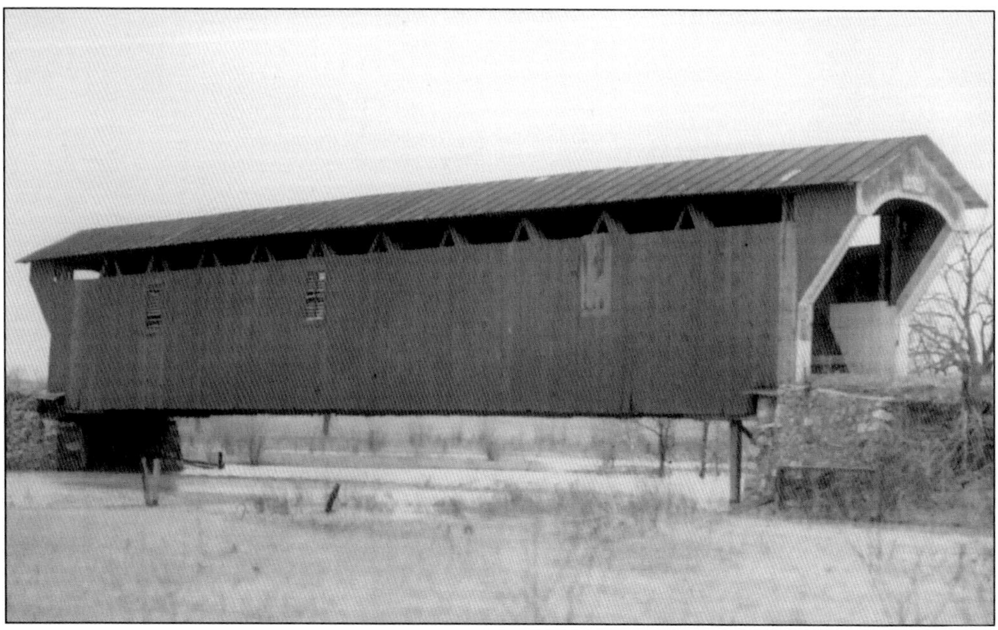

Houlton Bridge over Fish Creek North of Butler. The bridge was destroyed by fire.

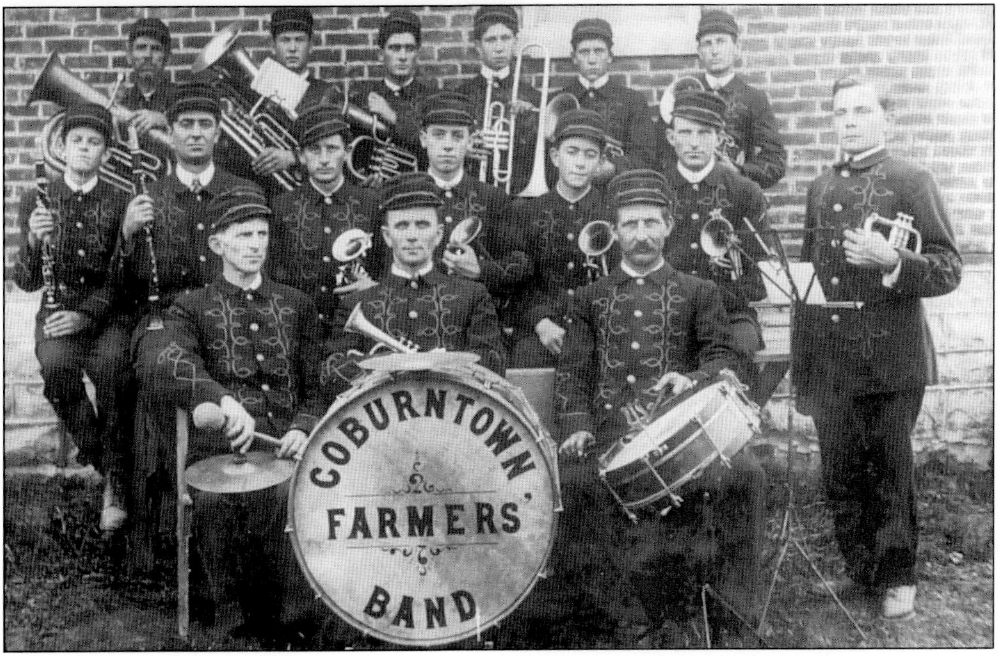

Coburntown Farmers' Band. The band had elaborate embroidered uniforms.

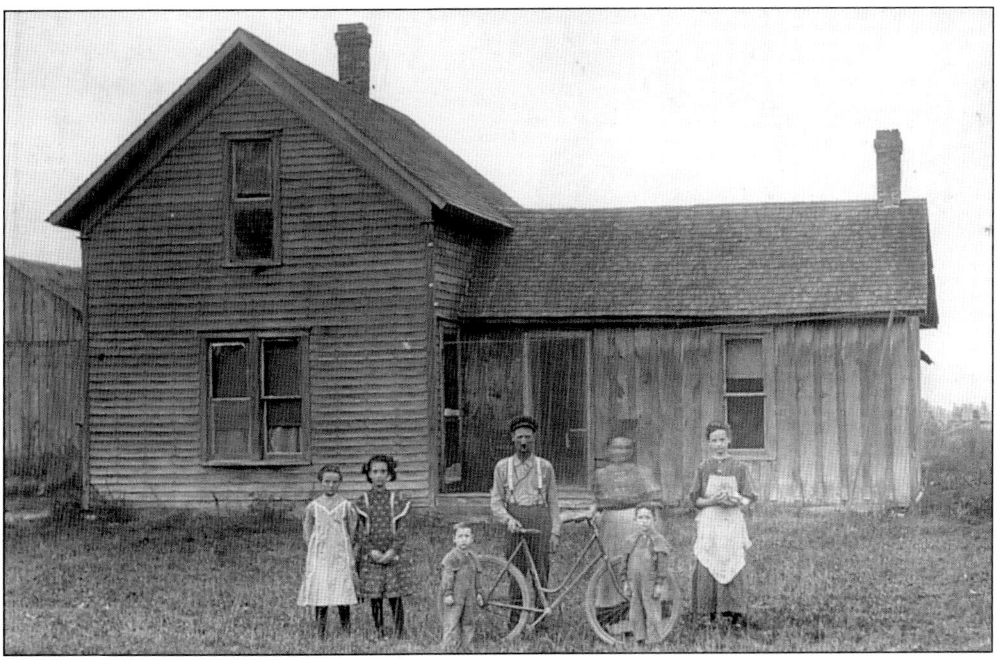

Farmhouse Family. An unidentified family poses in front of their DeKalb County farmhouse.

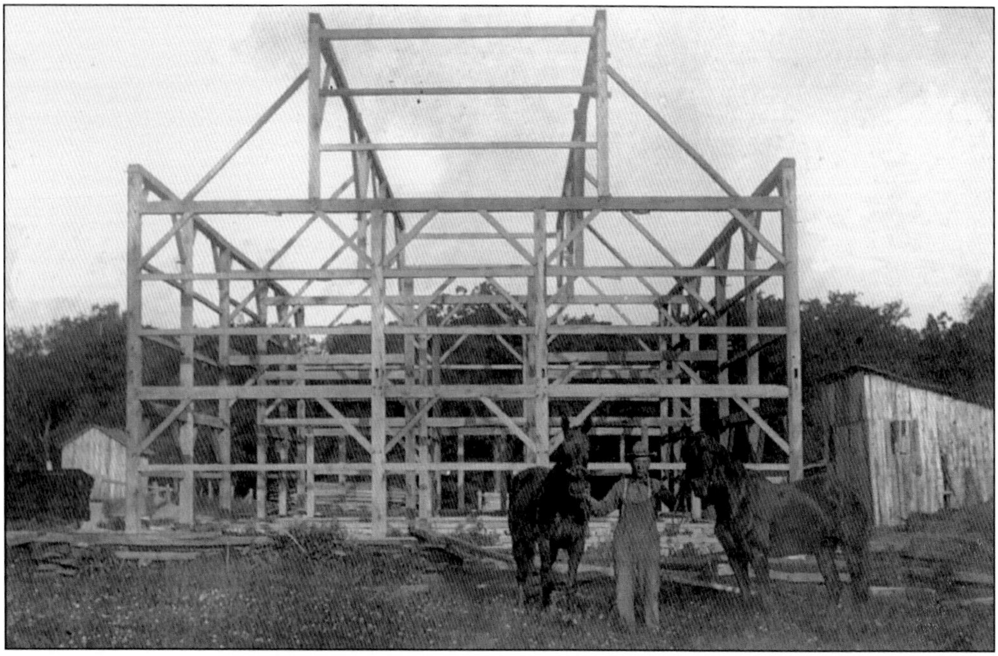

Barn Under Construction. This farmer proudly poses with his team of work horses.

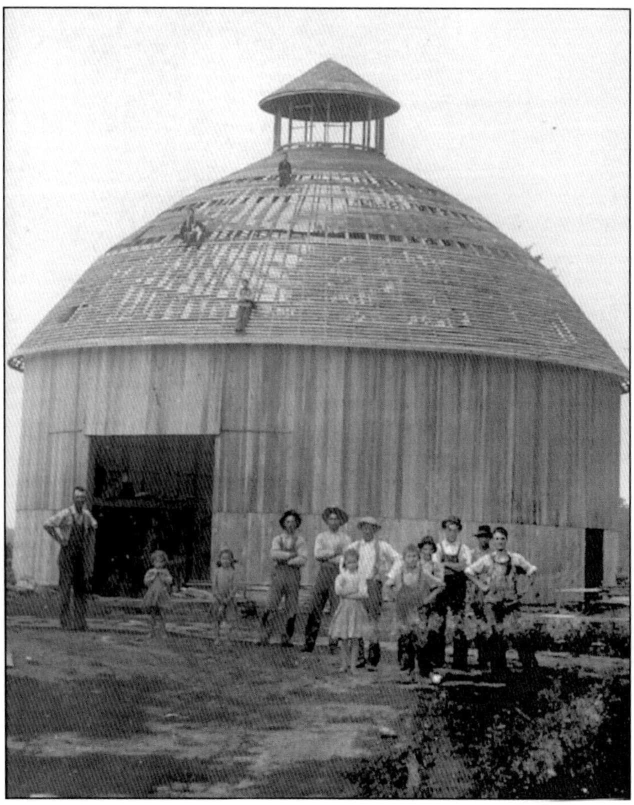

Round Barn Under Construction. The construction crew poses for a photograph. Note the workers on the roof.